Gregory Corso

Gregory Corso
Doubting Thomist

KIRBY OLSON

Southern Illinois University Press
Carbondale and Edwardsville

Library of Congress Cataloging-in-Publication Data
Olson, Kirby, 1956–
    Gregory Corso : doubting Thomist / Kirby Olson.
        p. cm.
    Includes bibliographical references and index.
        1. Corso, Gregory—Criticism and interpretation. 2.
Christianity and literature—United States—History—20th century.
3. Thomas, Aquinas, Saint, 1225?–1274—Influence. 4. Christian
poetry, American—History and criticism. 5. Belief and doubt in
literature. 6. Corso, Gregory—Religion. 7. Beat generation. I.
Title.

PS3505.O763 Z73 2002
811'.54—dc21
ISBN 0-8093-2447-4 (alk. paper)   2001049903

Printed on recycled paper. ♻

The paper used in this publication meets the minimum requirements of American National
Standard for Information Sciences—Permanence of Paper for Printed Library Materials,
ANSI Z39.48-1992. ∞

Contents

Acknowledgments vii

Abbreviations ix

1. Introduction: Corso and Christianity 1
2. Corso and the Great Chain of Being 31
3. Static Thomism or Progressive Romanticism? 55
4. Corso's "Perspective Through Incongruity" 88
5. Toward a Psychiatric Evaluation of Corso 100
6. Monstrous Aesthetics 130
7. Corso's Inquisition of Christian Metaphysics 148
8. Would You Rent Corso an Apartment? 153
9. Conclusion 163

Works Cited 175

Index 179

Acknowledgments

Gregory Corso's work and life have been central to my understanding and appreciation of literature. I studied with him at Naropa Institute in 1977 and have been a continuous reader of his work ever since. In the last year of his life, I sent him portions of this manuscript, and it was his warm and gracious encouragement that sustained my confidence that I was on the right track while I finished the volume. It is my regret that he was unable to read and comment on the final work.

Gregory Corso gave me permission to reproduce work from the following copyrighted materials.

American Express. Copyright © 1961 by Gregory Corso.

Elegiac Feelings American. Copyright © 1970 by Gregory Corso.

Gasoline. Copyright © 1958 by Gregory Corso.

Herald of the Autochthonic Spirit. Copyright © 1981 by Gregory Corso.

Mindfield: New and Selected Poems. Copyright © 1989 by Gregory Corso.

"Upon my Refusal to Herald Cuba," "A Difference of Zoos," "Writ on the Eve of My 32nd Birthday," "Saint Francis," and "God? She's Black" by Gregory Corso, from *Long Live Man,* copyright © 1959, 1960, 1961, 1962 by New Directions Publishing Corp. Reprinted by permission of New Directions Publishing Corp.

"Bomb," "Clown," "Food," and "Heave the Hive with New Bees" by Gregory Corso, from *The Happy Birthday of Death,* copyright © 1960 by New Directions Publishing Corp., are also reprinted by permission of New Directions Publishing Corp.

The second chapter of this book, "Corso and the Great Chain of Being," appeared in my volume *Comedy after Postmodernism: Rereading Comedy from Edward Lear to Charles Willeford* (Lubbock: Texas Tech UP, 2001), 45–73, copyright © 2001 Texas Tech University Press. I would like to extend my thanks to Texas Tech University Press for allowing me to reproduce the chapter.

I would like to thank Steven Shaviro, Mikkel Borch-Jacobsen, Raimonda Modiano, Michael Williams, Paul Remley, Brian Evenson, Mark Lester, and others at the University of Washington for marvelous conversations regarding contemporary theory, Gnosticism, and romantic poetry, among other topics. Charles Altieri's seminar on contemporary poetry at the University of Washington gave me a philosophical approach that I at first resisted but from which I've benefited. Corso scholars Michael Skau and another, anonymous reader have contributed by making numerous small and large suggestions for the book—many of which I adopted, making this a better book. I was fortunate to be able to offer a Corso seminar at the University of Tampere in Finland, which allowed me to go over this material with a dozen students and to see that it continued to exercise a powerful fascination even for students some fifty years younger than Corso in a country far removed from America. I would especially like to thank Riikka Olson, my wife, and our children, Lola and Tristan, for all the fun that sustained me over the many years I was writing this book.

All translations in the book are mine unless otherwise noted.

Abbreviations

AE	*American Express*
EF	*Elegiac Feelings American*
G	*Gasoline*
HA	*Herald of the Autochthonic Spirit*
HB	*The Happy Birthday of Death*
LL	*Long Live Man*
M	*Mindfield: New and Selected Poems*

Gregory Corso

1

Introduction: Corso and Christianity

A strict Catholic upbringing gave Gregory Corso a rich intellectual and spiritual heritage, but because he was put up for adoption at the age of six months, he was deprived of the ordinary emotional richness that family life provides. Shuttled between six families before he reached the age of ten ("When I Was Five" 29), Corso developed a sense of humor and an interrogative mind in these insecure circumstances, taking on Catholicism and yet doubting it at the same time, developing dark doubts as to the nature of his understanding of the universe. Corso's poetry references myriad metaphysical and intellectual systems, anticipating developments in postmodern thought and to some extent providing surprising new twists on rather sophisticated themes. For a poet blessed with a mere sixth-grade formal education, Corso's intellectual reach is great. His insecurity led to constant thinking, a thinking that in turn illuminates our own condition. The framework of this study is to place Corso's work into the larger matrix of postmodernist discourse. This work will draw upon Catholic theology as it is reacted to by Darwinism, alchemy, Gnosticism, surrealism, psychiatry, and contemporary critical theory.

Corso's work, like that of the other Beat writers, has been insufficiently studied, and yet it forms an impressive and original oeuvre. While bringing this poetry into productive dialogue with recent literary debates, the commentary will stay close to the poetry, with the illumination of it as the central focus of the text. In the growing conversation of Corso studies, in which two exemplary books already exist, the contribution of the present book is aimed at a metaphysical reading of Corso's poetry, an overlooked and understudied aspect of his writing, although some interesting work has already been done in this area by Michael Skau, Gregory Stephenson, Marilyn Schwartz, and others.

Today, scientists tell us we inhabit a materialist universe, but the poets posit something more. What does Corso see that goes beyond materialism? I believe his work can be read as serious philosophy that focuses on the nature of the universe. Corso's philosophical underpinnings are based on his questioning of what life can mean in a food chain. But before we address the larger questions, let us begin with some biographical background as well as a personal reminiscence in order to ground the discussion.

Gregory Corso is the most difficult writer of the Beat generation. Although some of his verses are seemingly simple and clear, the neglected majority of them are skillful, complex, arcane knots that one must go to great lengths to undo, if one can undo them at all. By "difficult," more is meant than just hard to understand or hard to take personally; it is some combination of these two. Corso was born into difficulty but somehow Houdinied himself out, and in his verses some of the psychological skills he developed are apparent. An orphan of the extreme lower classes and a prisoner in his teenage years, Corso survived as a poet to the age of seventy without the benefit of any help whatsoever from parents, family, or a college education, which would be taken for granted by almost any other poet of his generation. His endurance as a poet for fifty years without grants, teaching posts, or much critical recognition shows his brilliant capabilities of managing difficulty.

When I met Gregory Corso at Naropa Institute in 1977, I found him hard to take personally—he was constantly drunk and yelling curses at people—but I also found that in his quieter moods, he had an imagination so thoroughly profound that listening to him discuss the work of Edgar Allan Poe or the thinking of Pythagoras, the geometry of Egyptian pyramids, or the beauty of the fire contained in matches was the high-water mark of my student days at Naropa. As soon as I would begin to understand him, he would subtly change tracks and begin some other difficult discourse, too abstruse for my twenty-year-old mind to follow. Now that I have been reading his work for over two decades, I can see that it is this shifting iconoclasm that characterizes it. Corso wants to break free of any limiting thought, any kind of defining parameters, as his personality is often one of distrust. This is the unifying thread that runs throughout his poetry. His poetry slips free of the hold that any idea, person, situation, or institution might have on him, constantly challenging any taboos or any sense of normality that might happen to constrain him or try to constrain him, and yet at the same time there is a search for continuity and a place to call home. Most scholars emphasize his intellectual restlessness as opposed to his homesickness, and there is plenty of work that points in that direction: "Where does one stand who contends / a stand taken is a fall invited?" (from "Upon My Refusal to Herald Cuba," *LL* 57).

Corso's iconoclasm is readily apparent, but it is not the whole story. There is an innocent humor that he marshals in service of his various acts of mayhem. Corso is a disturbing individual, but he is also something else. At Naropa Institute in the summer of 1977, he created so much disturbance that he wasn't invited back the following summer. What follows is a partial inventory of his disruptions:

1. Corso smashed all of Allen Ginsberg's vintage jazz records from the 1950s, telling Ginsberg that he was helping him reach enlightenment because he was too attached to those records.
2. He threw a bag of black dildos into a feminist conference and said, "This is what you bitches need!" He then ran out of the conference into a car he had left running and sped through Boulder, Colorado, playing bumper cars with the traffic as he was chased by various members of the conference. I heard later that one of the feminists who had chased Corso later became his lover, and all was forgiven.
3. Corso fed his three-year-old child, Max Orpheus, from a bottle that he continuously refilled with wine.
4. He wore a camouflage jacket and red bandanna around his head, simulating a Vietnam vet, while carrying a ferret that occasionally nipped at his fingers, which were always bandaged.
5. He had a wife twenty years his junior, named Jocelyn Rothschild, who was always drunk and falling asleep or passing out in weird places, like the parking lot. Corso would have to come and get her, throw her over his shoulder, and bring her back to their apartment. At one point, another man appeared, who was a murderer wanted in seven states, and he claimed to be married to her also. Since she was rich, he wanted alimony. Corso, the murderer, and Rothschild walked around Boulder hashing it out, while William S. Burroughs Jr. followed them, trying to protect Corso from the murderer, who was armed with a shotgun. Burroughs held a length of chain with which he intended to strangle the alleged murderer if he went after Corso.
6. He lived in a Buddhist official's house because the man had said at a public talk that it was important to share. Corso helped himself to the man's food and bed for the summer.
7. He gave a series of talks, called "Socratic Raps," that were always given in an advanced state of inebriation; he changed tracks whenever they seemed to be getting too sensible. All the while he was lecturing, he would sit and obsessively tie and untie knots with a length of string.

The various students he slept with and other small crimes he indulged in are too numerous to note, but suffice it to say that wherever Corso went, trouble followed. He had shouting matches with the poet Larry Fagin, with various other faculty members, and with students. What I found impossible to explain was how he managed to create so little rancor with his antics. He was almost always immediately forgiven.

He spoke of strange things, such as the Pythagorean mathematics of Poe's verses and how shadows had infinite length. The principle of every conversation was that Corso could say any outrageous thing he wanted, but I could not ask "Why?" If I did, he would get furious. With almost any other person, I would have been angry at him for being so furious for no reason, but with Corso, I simply accepted the situation and the rules of the conversation, which constituted a double standard in Corso's favor.

Corso seems to be an exemplar of Bataillean heterology, forever escaping any kind of system, an iconoclast who is capable of destroying or eluding any system of thought, any system of recuperation. This is his specialty. While Ginsberg, Kerouac, and even Burroughs are fairly straightforward critics of the American system and have their own superior systems to replace it—whether with LSD and Blake, Zen and high-speed travel, or linguistic analysis and fragmentation—Corso is not in any sense a reformer of American society but rather and more importantly a chronic doubter whose center is Catholicism. Faith in God is the most insistent theme of his poetry, and whether or not this faith was misplaced is the major source of the lyric tension in his work.

Corso himself, in interviews, enhanced his image as a satanic rebel and perpetrated the myth of himself as a prankster without any kind of moral center. And yet, it is the claim of this book that in fact Corso was always fundamentally Roman Catholic and that this Catholicism provided him with a secure matrix to which he always returned. There is yet no biography of this poet, and so his childhood and adult years are not as easy to track as are the lives of Kerouac, Ginsberg, and Burroughs. However, Corso has himself published some autobiographical fragments, and it is here that he constantly alludes to his "strict Catholic upbringing" ("When I Was Five" 87). He dreamed and wrote poetry that had Catholicism as a central motif, which, he says in a letter, is "proof that I am not far from my religious heritage" (cited in Skau 29).

In his short essay "Notes from the Other Side of April: With Negro Eyes, with White," Corso discusses his childhood experiences with blacks. He mentions that at age five he met "another black angel—he was the janitor of an apartment building on the route to and from Catholic Sunday School" and that he ate all the man's cakes and read his comic books one Sunday afternoon "just like Goldilocks and the Three Bears, but I didn't go back for more. Because when I confessed it to the priest that Saturday he mentioned something about poisoned cakes strangers leave about for little crooks" (87).

Corso's autobiographical essay, "When I Was Five I Saw a Dying Indian," lists important foundational events in his early childhood. When he was five he attended "church first time" (29). This was shortly to become the most powerful experience of his young life. He writes:

> Those occasions I deem out of the ordinary all took place in my fifth and sixth year. Three had to do with my profound introduction into the Catholic Church. I had quite an imagination for so young a child, and what with the strange and mysterious teachings of Church—I was a live one for such occurrences as could be deemed *out of the ordinary.* (30)

The central intellectual experiences that Corso describes in his childhood all have to do with the church and its relationship to the food chain. For example, he put a cross on a dead cat he found in a parking lot and was told by a nun and a priest that this was a sin. The nun screamed at him while pulling his ears, "The crucifix is not for cats! Our Lord did not die on the cross for cats! It's a sacrilege to put the holy cross on a dead beast!" (30). In another incident, a little boy showed him a glass elephant as they sat in church, then appeared to drop dead. Corso drew the conclusion that the boy had blasphemed and had paid the consequences. "I never knew if the boy died or merely fainted; I do know that I never saw him again" (83). And later, Corso took Holy Communion, but the wafer got stuck in a tooth. "I literally believed that I had a bit of God's flesh and blood stuck in my teeth, like a piece of steak or something. I felt damned, like the worst creature in hell, I had God stuck in my teeth" (85–86).

These central experiences provided Corso with his most basic sense of life. Animals are not allowed into the church, and yet we eat them. God is allowed into our mouths via the communion wafer, but we are not supposed to chew it; it is to dissolve slowly in the mouth. Corso's art centers on these experiences, and throughout his work he defends animals and tries to create a sacred poetry in which animals have the sanctity of humanity. These religious experiences, along with his first orgasm and a memory of a dying Indian, resulted in some basic questions. Most important to him was, What is the line between animals, humans, and God? Other questions were, What is sex? What is death? These questions too are linked to procreation and the question of human animality.

Corso's "strict Catholic upbringing" can be read against those critics who accuse him of nihilism in order to provide coherence. When one reads his work, the importance of this matrix becomes clear. Corso attempted to deny his Catholicism, especially in some of his later work, and scholar Michael Skau writes, "In his later poems, Corso's rejection of the concept of God is emphatic" (27). However, Corso had the same relationship to Catholicism that Fred Flintstone had to his cat: every time he threw it out the front door, it came crawling back in through the window, and nowhere does Corso's Catholicism return more insistently than in his later poems. The final lines of his poem "Field Report" also make up the last lines of his *Mindfield: New and Selected Poems:* "like Holderlin sayeth I am closer to god / away from Him / Stop" (268).

Corso's Catholicism gave his otherwise iconoclastic existence a center, and if we look closely, it can be seen that this was all that he felt he needed to respond to—his own belief was the central drama of his poetry. He recognized problems, accepted them, described them—realistically—and stepped back without posing solutions. He never took up any new age religion nor became a leading spirit of any fads, whether it was hippies, ecology, or the punk movement. Corso always remained separate, aloof, and seemingly free. As such he is often seen as the monstrous, dark soul who cannot be recuperated but who is endlessly inventing new kinds of madness, new methods of unmeaning. His individual poems are not so much instructions for living, then, but mad constructs that do not permit assimilation, and this is what the general trend of the scholarship on Corso argues.

Many scholars have said that there is no system in Corso's work, just the record of a man who always felt he had to break out of any system, any contract, however slightly it might have impinged on his freedom. In an important article by Robert C. Timm on Corso, for instance, he writes that "[t]he Beat sense is not to create a new dogma, but to free the ego from the idea of dogma itself" (35), and the critic Gregory Stephenson writes in his book-length treatment of Corso's work that he is "not an expounder of doctrines, dogma, or systems. Indeed, he is disposed to be deeply suspicious of all that presents itself as being absolute, definite, fixed, or final" (cited in Timm 39).

He could put such iconoclasm very charmingly at the beginning of his career:

> **Dear Girl**
> With people conformed
> Away from pre-raphaelite furniture
> With no promise but that of Japanese sparsity
> I take up house
> Ready to eat with you and sleep with you
>
> But when the conquered spirit breaks free
> And indicates a new light
> Who'll take care of the cats?
>
> (*LL* 11)

It is appropriate that cats would be the pets that Corso would put at the end of the poem. Cats have the same kind of irreverent sense of non-attachment that Corso seemingly maintained. And yet here it is crucial to bring in another viewpoint, because Corso's is a vision that is not utterly free of morality. Morality is a hidden constant in the poetry. Corso is worried about the cats. He has a sense of responsibility to them and wonders who will take care of them. This is what makes the lyric tension in the poem. Corso is constantly seen as a lousy father, a breaker of communities, a "saint of divorce," as he puts it in his poem "Marriage" (*M* 62), but he is in fact among the most moral of poets with morality, almost perhaps against his wishes, at the absolute center of his thought. Corso wants morality to prove itself, and so he is always testing it against evil. Corso always wanted to believe in goodness, and this theme is never far from his mind. In "Marriage," originally published in *The Happy Birthday of Death* (1960), a sense of anarchy reigns throughout the poem, arguing against what Corso considers to be the stifling nature of the marriage contract and its institutionalized clichés, but against this anarchist tendency runs a countervalent desire to be good.

The poem opens: "Should I get married? Should I be good?" (*M* 61). The emphasis on "good," here, is crucial. It calls to mind Corso's Italian American Catholic upbringing. Corso sees being good as conformist, which is a trap, but it is also a temptation, something safe, something that will provide him acceptance and continuity, as he would gain communal support. He goes through all the hackneyed images of the marriage contract—the visit to the parents for the proposal, the offering of the cookies, and finally the priest's question, "Do you take this woman for your lawful wedded wife? / And I trembling what to say say Pie Glue!" (*M* 61).

The condensed images of nonsense throughout the poem that stand against the marital logic are like hard knots, but they can in fact be untied to understand a deeper poetic logic. "Pie Glue," for example, which seems like something nonsensical to say to a priest, also rhymes with "I do" and more importantly can be seen to represent Corso's terror at his penis being captured in the glue of a "hair pie," a slang term in the 1950s for a vagina. Thus, the narrator's ejaculation of "Pie Glue!" is not merely nonsense but an objection specifically to the problem Corso saw as being trapped with any one woman. Corso's love of any one woman, like his love for one God, was subject to doubt and caused him to be skittish. Later on in the poem, this is reiterated when Corso is busy "pasting Tannu Tuva postage stamps all over the picket fence" that divides his yard from the neighbor's. This act should be seen in light of the historic squabble in the late 1950s over Tannu Tuva, an autonomous region between Red China and the Soviet-controlled Republic of Mongolia. Wherever Corso goes, he is deterritorializing, making things ambiguous, freeing up images that have gotten hardened, breaking icons, and trashing reverence for anything and everything. He creates autonomous zones, but if one works at what he is saying long enough, a different logic appears, which is a reverence for life.

At the end of "Marriage," for instance, the famous lines appear in which Corso indicates that it may be possible, as it is for "She" (from the novel by H. Rider Haggard), that there is someone for him. The critic Richard Howard perceptively reads these lines as an indication of Corso's general willingness to choose "nothing but experience" and states that "Marriage" is Corso's most important poem because Corso seemingly describes his entire situation as "necessarily about choosing" (82). Howard is quite right, but he doesn't see that Corso's "Marriage" is also a rejection of a specific *kind* of experience, which is that of a traditionally sanctioned marriage, and in favor of another kind of experience, which is that of Faustian magician.

Corso opens his poem with a reference to his "faustus hood," which he rhymes against the word "good," and ends the poem with a female shamanic figure, She, equally outside the realm of ordinary rules and customs. The only possible mate for Faustus is She. She, in the Haggard novel, is an impossible woman—intelligent, fruitarian, but also a serial murderer who abuses the powers of the state to destroy thousands of servants at a whim and who uses her own immortality to dream of world power. By invoking this figure, Corso is certainly indicating that he is ready to choose a certain kind of experience. Using the double figure of She and Faustus, Corso invokes the magic of both women and men in order to forego normalcy and escape any kind of human contract in the name of wizardry and magic and pure sensation and the need to change out of every convention that can be handed to him. In this sense, the subtle image of the shoe at the end of the poem should be recuperated: "O but what about love? I forget love / not that I am incapable of love / it's just that I see love as odd as wearing shoes—" (*M* 64).

Shoes provide protection, as a marriage does, but they also keep a human being from feeling—or at least that is the logic in the poem. It is this ambivalence about shoes, as a kind of prophylactic, that runs through the poem. Institutions of any kind prevent inspiration, which is killed by dogmatic moralism. Nevertheless, Corso's conscience is always troubled by moralism, and this forms a constant undercurrent in his poetry, although he tries to explode any and every institution and stable value by turning them into highly charged nonsense. What Corso does in "Marriage" is protest against it as an institution, as a boring humdrum affair, and instead asks why the church does not resuscitate the marvelous, the realm of feeling, of joy, that Christ promised us. Corso is willing to be good, but not at the expense of lifelessness.

In a very deep sense, the institution that Corso fights against throughout "Marriage"—and throughout his career—is the Catholic Church and its Thomistic vision of a coherent and stable universe, though at the same time Corso has a deep reverence toward that same institution. While most of Corso's critics have seen that he works against stability, none so far have noticed that it is specifically Catholic stability against which Corso's work is positioned and which forms the most coherent framework through which to read his work. Born in 1930, he would have been introduced to the Thomistic conception of the universe, because Thomist thought was declared the official philosophy of the church in 1879 by Pope Leo XIII (and continues to have this status today). The great chain of being that St. Thomas Aquinas articulated, which places things at the bottom, then animals, then humans, who occupy an intermediate realm, and then various kinds of angels, and finally God himself at the peak, is challenged by Corso throughout his poetry. In his poems, he seeks to make animals into people and people into animals and often turns the narrator into the figure of a god. The strangeness of Corso's categorical leaps can be seen throughout "Marriage," which is a strategically chosen event in that it is one of the rites most strictly supervised by the church. Corso challenges not only the rite but also the Thomistic conception of the great chain of being by creating new creatures when, acting in the poem as a "scourge of bigamy," he breaks into "almost climactic suites / yelling Radio belly! Cat shovel!" (*M* 62). In yelling these epithets, he is explicitly breaking up the great chain of being, indicating that a belly can be like a radio and that a shovel can be in the same category as a cat. The inanimate can be animate and the animate, inanimate.

An overarching problem in Corso's poetics is the struggle between the Catholic Church and Darwinism. Christianity was stung by Darwinism, and Christians cannot explain it away. When Darwin challenged the Thomist conception of a stable order of categories with God as the highest and animals and things as the lowest, he posited a new notion in which species themselves could originate, could be created, as a kind of natural process in reaction to various environmental forces. Suddenly, the natural world was not as the Catholic Church had indicated. The entire Christian world was threatened, perhaps especially in North America with the Scopes trial and other events making the collision of viewpoints into an intense matter of public focus. The threat to the theological view is reflected very strongly throughout Corso's poetry. Putting this conflict into historical terms, Richard Cawardine writes, "During the late nineteenth and twentieth centuries Christian churches in [North American] societies had to face a variety of social and intellectual challenges emanating from immigration, urbanisation, industrialisation, war and Darwinian thought" (200).

In Corso's work, it is important that the food chain and the notion that we eat and have appetites are positioned against the spiritualized notions of St. Thomas, in which the entire universe is one good entity, overlooked by a beneficent God. In the poem "Marriage," the reality of the food chain weighs against spirituality in subtle and understated ways. For instance, at the wedding, he first imagines, "All her family and her friends / and only a handful of mine all scroungy and bearded / just wait to get at the drinks and food—" (*M* 61), implying a tension between the spiritualized world of the religiously sanctioned marriage and the realm of appetite. This distinction is made several times throughout the poem, such as when he projects another image of a marriage in which he has to deal with "a fat Reichian wife screeching over potatoes Get a job!" (63). In this image, potatoes are an inexpensive food, apparently all the family can afford, and the wife is tired of eating them and wants something better. They cannot live on spirit. But Corso's narrator moves back and forth between these images, telling the milkman to bring him "penguin dust" (63) in lieu of milk, and when his wife would like to cook something sensible like a "roast beef" but burns it accidentally, she comes to the narrator expecting sympathy and is instead met with "Christmas teeth! Radiant brains! Apple deaf!" (62). These rather puzzling images that at first seem to be total nonsense can be seen to mix rather cleverly the spiritual with the carnal: Christmas, a spiritual holiday, is not usually mixed with teeth; and the next image implies an advanced state of spirituality, but instead of using the word "spirit," Corso uses the term "brains" to indicate the biological terminology as opposed to religious terminology. The third image brings in an apple but then links it to the human body, through the word "deaf," again conflating different levels of the great chain of being. The Thomistic worldview of a spiritualized marriage doesn't make sense for this narrator, who is trapped between two paradigms, the Thomistic conception and the Darwinian viewpoint, between the religious framework and a scientific framework of appetite, with a pagan framework always hovering somewhere in the background, as it is in the stanza about how if there was a baby,

> Surely I'd give it for a nipple a rubber Tacitus
> For a rattle a bag of broken Bach records

> Tack Della Francesca all over its crib
> Sew the Greek alphabet on its bib
> And build for its playpen a roofless Parthenon
>
> (*M* 63)

This strange mixture of pagan Roman, Greek, Italian Catholic, and Germanic Lutheran elements reveals the grab bag of culture in Corso's heritage that he would pass on to his child, a mixture unified in that it is all part of Western culture. Corso is a classicist, much like Ezra Pound, another Catholic, but he is much more volatile than Pound, questioning institutions and their power rather than attempting to side with temporal powers. Corso is a synthesizer, taking incompatible elements and fusing them together, quite consciously, to reveal something of the frustration of a postmodern era in which many incompatible paradigms have met but haven't yet been able to be sorted out. Corso is not making a bricolage, however, in the Poundian sense, in order to reconstitute the best of society, but he seemingly puts together disparate elements in an attempt to emphasize the difference of their various parts and causes them to explode in friction. In the poem "Bomb," written in the same week as "Marriage," Corso creates a similar categorical mix-up at the end of the poem when he makes the bomb into both male and female. In a lengthy interview with Michael André in the journal *Unmuzzled Ox,* Corso discusses these two poems.

> I wrote "Marriage" the same time I wrote "Bomb." That was a funny week. I did "Bomb" in about three or four days. I had a ball with it, because to get the shape, I had to type it down on paper first, and cut it out, each line, and paste it on big construction paper. So the glue was all sticky on my fingers, and then I said the heck with it, the publisher can always line it up. (André 139)

André also asks Corso about Richard Howard's overview of Corso's poetry in *Alone with America* and whether he thinks that Howard had got him right. "No, I don't know what he meant," Corso responds (140).

What I don't think Howard understood is that the poems were meant to be love poems to things that were impossible for Corso to love: the bomb and the institution of marriage. Corso always mixes together things from different categories. He is not simply discussing his inability to choose. In fact, the poems are well built and solidly constructed, but they are about collisions of values, collisions of worldviews, between which the poet must scramble because his central set of values is Thomist, and yet he cannot understand evil from within this framework as he tries to argue that the entire world, even the bomb, is beneficent. Corso chooses "convulsive beauty" (the phrase is André Breton's) over any kind of convention. He mixes things that one should love and things that are unlovable and talks about them at the same time in order to break up the mechanical aspect of thought, to put the incomprehensible into a jargon, and to make jargon incomprehensible, but also to create untenable images that explode in Corso's customary iconoclasm. What holds them together is his notion that everything under the sun is good. The poem on the bomb ends: "magisterial bombs wrapped in ermine all beautiful / and they'll sit plunk on earth's grumpy empires / fierce with moustaches of gold" (*M* 69).

That the bombs are "magisterial" and "wrapped in ermine" would indicate that they were male in gender, since magistrates have until recently been mostly male, but being wrapped in ermine also recalls women's ermine stoles, revealing the sexual ambiguity of the image. That they had "moustaches of gold" would indicate a masculine gender. However, the line is preceded by the phrase "Know that the earth will madonna the bomb," which indicates a mother wrapping the bomb in her arms, as if the bomb is Mother Earth's favorite son. Bombs, Corso then says, are "all beautiful," an adjective that, especially in the late 1950s, was used only for women, never for men. The bomb is androgynous, then, as is the speaker in "Marriage" who links himself both to Faust and to Haggard's female shaman She.

To one extent, Corso's mixture of genders recalls the Jungian project of finding and enhancing the opposite gender inside oneself through the anima and the animus, something that Corso often referred to in his classes at Naropa as the development of the "he-she." The logic is that of putting together things that are impossible to fit together, which was Corso's logic throughout the poems— where he places together unlikely combinations of words such as "Flash Gordon soap" (from "Marriage") and "Pinkbombs will blossom" and "Elkbombs will perk their ears" (from "Bomb"). These impossible constructions themselves make a *frisson* in the reader's mind, a marriage that is also a bomb (in the sense of an explosive device rather than a dud). Corso's most prevalent strategy is aimed at testing the coherent worldview created by St. Thomas, which is never very far from Corso's thinking.

St. Thomas posited that the world was simple, that is, composed of one part, all made by God. Does the universe have simplicity or complexity? Is it unified, or is it a war of all against all? Even in the images of the bombs just discussed, Corso links animal life with bombs, presumably part of the object world and not belonging to the great chain of being, or belonging only to the bottom step, but Corso makes them all lovable, as the madonna cuddles the bomb as if it were the baby Jesus. Thus, in Corso's vision, in spite of the complexity of the inventory of all kinds of bombs, and all kinds of marriages and people, there is a tendency to want to think about unity. Marriage is itself a celebration of unity. The key to understanding the poem at a deeper level is the tension between the narrator's friends, fraught with desire, and the various women and all the clichés that attend them. Is unity possible? Yes, but only through magic. If Faust could marry She, then there would be enough magic in the air for unity to take place for the narrator. Somehow the narrator is worried that it will take magic for him to be unified to the world, and he doubts if he can find a mate. What if he turns sixty "and everybody else is married! All the universe married but me!" (*M* 64).

Corso's poem "Written in Nostalgia for Paris," also published in *The Happy Birthday of Death,* can now be seen as more than nostalgia for Paris the city; rather, it is nostalgia for a theological worldview that has vanished, best represented by the era of Thomas Aquinas, a Christian-centered era in which man was still at the center of the universe and love and beauty were the central preoccupations of civilized man. The poem opens with a short reflection on this period and the troubles that the people of that era lived through: "How lovely that childgirl was! / The street was wild with raiders / but France protected their youth" (*HB* 68).

In these opening lines, Corso recalls the invasions of the Norsemen at the end of the first millennium. He also makes a humorous parallel with the France of his own day:

> I ran to buy her a flower but a rioter
>   needed blood for the FLN;
>   St. Michel sold the flowers
>   but it was cut off by
>   the Garde républicaine.
>
> (*HB* 68)

The FLN (Front de Libération Nationale), which appears in many of Corso's poems of this period, was a group of Algerian freedom fighters who wanted to secede from France and had nearly succeeded by the time Corso had written the poem. Corso links this movement to the roving Norsemen of the Middle Ages and their barbarity. St. Michel is also a link between the medieval era and Corso's own particular experience of Paris. The Rue St. Michel is in the very heart of the city, an area in which the Cathedral of Notre Dame is situated. St. Michel is also a saint in the Catholic Church. The Garde républicaine cut "it" off, meaning that his action of buying the flower was suspended by the military police of Paris, who were trying to stop the riot referred to in the third stanza. The flowers, or the faith of the church as proposed by St. Michel, was stopped by a temporal entity of the state. There is in these opening lines a tension between political powers and Corso's love for a "childgirl"'s beauty. For Corso, there are sectarian battles raging everywhere, but inside of this struggle, there is another battle going on having to do with Corso's love for beauty, for a mystical and even medieval world.

> I ran up Notre Dame and called to an eagle
>   that I might glide its eyes
>   upon the childgirl's whereabouts,
>   and did! Wings to my eyes
>   I sightsailed down the sad Seine
>   and saw her mightily stand
>   against the fish-hooks of the fishermen.
>
> (*HB* 68)

In this stanza, Corso begins to question the line between human and animal and divine. The childgirl is an angel of mercy standing against the food chain and its carnivorous aspect in favor of the divine sanctity of all living things, a leftover of the aesthetics of St. Francis and St. Thomas, who are represented in the Cathedral of Notre Dame. The childgirl also calls to mind Victor Hugo's medievalist novel *The Hunchback of Notre Dame* and the hunchback's love for a young woman, whom he protects. In this sequence, the childgirl is a Christ figure, associated with fish, which reverses the notion of Christ as a protector of fishermen in favor of a childgirl who protects the fish themselves. "Angel of fish! I called! It was she the child!" (*HB* 68).

As if all animals are in league, Corso asks an eagle to help him locate the girl, and through the eagle's eyes he sees her radiant form protecting the fish. At this point, the narrator begins a strange medley that mixes the medieval notion of the "music of the spheres" with an ecological concern in a move that is a striking microcosm of Corso's ecological and theological concerns.

> The harp of carp, the flute of fluke,
>> the brass of bass
>> the kettle of turtle
>> the violin of marlin
>> the tuba of barricuda
>> hail whale!
>
> (*HB* 68)

In these lines, a musical theme animates the world's seas, bringing the fish realm into the realm of music, which at the time of Aquinas was meant to bridge the realm of the human and the divine. When music touches the realm of fish, there is a sanctification of fish, too, as they make music apparently to hail the whale, which would posit a utopian world in which all animals get along together instead of eating one another. The medieval notion of the music of the spheres is a common theme in St. Thomas Aquinas's theology. Eco writes in his book on Thomist aesthetics, "Music appears to be the art most intimately and specifically connected with the aesthetic, and with pleasure" (130–31), and so it is natural that Corso's poem should reflect musical animals as a central aspect of the medieval experience that he describes.

At the same time, there is a major problem enunciated in Corso's poem, which is also a central problem in the Thomistic worldview. As Eco puts it:

Gilson, again, has remarked that the characteristically symbolical outlook of the twelfth century meant that it was a century unable to observe nature accurately. Nature indeed was celebrated, but no one thought to observe it. . . . In the bestiaries and lapidaries of the time, the substance of the beasts and stones was reduced to their symbolical meaning; the material out of which they were composed did not matter. There was something missing in the twelfth century, and in the symbolical mentality as a whole, which caused this absorption of concrete reality into a universe of symbols. What was lacking was any conception, however slight, that nature had a structure of itself and was intelligible in itself. This was a conception that entered the Middle Ages only with Aristotelean metaphysics. When the medievals began to discover the ontological and formal reality of things—when they began, we might say, to scrutinize them with a living and passionate attention—the symbolical universe lost something of its substance. (*Aesthetics* 140–41)

In "Written in Nostalgia for Paris," Corso mixes the animal, the human, and the divine and shows them as all connected within the divine. He thus asks us to move back and forth between the symbolical realm of the church and the natural world, as if they make coherent sense together, which they don't, but Corso's "nostalgia" is for a time that they did. What Corso is hoping for is a world in which he can link aesthetics with an ethical world, but this can't quite be done, even though the narrator appears to think he has done it: "That I have followed beauty—reward to know / there's a God for fish / I echo the prayers of all seas" (*HB* 68).

This triumphant finish to the poem presents a worldview in which all things are considered sacred. Corso's narrator has followed beauty, against the strict logic of military might, sidestepping the politics of his own time in order to step into the medieval worldview and bring flowers to a female deity. Against the mercantile notions of buying and selling fish, or against the Darwinian notion of a purely physical world, Corso's narrator is still solidly within the realm of St. Thomas Aquinas. It is a strange worldview for a poet to have in our own day, but Corso, having grown up Catholic, was trying to get the viewpoint of ecology to fit with the zenith hour of the Catholic Church, found in the works and lives of St. Francis and St. Thomas. It is in this sense that his "Written in Nostalgia for Paris" can be seen—as a nostalgia for a time when there was a view of the universe in which everything had a part, all designed by God.

Curiously, an alternative version of this poem appears in the *Penguin Modern Poets* selection of poems by Corso in which the line "there's a God for fish" reads "there's God for fish" (*Penguin* 20). The difference in the worldviews that this article represents moves the poem toward a multiplicity of gods, as opposed to the one God of the Catholics, although in both poems the deity is capitalized. "There's *a* God for fish" seems to make the view of the poem rather pagan, although since the *G* is capitalized—not usually done with pagan gods—the actual theological worldview represented is somewhat ambiguous. The poem was unfortunately cut from Corso's *Mindfield,* so it is difficult to know what Corso's final take on the matter was, but what is important about the poem is to see Corso's attempt to link his nostalgia for the simple beauty of Thomas's music of the spheres and the narrator's thankfulness in having "followed beauty," which leads him to a divine notion of the universe, which only makes sense within Aquinas's aesthetics.

As E. R. Curtius writes, "When scholasticism speaks of beauty, the word is used to indicate an attribute of God" (cited in Eco, *Aesthetics* 6). The Franciscan conception of the world was that all things are beautiful. "The authors of the *summa Fratris Alexandri* were like their contemporaries in wanting to show that even monsters were beautiful, in that they are beings, because every being is beautiful and God creates nothing that is not beautiful" (Eco, *Aesthetics* 44). When we remember that St. Francis interceded with the emperor on behalf of the birds, we can glimpse a sense of this worldview, which is so apparent in Corso's poem.

Catholic apologist G. K. Chesterton writes in his study of St. Francis that

[t]he world around him [St. Francis], as has been noted, was a network of feudal and family and other forms of dependence. The whole idea of St. Francis was that the Little Brothers should be like little fishes who could go freely in and out of that net. They could do so precisely because they were small fishes and in that sense even slippery fishes. There was nothing that the world could hold them by; for the world catches us mostly by the fringes of our garments, the futile externals of our lives. One of the Franciscans said later, "A monk should own nothing but his harp,"; meaning, I suppose, that he should value nothing but his song, the song with which it was his business as a minstrel to serenade every castle and cottage, the song of the joy of the Creator in his creation and the beauty of the brotherhood of men. (122–23)

This vision of the vagabond minstrel, singing of the joys of creation, can be strongly discerned in Corso's Catholic worldview, to which he returns as often as he departs.

Today, now that God has disappeared, or has been challenged by scientific rationalism, beauty has waned. We could once say that beauty was theophanic, that in its appearance was the greatness of God. Without God, how are we to explain beauty? It has no logic. No realm of reason can contain it. What is beauty in a scientific world? Can poetry still coexist with Darwin? Can the realm of the divine still coexist with the rationalism of humankind? In this poem of nostalgia for Paris and its great medieval tradition, the fish are beautiful and have high hopes, too. However, today we are told that a fish has a memory of about eight seconds. For it to conceptualize God, or anything else, is out of the question.

Eco also asks about poetry after the disappearance of God. "What was to happen to poets, after the world was emptied of its mystical significance, and when it became uncertain under whose inspiration—God? Love? Something else?—the poet unconsciously spoke?" (*Aesthetics* 162). This is the question that looms within Corso's poetry and is the reason for his nostalgia. The ambiguity of whether or not there is a single God can be seen in Corso's hesitation in the two versions over the article "a" and over whether or not to capitalize "God." The angel of fish that the childgirl represents is both a Christian and a pagan figure and perhaps is also an allusion to Melusine, a woman discovered to be half-fish in a medieval fable held sacred by the surrealists.

Notre Dame was built on the site of a former Roman temple and suffered extensive damage from rioters during the French Revolution, which dethroned not only the king but also the Catholic Church as the official religion within France. Atheism was not born on that day, but it was made into the official thought. Corso's nostalgia is for a time prior to that, in which his early Catholicism was triumphant. It is something that Hugo looked backed toward as well in his *Hunchback of Notre Dame.* Corso takes that nostalgia and appends to it a concern for ecology, linking animal, human, and divine through the figure of the childgirl to create a new religion that not only includes animals, humankind, and the divine but also centers on a feminine deity (we could think of André Breton's *Nadja* or of the Catholic reverence for Mary) to create a renewed sense of hope out of nostalgia for a past that had a complex and coherent myth, destroyed by the "raiders" or barbarians and represented by Darwinian rationalists, Marxists, policemen, and the political urgency of the FLN. This attempt to create a new myth was never discarded by Corso even in his later poems. It represents a major attempt to revivify the pagan childgirl myths of the early Mediterranean cultures within a Catholic framework, an attempt that would recur in Corso's work countless times. Even if it never quite caught on in the general culture, it was an attempt to create his own personal synthesis of surrealist and Catholic myth, perhaps too hermetic to be understood by the average atheistic reader, who may have grown up without any notion of either religion or divine beauty whatsoever.

It is often said that Corso received only a sixth-grade education. But he had another education in the church, and this seems to have been his aesthetic education as well. All his life he struggled to make this viewpoint make sense within the Darwinian paradigm, and thus when we look at his poems we can see them within this framework, even when they are sometimes reactions against this framework.

Even though he was a Catholic, Corso was also a child of the street, and his radical inclusion of the dirty languages of the street into high poetry is part of his religious iconoclasm. Words like "fuck," "cunt," "masturbator," "dildo," and "shit" were present not only in Corso's everyday speech at Naropa Institute but also throughout his poetry, often surrounded by flowery, more elegant language strictly reserved for poetry and by words that he invented, such as "flowerian" and "frankensteining." Corso is an alchemist of language, and he uses every word available in order to create a golden language of resistance to the psychic pressure to conform. His language is a matter of exploding conventions, putting disparate elements together only in order to explode any possible moral frame whatever, but he does this seemingly in favor of a higher morality, a personal morality, a morality of an older Catholicism that has been rigidly repressed by a Puritan government, which was in turn instantiated against Catholicism and its excesses. In a radio interview in Boulder, Colorado, Corso continually used four-letter words, even while being reprimanded by the deejay; he was finally turned off the air. Meanwhile, Corso demanded to be allowed to use this language, saying everybody uses it:

Corso: Well, I think human beings say "shit," man, I really do. Human beings use it naturally. . . . We're talking about a particular subject, right? Uh, what is it called? Release? Excrement?

Deejay: Why don't we not . . . yeh . . . why don't we not? (Corso, "Radio Interview" 22)

Mikhail Bakhtin discusses the use of nonliterary languages in *The Dialogic Imagination* in terms of the way they resuscitate the more formal and somber literary language.

> The novel senses itself on the border between the completed, dominant literary language and the extraliterary languages that know heteroglossia; the novel either serves to further the centralizing tendencies of a new literary language in the process of taking shape (with its grammatical, stylistic and ideological norms), or,—on the contrary—the novel fights for the renovation of an antiquated literary language, in the interests of those strata of the national language that have remained (to a greater or lesser degree) outside the centralizing and unifying influence of the artistic and ideological norm established by the dominant literary language. (67)

Corso is extraordinarily sensitive to what cannot be said, what is taboo, in any given situation, and he moves toward those areas instantaneously and without remorse. Like Bakhtin's novelist, challenging the boundaries of the novel, Corso challenges the boundaries of social discourse, as he did during the radio interview and as he does within poetry. He often spoke of assholes, tits, cunts, pricks, and so on, but he never meant to put down these things; rather, he intended to recuperate them into a divine logic in which beauty was everywhere. Like the other Beats, Corso thought the body was innocent, not guilty as it has often been held to be in Puritanical Christianity. In the introduction to Peter Orlovsky's book of poems, Corso writes, "He [Orlovsky] hails the human asshole as divine—He offers humankind an anatomical compassion for that bodily part long maligned, shame-wracked, and poetically neglect" (Orlovsky 7).

This strange acceptance of the body places Corso squarely among the millenarian poetry of the Beat generation. Corso was not Manichean. His thought was that the universe is good throughout, and he seems to move against Manicheanism just as St. Francis and St. Thomas reacted against the Catharist heresy (which was Manichean) in reasserting the idea that everything, even shit, was good. To the medieval church fathers, who sought to eradicate the notion that some of God's world could be bad, St. Thomas wrote that "God creates nothing that is not beautiful" (cited in Eco, *Aesthetics* 44). Even women's beauty was not to be condemned, as it was in the Protestant tradition. As Gilbert of Hoyt wrote, "breasts are most pleasing" (cited in Eco, *Aesthetics* 12). Presumably, there are no parts of the body that were not thought to be created by God.

Corso moves back and forth between accepted and unaccepted categories of being, mixing them up and laughing, troubling the conscience of ecological poets and hipsters alike. He is not the spokesman of any generation but rather the artist, constantly warring against any totalizing system, showing what others would flush, desiring to show that all is good. Corso is thus unrecuperable into any kind of Manichean system but rather can be seen as having an ongoing war against the majoritarian language of good and evil—and any language that segregates and is in danger of becoming majoritarian—in order to challenge consensus materialist reality. Against conventional thinkers, Corso destroys conventions in order to let in something anomic and irrational and iconoclastic, which is the idea that everything is good and that everything should be loved, even the atomic bomb.

When Corso struggles with the dominant cultural forms, it is always a good-humored struggle, and his Thomistic origins could go a long way toward explaining this. What seems like a terrible linguistic battle between classes in a fight to the death in the world of Mikhail Bakhtin is for Corso something as lighthearted as the way that St. Francis threw his arms around the neck of a leper. It is in this sense that Corso argued with the radio broadcaster, not as a fight to the finish but in a spirit of fun and joyous if irrepressible play. It is for this reason that Corso's transgressions are nearly always forgiven, as they seem so innocent, finally. As Chesterton wrote in his study of St. Francis:

> It was in a wholly happy and enthusiastic sense that St. Francis said, "Blessed is he who expecteth nothing, for he shall enjoy everything." It was by this deliberate idea of starting from zero, from the dark nothingness of his own deserts, that he did come to enjoy earthly things as few people have enjoyed them; and they are in themselves the best working example of the idea. For there is no way in which a man can earn a star or deserve a sunset. (*St. Francis* 88)

It is important to keep this cheerfulness in mind when we think of Corso through the lens of another doctrine, such as Bakhtin's Marxism, for although it may be illuminating, it may also cause us to lose focus on Corso's own starting point.

Bakhtin writes, "What we have is a never-ending folkloric dialogue: the dispute between a dismal sacred word and a cheerful folk word" (76). Bakhtin refers to linguistic struggles within the medieval era, in which the folk languages sought to contest the sacred word of Latin clergy through incorporating and surrounding it with the local languages, often more vulgar and more direct. This is part of Corso's struggle throughout his poetry and also one reason he has never been accepted within the reverential canon, except within the canon of Beat literature, which is marked by its rejection of official culture. The short scrap between the deejay and Corso went on after Corso was taken off the air, as the deejay bantered with various audience members, some of whom were glad for a return to Joni Mitchell while others argued that Corso was a great "poet," which was something much more important than a "deejay"—again questioning the hierarchy of who should be allowed to set the standards of speech. Michael Holquist writes in the glossary to *Dialogic Imagination* that in Bakhtin's work,

[i]deologies "battle it out in the arena of the utterance." Novelness "invades" privileged discourse. . . . Behind this aggressive talk is Bakhtin's concern that the reader feel the forces involved here as bodies, in concrete competition for limited supplies of authority and territory. (431)

The deejay explains himself to his listeners:

I just feel that if poets are here to communicate, and especially if they are here to glorify our language, then perhaps even these words could be put in contexts that were more artful. I think there are many people who feel as I do. (Corso, "Radio Interview" 24–25)

This struggle for authority is not just between a radio deejay and a poet but rather between two different bodies or organizations. It is between the federal government and a Catholic poet who sought to challenge that government's rejection of excrement. The deejay wasn't just speaking for himself; he knew that behind him was a whole realm of legal watchdogs. The business in which he worked was very strictly controlled by the Federal Licensing Commission. Had he allowed Corso to continue to speak, the state would have shut his radio station down. Corso must have known this, but he nevertheless chose to speak in the fashion he did. This kind of refusal to accept institutions as they are is perhaps indicative of a larger rebellion against the standardizing, centralizing grip of the American state in American culture and thus can be seen on a smaller level, as another uprising of the "folk" in Bakhtin's terms, or it is perhaps just an arrogant refusal to allow the "folk" to set their own standards, but it can be best seen in St. Francis's refusal to allow the bourgeois attitude to become his own attitude. There is always in stories of Corso a certain brio, a certain zest for life, which one could also see in St. Francis. As Chesterton writes of St. Francis, "The sense of humor which salts all the stories of his escapades alone prevented him from ever hardening into the solemnity of sectarian self-righteousness" (*St. Francis* 186).

Corso takes the position of both aristocrat and lowlife in the altercation, as does the deejay. Corso tells the deejay that he has the right to use any language he wishes, "as an old master of language" (Corso, "Radio Interview" 24), but he is also linked to the lower classes by the deejay's rejoinder, who says after he put Corso off the air, that "beat may look beat when you're twenty and you're thirty, and when fifty you might look like a bum." The deejay quickly recovers from this classist arrogance and says, "That's not meant as a blanket put down" (25). But the struggle over who should be able to determine cultural authority is quite amusingly the constant in this altercation, as it is throughout Corso's poetry, where Corso, an Italian Catholic orphan from the streets of New York City, links himself to François Villon, Shelley, various German romantics, Mozart, and Cellini and references high art contexts such as museums and symphonies in order to be able to discuss his street life and gain respect for aspects of the world that have been rejected by high culture. The strategy is hilariously insistent and surprisingly successful. Already in Corso's first poem in his *Mindfield,* there is the strategy of bringing down the high and mighty by showing the struggle between the two cultures, but as always he does so with a certain salty humor.

> **Greenwich Village Suicide**
> Arms outstretched
> hands flat against the windowsides
> She looks down
> Thinks of Bartok, Van Gogh
> And New Yorker cartoons
> She falls
>
> They take her away with a Daily News on her face
> And a storekeeper throws hot water on the sidewalk
>
> (*M* 3)

When seen from the context of the war Corso is carrying out from within his own cultural milieu and of the struggle between elite and vulgar or local languages that Bakhtin sketches out in his work, the woman's fall from high to low has more value than merely humor. There is also morality at stake. In a certain sense, the *Daily News,* the journal of the New York rabble that has no cultural prestige and limited circulation outside of New York, cannot compete with the international high art constructs of Van Gogh and Bartok and the *New Yorker,* but it has a certain cheerful functionality, and everybody who dies in New York City ends up in the paper's obituaries. High art couldn't keep the Greenwich Village resident alive, so what use was it? The upper-class woman who fell dreamed of immortality in terms of high art, but the following morning she was yesterday's news. And, too, everybody who dies ends up just as dead as the next person, and thus all distinctions between people are ultimately quite small. Corso's worldview isn't Marxist; it is Thomist. If he had been a Marxist, there would have been profound bitterness toward the upper-class woman reflected in the poem. However, there is no such bitterness or contempt. This is where Corso departs from Bakhtin, who was writing within a Marxist framework and showed hatred for the upper classes in his writings. Corso's poem has no trace of this. It simply records what happened. How would this Thomist or even Franciscan background translate into today's political terms? Chesterton writes, "Everybody knew, of course, that Franciscans were communists; but this was not so much being a communist as being an anarchist" (*St. Francis* 178).

Bakhtin wanted to provide a special place for the novel within literary discourse and show how different it was from the higher genre of the poem in that it included polyphony. In this way the novel was more anarchistic, or less inclined to create hierarchy, than was the higher world of poetry. The poetry of the Beat school is precisely anarchistic and novelistic in this sense, not wanting to be included in a self-enclosed higher art world but to interact and dialogue with the various languages of contemporary life. Hence its popularity: it was the first poetry to reach a wide audience in decades. Corso discusses this in his interview with Michael André:

Corso: Back in the fifties poetry wasn't going at all. Yale's Younger Series would sell 300 copies. Then after Ferlinghetti's and Ginsberg's books got going, and sold tens of thousands . . .
André: And how do your books sell?
Corso: Well, I know only by their printings. Some have had ten printings, some only one. But I don't know how many copies Laughlin comes out with a printing. I think 10,000 maybe. Ferlinghetti or Ginsberg, their things go into like 100,000. Mine not that much, but they keep on going, every year I get from these three books maybe two thou, something like that. (149)

Many critically acclaimed novelists would be satisfied with such runs, as the literary novel becomes more and more the work of the rarefied artist and less a popular art form. Corso's is the voice of the street, and it includes within it many voices, many folk rhythms, such as the poem "Song," which begins:

> Oh, dear! Oh, me! Oh, my!
> I married the pig's daughter!
> I married the pig's daughter!
> *Why? Why? Why?*
>
> (*M* 6)

This is certainly not an autobiographical confessional poem or a poem out to impress the reader with the writer's education but is almost the voice of a nightmare cartoon, which ends with the narrator taking the pig's daughter to the slaughter and asking again, "Why? Why? Why?"

Exactly who is speaking in Corso's poetry? Who is Corso? Is he an Italian American street urchin, or a member of a famous avant-garde, or an uneducated lunatic, or a self-made magician, or all of these? Bakhtin questions who is speaking in "[t]he laughing, parodic-travestying literature of the Middle Ages . . . which grew out of local folklore" and asks whether the author is "quoting with reverence or on the contrary with irony, with a smirk?" (68–69). Corso's appropriation of high discourse is questioned by his marshaling of low discourse, as in the usage of the crazily rhymed Mother Goose–type "Song" just cited. He makes use of Old MacDonald in "A Pastoral Fetish," and in "Sea Chanty," he makes use of pirate chants. Corso is never very far from popular consciousness, drawing on daily concerns when he writes poems to fallen cultural idols such as Elvis Presley and John Lennon. In every instance, however, he pulls back from becoming a popular poet playing to the crowd through his iconoclasm. He doesn't express the popular mentality so much as he questions it, but he doesn't do so from a snobby, upper-class perspective. He almost cannot help from making fun of everything he touches, and thus he never earns the complete love of an audience in return, but his fun is never cruel and always has a portion of humanity in it, showing a certain love affair with the cosmos. Corso, in essence, is an intellectual clown, and it is the charming figure of the clown that marks all of his work and is the subject of his second-longest poem, titled simply "Clown." Corso teases and tickles rather than comforts, always maintaining a distance from any ideology and any audience, pleasing only himself but remaining within a positive, life-affirming framework.

Critic Charles Altieri writes, "If we want to understand a general situation that contemporary poets might share, we need to construct a hero, however provisional a one, as our emblem for cultural pressures manifesting themselves in individual choices" (*Self and Sensibility* 1–2). In the poem "Clown," Corso seems to ask himself why he took up the model of the clown in the first place as a persona for his poetry. Others might see more serious figures as heroes, but Corso sees the businessmen, the knights, the aesthetes as being pre-embarrassed, and perhaps all that is left is the dubious figure of the clown. Corso positions the clown as a hero and the serious figure as a kind of idiot.

> I've no plumed helmet, no blue-white raiment;
> and no jester of-old comes wish me on.
> I myself am my own happy fool.
>
> . . . .
> And why do they say be a man, not a clown?
> And what is it like to be a man?
>
> . . . .
> It is time for the idiot
> to pose a grin and foot on the dead lion
> (the embodiment of the clownless man)
> Time to grow a mustache; suck gin;
> and win the hard-to-get lady.
>
> (*M* 76–77)

Corso here compares the clown to the idiot—the macho British exploiter of Africa who poses with his foot on a dead lion. The clown, he implies, is better. Why? Because the clown is linked to nature and to nature's cycles.

> If the clown were dead
> the month of August would be weighed
>   with sacks of sour wheat.
> Dead the clown, there'd be havoc!
>
> (*M* 78)

All the other models for the poet seem wanting: the hero, the businessman, the aesthete, all of them seem to have been destroyed by various critiques. All that is left is the clown. Without humor, wheat, the staple of life, would go bad. It is again necessary to show Corso's proximity to the tradition of St. Francis. As Chesterton writes of St. Francis, "[I]t is enough to record that while he wandered in the winter forest in his hair shirt, like the very wildest of the hermits, he sang in the tongue of the troubadours" (*St. Francis* 67). The Franciscans developed the notion of the jongleur, who was part troubadour and part clown. Chesterton writes:

> The jongleur was properly a jocular or jester, sometimes he was what we should call a juggler. Sometimes he may have been a tumbler; like that acrobat in the beautiful legend who was called "The Tumbler of Our Lady," because he turned head over heels and stood on his head before the image of the Blessed Virgin, for which he was nobly thanked and comforted by her and the whole company of heaven. In the ordinary way, we may imagine, the troubadour would exalt the company with earnest and solemn strains of love and then the jongleur would do his turn as a sort of comic relief. (*St. Francis* 81)

Corso throws away every other image of man except the clown, seemingly keeping this for himself, and thanks God that this "charlatanry" is part of his "organic pyx" (*M* 84). In his much later poem "The Whole Mess . . . Almost," he throws away Truth, Beauty, Faith, Hope, and Charity, as well as money. He even throws Death out the window:

> Laughing I threw it out, kitchen sink and all
> and suddenly realized Humor
> was all that was left—
> All I could do with Humor was to say:
> "Out the window with the window!"
>
> (*M* 200)

Like St. Francis, who threw away all his worldly belongings and lived like a pauper with an old coat drawn around him with a rope, Corso too wished to live as a Franciscan might, with very little in terms of possessions, throwing away even mental baggage. Corso's poetry might end on that note, but it doesn't. His iconoclasm, his humor, seem destined to stick around for some time because they insistently question morality instead of stating it or demanding it. Much of the moralistic poetry of the 1960s appears to be dated—the serious concerns with nuclear war and people's rights placed poets like Allen Ginsberg and Lawrence Ferlinghetti very high in their own time, but those poems are increasingly forgotten, and more intimate or humorous parts of their work are what remain fresh. Richard Eberhart wrote in 1956 that

> San Francisco teems with young poets. . . . Its members make a living at odd jobs. Ambiguity is despised, irony is considered weakness, the poem

as a system of connotations is thrown out in favor of long-line denotative statements. Explicit cognition is enjoined. Rhyme is outlawed. Whitman is the only god worthy of emulation. (24–25)

While Corso was in San Francisco at this time, his work is often ambiguous, ironic, and rhymed. Against the flat programmatic statements of many San Francisco poets, Corso's poetry is extremely subtle and difficult to puzzle out, or even to place in any kind of lineage. Corso's work, nonaligned with any specific program of his own time and more easily linked to that of the jongleurs, still has a freshness and an aesthetic urgency to it, as do many of the smaller poets of the latter twentieth century who do not seem to directly address the issue of politics, as poets like Vachel Lindsay or Carl Sandburg did in their own day, so much as concentrate on that which seemed funny or beautiful to say from the eternal perspective. Corso was not the spokesman of his generation, and he wasn't interested in finding out how he felt about specific political matters. He was the clown, and his work thus has a clear reference to his time but is not gone with yesterday's newspapers, because his themes are timeless.

Because of his clownish poetry, we do not link Corso with serious religion. Among the Protestant traditions dominant in America, laughter is not an important aspect of church-going, and the priests rarely act in the same way as stand-up comics. But in Catholicism, there is an ancient tradition of humor in the pulpit. As Catholic theologian Karl-Josef Kuschel writes in *Laughter: A Theological Reflection*:

> Here a look at history helps to break down constraints and to counter the deadly serious solemnity which has found its way into the liturgy of the churches. For in German-speaking countries for centuries preachers at the Easter mass used to provoke the congregation to violent bursts of laughter—not even being afraid of obscene pantomimes and doubles entendres. This was called *risus paschalis*, Easter laughter. (84)

There is something like this in Corso's verses, which retain a strong Catholic bearing, but this bearing is increasingly unrecognizable after many centuries of influence by the "deadly serious solemnity" of the Protestant churches on Catholic traditions.

Kuschel continues his reflection on laughter in the Catholic churches:

> Why is laughter so tabu in the liturgy? Are Christians afraid of their own laughter or of the laughter of God? Or have they so little faith that they do not even have anything to laugh at? Do they believe that liturgy and laughter do not belong together, because God might find this offensive? How reduced a picture of God that would be! Wouldn't this be to confuse one's own morality with the living reality of God? Didn't the Christian Easter liturgy in particular from earliest times take up a saying from the psalms and relate it to the day of the resurrection of Jesus Christ: "This is

the day which the Lord has made; let us rejoice and be glad in it"? But if this is to be more than a nice quotation, one might ask: what has become of jubilation and joy in today's liturgy? (87)

Corso's work maintains a strong Catholic identity and attempts to reawaken "Easter laughter." It is partially for this reason that his work has such a strong constituency and the reason for which it will remain popular for a long time to come. How confidently can I assert that Corso will survive the more politically obsessed voices of his era? Derek Parker in 1970 compared Corso to the various poets of the Beat generation: "He has shared in the over-publicity which has dogged them, but only Ginsberg seems more likely to survive as a lasting, insistent and memorable voice" (237). Critic Michael Skau, in his full-length study of Corso's oeuvre, makes a short inventory of those who praised Corso over Ginsberg at the beginning of the Beat movement:

> In 1960, G. S. Fraser could assert that "Corso's verse seems to me to show more talent than Ginsberg's," and John Fuller too asserted "Corso's superiority" over Ginsberg. . . . Hayden Carruth, in 1963, called him "an exceedingly talented poet who has written perhaps two dozen really good poems." Kenneth Rexroth wrote, "in my opinion Gregory Corso is one of the best poets of his generation." (128–29)

However, Corso's vividness and memorability have been offset, Skau writes, by his declining production and his refusal "to assume the politically engagé stances of Ginsberg and Ferlinghetti and devote himself to the politically correct ecological focus of Gary Snyder, positions that have helped to vaunt these poets into popularity and allow them to remain there" (129). The opposition between Ginsberg and Corso could be seen now as the opposition between a writer like Vachel Lindsay and a poet like Marianne Moore or Emily Dickinson—the one involved in the public debate of his time and greatly valued in his own day as a moralist and reformer and public agitator, and the others ever more intimate, religious, comic poets, more difficult perhaps, but who were just as reflective of their time and whose reputations and influence have slowly grown. Jean-Jacques Lecercle writes of a similar reversal of evaluation after the Victorian era. We can no longer take seriously the poetry of the great Victorians such as Alfred Tennyson or Charles Swinburne, but Lewis Carroll and Edward Lear are still fresh and readable, even though they were minor poets who worked in a minor vein (children's verse) in their own day.

> The exotopy of nonsense subverts Victorian values in that it mocks their sentimental, or self-righteous, seriousness (and it is a sad fact that, nowadays, any of Dickens' villains is more acceptable to the reader than that preposterous bore, little Dorritt—we prefer to read about Mrs. Jellyby, because she is ridiculous, than about the saintly death of Jo the roadsweeper, because we can no longer bear the pathos). And yet it also preserves what

is essential in them, in the form of rules of language and social behavior—we still recognize our modern preoccupations in the dialogic struggles in *Alice's Adventures in Wonderland.* (*Philosophy of Nonsense* 222)

In a similar way, Corso's very lack of a political program combined with his ridiculousness make him readable today. Many students like his poetry and instantly respond to it, and in large introduction to literature classes, they often pick his poetry to write essays about over the work of Allen Ginsberg, who is seen as the political propagandist of his generation. Ginsberg's poetry is more easily forced into the overdone politicizing of which the more intelligent students are rightly tired, because promoting gay rights, workers' rights, anti-pollution, and other ideas is too predictable. When Ginsberg was writing, very little poetry was overtly political in its orientation, and *Howl* was a fresh voice. Today, humanities education has overemphasized a politically correct reading, and this distracts from the considerable humor and sharpness Ginsberg also possessed. Reading him today on Vietnam or Ankor Wat or nuclear power is much like reading Vachel Lindsay on the politics of land reform or on the presidential campaign of William Jennings Bryant, as generous and insightful as those poems were in their own day.

Corso, too, has in mind a certain generous program, but it is put across with the humor of a clown, and it is the freshness of the humor that we remember rather than any particular message. Ginsberg is already found to be too self-righteous, too strident, too interested in things that now seem hopeless aspects of the hippie movement, such as finding God in LSD and spreading the good word of various Indian religions. Finally, there is often no depth seen in his ideas, no irony, no hidden recesses; it is all meant to program readers toward Ginsberg's viewpoint rather than lead them to question their own viewpoints, which is Corso's stance. Ginsberg's short-lived but very intense importance may come at the price of a longer oblivion, while Corso's star may continue to rise, as it is based on doubt and on standing against the popular currents of his time in favor of deeper traditions. Ginsberg was an important writer and was capable of creating great poems, but he was such a public personality and so intensely wanted to be understood that it is easy to put his work down as pamphleteering. Many of his critics have done just that. Ginsberg's work hasn't been well served by his critics. There is enormous mystery remaining in his body of verse, but he has never had the critics he deserved, nor have any of the other major Beat writers. They were caught up in issues of their day, and most of their critics, pro and con, are only interested in those issues. A larger philosophical and religious matrix is necessary to understand these writers. Corso, on the other hand, doesn't fit into any narrow political scheme and is not so easily shoehorned into a concern over lobbying for minority rights; for this reason, he has had fewer critics, but they have opened more scintillating questions.

Alfred Kazin, writing of Emily Dickinson, suggests a way of looking at Corso. "Not being a romantic or transcendentalist, she did not find Nature a consoling simile for Deity. Nature was a daily event. It often struck at her with a force that only she would have split into different realms of feeling" (123). Like Dickinson, Corso has not taken up any of the major preoccupations of his time. He is an original whose great strength is in looking at things through an ancient tradition. To understand Corso is to have to think long and hard about what he's saying. Kazin writes of Dickinson, "She saw things in Nature positively raining blows. . . . Her gift shows itself in an attachment so driving that it can excite and exhaust the reader, as it plainly did her" (125). Dickinson's strange and solitary existence, living all her life in the same place, would seem to contradict Corso's existence, spent as it was in traveling, living in a great number of countries, and knowing thousands and thousands of people, among whom there were probably hundreds if not thousands of lovers. Nevertheless, Corso remained a solitary unknown, unwilling to adapt himself to any program, even to the orthodoxy of his contemporary Catholicism. Kazin writes of Dickinson, "Yet she now seems to have been the subtlest, cagiest, most unafraid spokesman for a wholly personal, unspontaneous faith at a time when church-dominated Amherst, its spires as frequent as its red barns, seemed unmindful of orthodoxy's hollowness" (125).

To praise Corso at the expense of his contemporaries may seem callow, and yet criticism is canonization. This book is an attempt to make room for Corso in the postmodern canon on the basis of the profundity and intensity of his questions, which until now have been largely overlooked. Corso has been dismissed as a lightweight Beat or as a nihilistic nonsense writer; he is neither. While Ginsberg and other Beat writers have been extensively cited by postmodern French writers (especially Gilles Deleuze, who was well versed in American literature), Corso is unknown in postmodern circles. He is a peculiar and unorthodox Catholic whose thinking is original and yet intensely responsive to its tradition. After those orthodoxies that have upheld great reputations disappear, only the peerless solitaries will remain, and Corso is the prince of the solitaries, although ironically he lived within the great movements and events of his time. Imagine a poet like Dickinson moving in and out of the great events of her time, yet retaining her witty and flexible perspective, and you have something very much like Gregory Corso.

At the end of the Michael André interview, André asks Corso whether he was ever interested in Indian religions: "I don't think I am interested in any religion. I mean, I like to know all I can of all the religions, but not as a thing to fall into, I don't think that's possible" (158). Corso has no such interests in recuperating exotic religions, as did Gary Snyder and Allen Ginsberg; just dealing with Thomism was a full-time occupation. So was getting to know the history of Western art. Jim Philip writes that

> [p]erhaps the best way to recall Corso's deep concerns, and his sense of what connects him to others, is to consider that significant group of poems in which there is conversation with other writers, artists, musicians, and their works. Much could be said about the selection and juxtaposition of these figures, who range from François Villon to Charlie Parker. (72)

Philip then goes on to discuss Corso's poem on Uccello, which, he writes, "is a work as multifariously responsive to the origins of modernity, as his own has been to its culmination" (73). Corso, Philip writes, remains hesitant and humorous, a loner, throughout his work. "Here at least we are in the presence of the interrogative, as opposed to the affirmative" (62). Philip contrasts Corso with Burroughs's and Ginsberg's introductions to *Mindfield,* which he claims reek of advertising and self-promotion.

> The questions, the sources of anxiety, but also of qualifying humour, are many and varied. What gives an underlying movement to the passage is the restlessness of the older man who has found that age has not brought with it settled wisdom, but rather, as he puts it earlier in this long and interesting poem, "a multitude of various thought." (62)

Corso says in his interview with André: "Moralizing on things, this social shot could not be for me. I said, 'That's what it is and that's what's happening,' and I let it jump" (139). Corso's writing is more insistently private, a record of his iconoclasm and his need to stand outside the dialogue of his time and to see what was happening without imposing any kind of moral program. This is not to say that Corso's work is in any sense devoid of morality: to read it is to be forced into moral questioning. Corso's language is more surprising than Ginsberg's, more refreshing, and his routines odder and less motivated. They are also much less devoted, in the final analysis, to being recuperated as saintly by the literary industry. In Bakhtin's sense, they are more resistant, more thoroughly vulgar, and thus have an irreverent insouciance that, as Lecercle points out in the case of Lewis Carroll and Edward Lear, seems to age well.

Bearing this in mind, it is important to look at some of Corso's themes and to see what a curiously refreshing morality and aesthetic is at work. His most important theme is the great chain of being: can all animals be considered equal within it, and is there a God behind this menagerie? To this extent, his starting point is the thinking of St. Francis and St. Thomas. It is a worldview that provides a framework for all of Corso's poetry and most especially in his thinking about food.

Many of the Beat writers were interested in St. Francis. As Norman Podhoretz wrote of the Beats, "They talk endlessly about love; they are fond of Christian imagery, and especially fond of appealing to St. Francis in support of some of their ideas" (34). Bruce Hunsberger writes, similarly, that "Ferlinghetti, Brother Antoninus, and Kerouac frequently mention St. Francis in their poetry . . . . [P]overty, humiliation and suffering [are] accepted without rancour and even with a kind of joy" (160).

In the notion of food, however, Corso found something that seemed to stick in his craw. If we are supposed to love all beings, as St. Francis intended, and if all animals are considered our brothers, why do we bake and eat them? The notions of whether an animal is good or bad and whether eating is a spiritual activity come to the fore in his work, provide a powerful tension between two paradigms, and form the central core of his lyricism.

Arthur Lovejoy, in *The Great Chain of Being: A Study of the History of an Idea,* writes that the attempt to make sense of eating within a world that was wholly divine goes back at least to Plotinus and has hundreds of interpreters up until our own day. None of them seem to make any sense. Lovejoy writes that one of the ways out was to argue for diversity, that is, that God's plan was to allow the existence of every possible configuration of good and evil—"this world to be good must include every conceivable evil" (64)—but this thinking does not square with that of Aquinas, who didn't admit evil as part of God's plan. There were others, like Abelard, who argued that

> as a picture is often more beautiful and worthy of commendation if some colors in themselves ugly are included in it, than it would be if uniform and of a single color, so from an admixture of evils the universe is rendered more beautiful and worthy of commendation. (cited in Lovejoy 72)

The notion of a vast diversity, stemming from God, is perhaps most forcefully presented in Plotinus. Lovejoy summarizes Plotinus's viewpoint:

> The existence of the carnivora and of their victims is indispensable to the abundance that cosmic Life whose nature is to "produce all things and to diversify all in the manner of their existence." Conflict in general, adds Plotinus, is only a special case and a necessary implicate of diversity; "difference carried to its maximum *is* opposition." And since to contain and to engender difference, "to produce otherness" is the very essence of the creative world-soul, "it will necessarily do this in the maximal degree, and therefore produce things opposed to one another, and not merely things different to a degree falling short of opposition." (65–66)

What Corso makes of the lion and the lamb and their possibility of peaceful co-existence partakes in this problem of difference and diversity, specifically as it is addressed very clearly in the system of St. Thomas, as he tries to build a romantic-surrealist worldview that updates the Catholic Church while retaining the Catholic feeling of the beneficence of all things. Throughout his writing, Corso courts paradox, unafraid to play the fool and to believe in the impossible, and thus explicitly Catholic references remain throughout his poetry, even though he puts hard questioning to that system and remains what many in our materialistic age would consider a "foolish Christian."

Catholic theologian Karl-Josef Kuschel writes that Christianity has been considered a game of fools from the beginning. "Paul, too, was aware that discipleship of Christ and folly belong together. His gripping fool's speech (in II Corinthians) makes this clear" (90). Kuschel goes on further to say that

> Jesus's joy was evidently indestructible, as is proved by the history of his followers. And this indestructibility found its expression in a belief in the

resurrection of the crucified Christ by God. In this way the earliest community expressed their conviction that lamentation and mourning do not have the last word. (83)

Corso's strong Catholic tradition and belief is pointed to but never quite accepted by his critics. Not wishing to expose Corso to ridicule, his Christianity has been downplayed, as if it were something that he ought to have moved against as a mature adult. But this folly remains throughout Corso's oeuvre. In an age in which almost any paradox can be accepted, the paradox of a loving God having placed us on an ambiguous planet is laughable. And yet bitter, mocking laughter has devastated Christianity from the beginning. As Kuschel writes:

> Jesus continues to be laughed at to the end. Even on the cross he evidently had to listen to laughing contemporaries—in particular the rulers among them—who inevitably felt the discrepancy between his beginnings and his end: "He saved others; let him save himself; if he is the Christ of God, his Chosen One." (80)

Kuschel notes that "artists like James Ensor and George Rouault have with some justification depicted Jesus in the garb of a clown. They could not have described the deep significance of his life more aptly" (80). American theologian Harvey Cox describes Jesus in the following terms:

> Like the jester, Christ defies custom and scorns crowned heads. Like a wandering troubadour he has no place to lay his head. Like the clown in the circus parade he satirizes existing authority by riding into town replete with regal pageantry when he has no earthly power. Like a minstrel he frequents dinners and parties. At the end he is costumed by his enemies in a mocking caricature of royal paraphernalia. He is crucified amid sniggers and taunts with a sign over his head that lampoons his laughable claim. (cited in Kuschel 80)

Corso was part of a movement that opened out to other systems and ways of life. Allen Ginsberg and Gary Snyder were Buddhists, while William Burroughs dropped his early Protestantism and seemingly ended up worshiping cats, in the manner of the ancient Egyptians. Corso alone remained true to the paradoxical origins of his faith, even though he himself often put this faith down and ridiculed it. His greatness as a poet is dependent on a deep reading of Catholicism, on the Bible particularly, and his life's work can be seen as a dialogue with that tradition—reopening the question of humor and returning the church to its joyous origins.

2

Corso and the Great Chain of Being

Corso is often thought of as a comic sidekick to the more serious Ginsberg. As the leader of the Beat movement, Ginsberg received lavish critical attention, and it is no longer doubtful whether he will be included in the mainstream canon. Corso's "zany" work places him as a lightweight Beatnik, remembered outside the movement for his poem "Marriage" and inside the movement largely as a problematic character for whom the other Beats felt the burden of responsibility. During a gathering of the Beats in Grand Forks, South Dakota, in 1974, Corso was described by Ginsberg rather disparagingly as "the last Beatnik," and Gary Snyder labeled him a "casualty" (Knight and Knight 7, 23), along with Lew Welch and Jack Kerouac, as if Corso, too, had died—even though he was there at the conference! Corso's work has been consistently misread, even by his own close friends who do not see the seriousness of his themes. Timm and others have reduced him to merely a nonsense poet or a challenger of traditions. Corso is a Catholic writer, and his doubt is part of his deep faith. Questioning the doctrine of the great chain of being, Corso's humor addresses the conceptual boundaries of what it means to be animal, human, or divine, and he rearranges these categories, creating incongruous creatures that are half-animal and half-divine, showing both the divine and the animal within the human. The reasons he does this are seemingly obvious and yet have never been noted by any of Corso's perceptive critics.

Throughout his poems, Corso takes on the difficulty of being ethically human within nature, a theme touched upon frequently by postmodern philosophers. But Corso seems to outstrip even them in terms of his ontological transgressions and his understanding of their ramifications, thanks to his initial orientation within the Thomist system, which outlines these categories and their various faculties quite clearly, if rarely as succinctly as Chesterton. In this chapter, I will try to uncover the way Corso works against and within this system by focusing on his investigation of the ontological categories of animal, human, and divine and of what category is permitted to eat the others.

The basic question, as Corso puts it, is, can we be ethical when we must eat other creatures in order to live? If other creatures have the right to co-exist with us and to be considered as subjects, but humans must eat other creatures in order to survive, is there a possibility of ethics and morality in our world? The obvious answer is no. Corso's work for several decades was to see if he could find a loophole in this pessimistic theodicy, or theological explanation of evil, but he could not and often lapsed as a result into an almost Gnostic nihilism, in which grace was anywhere but here on this planet. The result of Corso's investigation is that he has been ignored, because his ecological suspicions do not accord with the contemporary optimism regarding the food chain as it is perceived by various pragmatic poets of the nature school.

At a midpoint in Corso's career, he began to write poems in which animals appear without humans. Completely overlooked by any of Corso's commentators thus far, and yet retained by Corso in *Mindfield: New and Selected Poems,* the short poem "Active Night," from the 1962 collection *Long Live Man,* contains many secrets to Corso's vision:

> A tarsier bewrays the end of an epical rain
> Burying beetles ponderously lug a dead rat
> A moth, just a few seconds old, tumbles down fern
> Bats are drinking flowers
> The lonely tapir walks the river bottom
> And up comes a manatee with a sea-anemone
>   on its nose

(M 114)

In this poem, set in the Malaysian rain forest, a variety of animals return to their feeding after a long, pensive wait. A tarsier's appearance "bewrays," or prophesies, the end of the rain. The action and diction turn to New York street talk with "lug a dead rat" as the end of the "epical" rain is reached. This ecosystem functions much like a utopian nightlife scene—every individual going about the business of pleasure—hence its title. Since groups mean the death of the individual to Corso, the two groups presented here, "burying beetles" and "bats," are explicitly or implicitly linked to death. The burying beetles, like pallbearers, lug a dead rat to a softer place, where they will then bury it and live off the fly larvae that will develop inside its underground carcass. The bats, with images of vampires flitting through our cultural image bank, in this instance "drink" from flowers, a sexy image, in which the bats, simply by following their natural instincts, end up all doing the same sweet thing together.

Corso's initial hypothesis seems to be that if everyone just minds their own business by following their own nature, then everyone can be content within nature. But the last few lines debate this conclusion. A tapir, a smaller animal related to the rhinoceros, is walking along the river bottom, feeling lonely, when he sees a manatee surface—with a sea anemone on its nose. The sea anemone, which eats small sea creatures, has apparently mistaken the manatee's nose for something to eat, and the manatee surfaces in this humorous close, an ending akin to a mousetrap on a clown's nose in a tiny circus. The tapir, we may assume, now relishes his loneliness, as his nose at least is not being chewed by someone else, so perhaps, the poem seems to say, it is better to be lonely. Corso, in a sense, denies the very possibility of community between species in the poem. Although the poem has a circus feeling, there is a bitterness at the heart of it in that creatures are forced to perceive each other with suspicion.

In the above poem, Corso appears to question the anarchism of the San Francisco Beat movement. For decades before the arrival of the Beat writers in San Francisco, Kenneth Rexroth and others had prepared the ground for philosophical anarchism through offering extensive lecture series. Ginsberg, among others, believed in noncompetition between writers and in hedonism, in which pleasure was the only end-goal of any relationship, as a coherent philosophy. Chesterton, already at the beginning of the twentieth century, was able to write that right-wing anarchist Herbert Spencer's books "became sacred books for a rising generation of rather bewildered rebels, who thought we might perhaps get out of the mess if everybody did as he liked" (*Victorian Age* 106).

Corso doesn't follow the libertarian program on the right or an ecological program on the left, nor does he accept the philosophies of "do whatever you want" that have swept through the West. He interrogates them, rather, in the poem "Active Night." Long before this poem was written, Corso had already written against an optimistic Gaia concept of nature in "A Pastoral Fetish," which appeared in his first collection of poems, *The Vestal Lady on Brattle* (1955). This book was the only one to have at least one poem in it written before Corso had met the other members of the so-called Beat generation (he met Ginsberg in 1950, and "Sea Chanty" had been written in 1945), thus showing that his anti-ecological suspicions were not conceived against the other Beats but were part of his original vision of nature and society. Poems such as "Sea Chanty," "Song," and especially "Pastoral Fetish" are the most obvious examples of this tendency in Corso's early verses, but nearly all of the early poems touch on this same theme. As Gregory Stephenson says:

> The central motif of the poems in this collection *[The Vestal Lady on Brattle]* is that of a predatory devouring or destruction of innocence and beauty. This theme is first treated in the title poem of the collection where an aged woman devours a child; a vampyric, cannibalistic act that is apparently part of her daily regimen. In "You Came Last Season," a lover consumes his beloved, while the poem "Coney Island" presents a comedian-crab and a fungi-man whose common and consuming interest is eating the feet of the

bathers on the beach. The sea itself is seen as a cruel devourer in "Sea Chanty" in which the narrator's mother is first eaten by the sea and is then unknowingly eaten by the narrator himself. In "Song," it is the "pig's daughter" who is to be betrayed, killed, and eaten by her husband. Other predators in these poems include the mouse-eating mandrill in "Vision Epizootic"; the "drooling Desirer" with his "long greasy coat, and the bloodstained fingernails" who stalks his human prey in "The Early Morning" . . . and the perverse, flower-murdering Old McDonald in "A Pastoral Fetish." (11–12)

A Pastoral Fetish
Old Mac Donald wears clod-hoppers
in his walk through field of lilac and dandelion
A storm-trooper, like a Klee tittering machine, he stomps:
Crunch one lilac here; crunch another dandelion there,
here, there, everywhere (he's got no mercy at all)
crunch crunch here and a crunch crunch there
crunch everywhere . . .

There comes a time when he's got to stop
take off his shoes; go to bed . . .
ah, that's when Old MacDonald's in his glory.
Green blood and mud-caked leather he digs the most.
He makes it a habit to sleep his nose by his toes
so that all night long he could snore in the sticky smell
of murdered lilac and dandelion.
It's the old bastard's greatest kick

(*M* 13)

Comparing the nursery rhyme figure of Old MacDonald to a Klee storm trooper and calling him an "old bastard" subverts the innocence of the children's genre and gives the poem an adult realism. It also calls art into question through the juxtaposition of the work of Paul Klee and Nazis as well as through the mixing of children's rhymes with psychokillers' actions. In a sense, Corso stomps on the innocence of childish rhymes and shows the bitter truth of life in a food chain, in which flowers can be murdered and nobody can say anything about it, because even today plants do not have subjectivity, and they are unlikely to get it before a court of law, even if animals are well on their way. The fun of destroying nature is something that almost everyone has felt—stomping on beauty, pulling the wings off insects, shooting guns at birds. It is something wired into people, who are, after all, predators with teeth and hard nails and stomachs they are forced to fill. The poem is not simply comic, not simply intended for laughs, however. It calls into question ontological categories of human, plant, and animal and asks us to ask again which should have rights.

The long philosophical tradition from Plato to the church fathers through Martin Heidegger denies animals the power of rationality and speech in order to rationalize our dominance over them. Critic John Lewellyn writes of Heidegger:

> [H]is problem here is very much Kant's problem: how to understand the classical definition of man as a rational animal without implying that Dasein and the animal are species of a shared genus. The same problem surfaces in [Emmanuel] Levinas's remark "We understand the animal, the face of an animal, in accordance with Dasein." Levinas, Heidegger and Kant are all preoccupied, like the Stoics, with the problem of safeguarding the dignity of man. (83)

Corso's perspective is mostly Catholic, but his poetic investigations sometimes veer toward Darwinism, which has had an impact on virtually every domain of humanist philosophy. Humanism assumed that humans do not have continuity with the animals. Darwinism conclusively proved, through DNA tests, that the paternity of the human species is linked to animals. We not only are animals but eat them, too, making us into cannibals.

Corso's humor consists largely of continually unmasking the foundational truth that we live in a food chain and must eat other creatures in order to live. The food chain, though never named as such, emerges in his earliest poetry, such as the poems "Song," "A Pastoral Fetish," and "The Sausages" from *The Vestal Lady on Brattle,* inscribing the unassimilable and disturbing content of the food chain within the feel-good rhymes of childhood. Within the self-cannibalizing convoy of subjects known as a "food chain," Corso relentlessly questions the possibility of a logical ethics, and the most he can achieve is an absurdist aesthetics. In the later poem "This Was My Meal," from the collection *Gasoline* (1958), Corso writes:

> In the peas in the upside down letters of MONK
> And beside it, in the Eyestares of Wine
> I saw Olive & Blackhair
>   I decided sunset to dine
>
> I cut through the cowbrain and saw Christmas
> & my birthday run hand in hand through the snow
> I cut deeper
>   and Christmas bled to the edge of the plate
>
> I turned to my father
>   and he ate my birthday
> I drank my milk and saw trees outrun themselves
>   valleys outdo themselves
>   and no mountain stood a chance of not walking

Dessert came in the spindly hands of stepmother
I wanted to drop fire-engines from my mouth!
But in ran the moonlight and grabbed the prunes.

(M 39)

"In the upside down letters of MONK," the poem begins. As Sami Laakso, who took a seminar with me devoted to Corso's work, pointed out, if we turn "monk" upside down, we get the word "know." What is it that monks would know if their world were righted? It is that we eat. When the narrator cuts through the cowbrain he sees Christmas—a critique not only of Christianity but of the traditional foods we eat at Christmas. Everything is busy eating in the poem, pleased with the taste of other things, and there is real fear as the father eats the child's birthday. Trees take off running, even mountains run to escape the general mayhem, and finally, even something as insubstantial and traditionally poetic as "moonlight" runs in and grabs the prunes.

Corso does not simply accept the ethical face of humanity. He would never accept the project of Heidegger and Levinas of "safeguarding the dignity of man." Cannibalizing other beings, something we must do by our very nature in that there is nothing we can eat that didn't first have a life of its own, seemingly undoes any morality we might claim to possess as soon as we grant spiritual being to other creatures. Morality is, Corso avers, merely a series of conventions or masks. Eating is a public secret that we must repress in order to continue the fiction of living in an ethical world.

In his novel *American Express,* Corso presents a scene in which a seal trainer's seal is stolen from him at a party and cooked. The seal meat is then passed around. Very quickly, the seal disappears. The seal trainer remains in the room, and after the orgy of consumption is accomplished, he is accused of having partaken:

"You ate it all!" Vatic accused Sgarlotto.
"Would I eat but a morsel? I could not. I too am hungry, but ate nothing. A sacrifice of the stronger need—disposed in ethics—the animal was my pet, sir." (128)

A few pages later, Corso pushes the cannibalistic theme even further. A statue of Christ is smashed, cut into small pieces, and cooked in oil. "'Carroll,' I said, 'have you ever thought of frying bits of Christ?' I had chopped off an entire foot and he watched it fry with horror in his eyes" (139). The implicit reference to the practice of communion is obvious.

Corso's character Mr. Plow argues that

[m]an can live without food. There are ways. But these ways are held back. There are certain forces, the restaurant industry in particular, that put all their effort into keeping these ways out of man's consciousness. Farmers, cattlemen, the entire scheme of eating would crumple were the ways exposed— (*AE* 133)

These lines are some of the few that Corso marshals against the general slaughter of everything by everything, a wall-to-wall bloodbath of eating and carnage spread from one end of Corso's art to the other over a period of more than forty years, from the first poem, "Sea Chanty," written at the age of fifteen, to the drawing of knights slaughtering each other, titled "Life Is a Battlefield," at the end of *Mindfield.* Unrelentingly, this is Corso's theme, which is mitigated, as Stephenson writes, by "love, humor, compassion . . . and the imagination" (19). But which is predominant in Corso's vision—the slaughter or the love? It seems that slaughter wins as long as we are materialists, just as it does in life, eventually, but Corso does hold out the hope of an afterlife and, with it, a sense of a spirit that can rise above the food chain and act beyond the nature that is granted to animals.

In "A Dreamed Realization," from *The Happy Birthday of Death,* Corso writes:

> Back there in God creatures sat like stone
> —no light in their various eyes.
>
> . . . It was Life jabbed a spoon in their mouths.
> Crow jackal hyena vulture worm woke to necessity
>
> (49)

The price of life, which is death, is also distressingly recounted in "Food," in the same collection. Even if in this short section the narrator abstains from eating, this abstention can be only momentary, an ethical pose permitted by a full stomach.

> The farmer will never love me
> Nor I, he.
> I'd rather go hungry
> Than assist his chicken slaughter,
> Attend his State Fair,
> Or screw his famous daughter.
>
> (*HB* 33–34)

In the second section, the narrator goes wild, indicating that the first half of the poem was Lent, which was only meant to play up the second half, which is Carnival.

> Goose legs stream from my eyes!
> I plunge my hands into apegrease!
> The plate avalanches!
> Baked lions, broiled camels, roasted fennecs,
> Fried chairs, poached mattresses, stewed farms!
>
> (*HB* 35)

Corso writes often of zoos in poems such as "Berlin Zoo," "Puma in Chapultepec Zoo," and "A Difference of Zoos," because they accentuate the captivity of animals, but he always implies that the metaphor is easily reversible to show the captivity of the animal-like instincts in humans. Corso shows a special affinity for those creatures that lie somewhere between humans and animals, in that zone that Gilles Deleuze and Félix Guattari call in *A Thousand Plateaus* "Becoming-Intense, Becoming-Animal," because they help to erase the humanist line that reserves a special place for humanity.

> **A Difference of Zoos**
> I went to the Hotel Broog;
> and it was there I imagined myself singing *Ave Maria*
> to a bunch of hoary ligneous Brownies.
> . . . .
> I sang *Ave Maria*
> for the Heap, for Groot,
> for the mugwump, for Thoth,
> the Centaur, Pan;
> I summoned them all to my room in the Broog,
> the werewolf, the vampire, Frankenstein,
> every monster imaginable
> And sang and sang *Ave Maria*—
> The room got to be unbearable!
> I went to the zoo
> and oh thank God the simple elephant.
>
> (*M* 111)

In the final line, Corso thanks God for the comparatively simple elephant. Corso's Italian Catholic upbringing, which upheld the dignity of humans but, at least in the lives of certain saints such as St. Francis, also upheld the dignity of animals, is a major source of lyric tension in Corso's work as it contrasts so painfully with the actual nature of the world. In the poem "Saint Francis," Corso writes:

> I praise you your love,
> Your benediction of animals and men,
> . . . .
> I see you with eagle,
> Penguin, vulture, seagull;
> Nor be it a bird
> But an elephant, a herd!
> All on your goodly compassionate shoulders.
>
> (*LL* 36)

If we are all fragile beings placed in an immanent world, rather than immortal beings in a transcendent one, questions of morality arise with the problem of mortality. If we must treat this world with respect, since there is no possibility of an afterlife, we are yet simultaneously prevented from doing so by having to eat our neighbors: the animals and vegetables. In the poem above, St. Francis does very well with birds on his shoulders, but then Corso piles on the heavier facts of the food chain: not just one elephant, but a whole herd, and one can imagine the saint being crushed into a blood pancake.

Recently, the way out of this horrible realization that "life is a battlefield" has been to grant animals subjectivity and to argue for vegetarianism. If this alarming trend continues, there will probably be laws passed against eating meat, just as there are laws against eating people. It all began innocently enough. For two millennia, male European philosophers held that women possessed limited moral understanding. Aristotle wrote in *Politics,* "For the slave has no deliberative faculty at all; the woman has, but it is without authority. . . . The courage of a man is shown in commanding, of a woman in obeying" (*Aristotle on Man* 270–71), and he cites Sophocles to the effect that "[s]ilence is a woman's glory" (271). In the *Summa Theologica,* St. Thomas argues along with Aristotle that women have "a defect in the active power," perhaps coming from some "external influence, such as that of a south wind, which is moist," which precludes them from the clearer, drier reasoning necessary for moral judgment (Aquinas 880). Today, such chauvinistic thinking is considered more and more antiquated, as Western democracies have accepted for at least fifty years the right of women to vote, to be educated, and to hold increasingly complex professional positions, including the presidency. Now to grant souls to men but not women is ridiculous. But must we then grant all of nature a soul?

A paradoxical double-movement is taking place in ecofeminist discourse, the contemporary French philosopher Luc Ferry says, in which women are held to be more "natural" than men. This would thus undermine women's right to "rationality" and "humanity," consigning them to the precise roles that Aristotle laid out for them 2,500 years ago—irrational, emotional beings whose "irrationalism" consigns them to certain positions outside the logos.

Ferry is a contemporary enlightenment thinker concerned with the destruction of human subjectivity among postmodernist philosophers and argues for rights among the human genus that he would deny to animal species. "To assert that women are more 'natural' than men is to deny their freedom, thus their full and whole place within humanity" (Ferry 126). Without full human subjectivity, women will have the same status as animals, which Ferry argues must not be accorded the same privileges as humanity. Rights and the idea of women's subjectivity were launched by the early feminist movement, properly, Ferry believes, only to be challenged unwittingly by more recent ecofeminists who would place women back among the animals.

Should animals have the same rights as women? Ferry sees this as preposterous. The animal rights movement is now trying to extend the notion of subjectivity and rights to other mammals and even trees, which, Ferry thinks, makes the entire idea of rights ridiculous. Which way is it going to be? Is humanity going to extend rights to women and animals, thus granting everything subjectivity, or will men also be stripped of rationalism and stripped of rights? To grant everything the right to vote would be fun, but would it mean anything to grant a worm the right to vote and hold office?

Without the ontological category of subjectivity, of a precious autonomy outside the food chain, there can be no vote granted. A worm would have to speak, as would a tree, in order to take its place in the legislature. Humanity, and nowhere more so than in the Thomist tradition, has always found reason to be what set it apart from the animals. Chesterton states:

> To be brief, in all humility, I do not believe that God meant Man to exercise only that peculiar, uplifted and abstracted sort of intellect which you are so fortunate to possess: but I believe that there is a middle field of facts, which are given by the senses to be the subject of the reason; and that in that field the reason has a right to rule, as the representative of God in Man. It is true that all this is lower than the angels; but it is higher than the animals, and all the actual material objects Man finds around him. (*St. Thomas* 22)

The decisions we make over rights for each category of creature, Ferry asserts, are not whimsical philosophical debate but will affect the legal realm and the way every category of life is treated in the future. What counts as food, and what is exempt from being eaten; what will be treated as object, and what will be treated as subject?

Christopher D. Stone's landmark article, "Should Trees Have Standing? Towards Legal Rights for Natural Objects," appeared in 1972 in the *Southern California Law Review* and was later reprinted as an influential short book (cited in Ferry xvi). While the notion of radical democracy for all beings continues to spread, Corso works in the other direction, a direction of many postmodern scholars, in arguing that humankind does not possess rationality, whether or not it is merely animal. Corso has gone further than any of the postmodern philosophers in asserting the animality of people, and thus he seems, from his earliest poetry on, to implicitly accept cannibalism. But there is in this acceptance the kind of moral teasing that Corso always carries out, a teasing that awakens uncomfortable questions of ontology and almost forces one back to Christianity to find a way out. Corso sometimes seems to argue that if animals do not have subjectivity, then neither do humans. Meanwhile, animal rights activists assert that "all animals are born equal and have equal rights to exist" (quoted in Ferry 3).

Ferry sees this spreading of ontological subjectivity as a continuation of the French Revolution of 1789 (3), a spreading of a radical democracy that he thinks must be curtailed, if it is not to end in nonsense.

> Law is always for men, and it is for men that trees or whales can become objects of a form of respect tied to legislation—not the reverse. . . . The most common response among [ecological] fundamentalists is that it is the "biosphere" as a whole, because it gives life to all beings, or at the very least

allows them to sustain their existence. But the biosphere gives life both to the AIDS virus and to the baby seal, to the plague and to cholera, to the forest and to the river. Can one seriously claim that HIV is a subject of law, equal to man? (139–40)

Ferry asserts that humanity has greater freedom than animals, and this makes us separate and special, above the general slaughter. Animal cultures, he says, persist over thousands of years without any change. Human cultures are constantly changing, constantly evolving, and thus we have a freedom that distinguishes us from animals,

> for unlike an animal, which is subject to the natural code of instinct particular to its species more than to its individuality, human beings have the possibility of emancipating themselves, even of revolting against their own nature. It is by so doing, that is, by breaking away from the order of things, that one gives proof of an authentic humanity and simultaneously accesses the realm of ethics and culture. (115)

Is Ferry's argument more than simple conservatism, a hope to keep things as they are? If nobody has rights, then the world is a free-for-all, in which murder is as legitimate as negotiation. If everything has rights, then to step on a flower inadvertently would mean that one could be charged with murder. Is there a balance that we could strike between these two extremes?

Ferry wants us to see that human beings are able to think over a certain period of time, outside of instinct, outside of natural needs, which allows us to create a culture, a legal realm, thanks to the length of our memory (a pigeon, by comparison, has a memory of approximately twelve seconds [Kendrick]). Our speech and the length of our memory permit us to think and communicate important moral concepts that other animals cannot access.

It is Gregory Corso's cynical laughter over this so-called separation of humans and animals that led him to write a poem in praise of the animalistic aspects of man during the first hours after President John F. Kennedy's assassination. In the first part of this poem, Corso sees murder as legitimate, as a part of a long tradition going back to Rome, back through the animal species, back to the very beginning of life. Corso doesn't see anything "emancipating" in man throughout the greater part of this poem. There are no ethics because there is no such thing as an "authentic humanity" and so no such thing as an authentic culture, either. The radiant moments of humankind are dimmed by its blacker moments, which are part of our legacy in a natural world. This doesn't mean he's happy about it: it's devastating to him, even if it is also funny:

> Come you illiterate creepy dumbbells harken the cry of
> the *true* Assassin
> I damn! I hail!
> I summon the Blessed Lord of the Ice Cold Nanook Country

and eat raw seal meat with Him!
I curse the earth in Space and in Time!
I pee upon the Evolution of the Rocks!
I weep upon the first living things!
Bang my fists on the unknown age of the world!
I vomit up Natural Selection and the Change of the
Species!
I laugh like a sick dinosaur o'er
   the invasion of the dry lands by Life!
I smirk at the butterfly like a pimply-faced stumble-bum!
By the wings I yank by the wings the wings the lovely wings
By the throat I smote the Age of the Reptile!
So too the Age of the Mammal!
So too O very much so the Ancestry of Man!
Man descended from a walking ape!
I awake the lazy greasy Neanderthal and spit in his big sad
   stupid eye!
I pummel my Colt .38 into the iron skin of the Palaeolithic
   muralist!
I look contemptuously down upon the screwed-up Neolithic
   creep!

(from "Lines Written Nov. 22,
23—1963—in Discord," *M* 141)

Corso sees the good in people, the democratic, freedom-loving part, as being hopelessly eclipsed by a demonic, animalistic agency that has made its way into every living thing. "I have made goats of every King every Pope every puny club-footed Elect" (*M* 141). Corso sees even God himself as being merely an animal, or as having animal faculties, in the poem "God Is a Masturbator" (*EF* 112). There is nothing that is not immanent and nothing that is not damned and fatally flawed and utterly animalistic to the core, Corso implies, and yet at the end of "Lines Written Nov. 22, 23—1963—in Discord," Corso contradicts this perception:

When a captain dies
The ship doesn't sink
And though the crew weeps the loss
The stars in the skies
Are still boss.

(*M* 143)

Corso is not willing to accept the human dignity of the "face" as posited by Heidegger and Levinas; and yet he has been unwilling to dispense with all spiritual traditions and regard humans as vicious and unredeemable animals, as the end of the above poem demonstrates. Cultural institutions outlast single individuals and provide a kind of stability to humanity, a stability that animals attain through their unchanging qualities. The heavens still exist and still have power over humankind.

While Levinas, Heidegger, and Kant are preoccupied with "safeguarding the dignity of man," Corso increasingly questions the "face" of this civilized, alienated man and posits a lurking rapist who murders innocent schoolgirls, and yet he is never comfortable simply condemning humankind. "The kind man behind the kind man / Is the kind of man who could and can" (*EF* 77), writes Corso about British sexual psychokillers.

As Corso distances himself from his early Catholicism, his writing grows darker, he turns to heroin and drink, and his output diminishes at the same time as he begins to explore Gnosticism and other heresies and to develop a Manichean worldview. Corso does still offer optimistic lyric efforts into the 1970s and 1980s, but the poems seem to depend on human magic rather than on a vision of nature as being wonderful all by itself; for example, see "Sunrise" (*M* 166), in which Corso depicts the poet as Hermes, or "Alchemy," in which Corso sees nature itself as an alchemist, uniting a Franciscan view of nature with his later more magic-oriented vision: "A bluebird / alights upon a yellow chair / —Spring is here" (*M* 202).

St. Thomas's entire theology was built on defeating the Manichean heresies by proclaiming that all of creation was divine and that Satan, who had been created by God, was the originator of evil. Corso gradually fell away from this worldview and began to see evil as an aspect of the world that could never be gotten rid of. The central problem for him lay in eating. If we eat other creatures, then this entire world has to be evil.

From 1958 to 1962, Corso produced three ebullient volumes in four years. Corso says in his interview with Robert King in *The Beat Vision* that he began to take drugs at the age of thirty-three, which would have been in 1963 (179). Was this in response to the Kennedy assassination, which threw him into "discord," or was his moral disarray already in effect when the assassin(s) destroyed the first Catholic president? After 1963, there have been only two complete volumes of Corso's poetry, and these later poems (when they are successful, such as "Of One Month's Reading of English Newspapers" on rape) are even more bitter, as the qualifying aspect of humor is often muted or even extinguished.

It would be a mistake to see Corso as having had one event or one moment in time in which he changes from optimism to despair. "Of One Month's Reading of English Newspapers," printed in *Elegiac Feelings American* in 1970, was originally published, according to Michael Skau's bibliography, in the *Evergreen Review* in 1962 (206). In fact, Corso veers between wild optimism and dark pessimism throughout his career but never loses faith in poetry. A continuity appears in his work, and if anything his poems are characterized by too much faith in people, even if he occasionally gives in to dark doubts.

Corso himself claims in *The Riverside Interviews* with Gavin Selerie that the missing middle period in his work came not from a lack of faith in poetry or in God but rather because a woman stole it.

Corso: It was in two suitcases and I had all my letters from Kerouac and every-thing and I was living in this fucking Chelsea Hotel in New York City. A supposed friend, a woman, who's a very rich lady and all this shit, a poet named Isabella Gardner, got hold of it; once it was in her hands, it was gone.

Selerie: What did she do with it?

Corso: Well, she was very jealous of me, you see, 'cause there again . . . Remem-ber I gave you my background—Prison guy, schoolkid, and yet I was having the ball-game with the poetry. I was really collecting, I was making it, I was writing the goodies and she knew that that was my book. So there was a big gap—1970–1974, four years' work, gone. I got so fucking pissed at that shit, man, I said, "*Forget* it" for two years. That led up to 1976 and I said, "Hey wait a minute, the poet's not gone. They can fuck my poetry around but they didn't fuck the poet around." (32)

The interview continues and Selerie again says, "You tend to have long inter-vals between publishing books."

Corso: I told you—the losses—they're stolen.

Selerie: That explains all?

Corso: Yes. (33)

The apparent break in production was not because Corso could not find a transcendent truth, and although he could not find the actual world to his taste either, as long as there remained the "drudgery and insult of food" (*AE* 104), his poetry was continuous, even if the publishing wasn't. Unlike the more popular American eco-poets such as the Luddite Wendell Berry or Zen naturalist Gary Snyder, who find delicious truths that we can live with and then point the Way, Corso finds despicable truths that he cannot live with and reveals his fruitless attempts at ethical reconciliation, but he never stopped writing.

Corso is treated with concern by Gary Snyder in an interview in *The Beat Vision* collection. Snyder suggests a confrontation with Corso because Corso doesn't share the consensus vision that the Beats were coming to in the 1970s.

It's very interesting that we find ourselves so much on the same ground again, after having explored divergent paths; and find ourselves united on this position of powerful environmental concern, critique of the future of the industrial state, and an essentially shared poetics, and only half-stated but in the background very powerfully there, a basic agreement on some Buddhist type psychological views of human nature and human possibili-ties. (Knight and Knight 3–4)

Corso doesn't fit into any of this—denying the relevance of organized reli-gion, denying a critique of anything. He writes down what he sees and is not a social reformer at all. On the other hand, "in some ways I'm a good Maoist," Snyder says (15), echoing the Maoist program of a cultural revolution that was popular at the time (1974), while Corso isn't with the program at all. Snyder considers him to be a problem.

> I haven't really tried to deal with where Gregory's at; but he's had a lot of self-created hard times. . . . But we're all responsible collectively in some sense for Gregory, so what I would like to do is all of us (Lawrence, myself, and Allen and so forth) sit down and have a collective meeting with Gregory. That's what I'm going to suggest, too. I've learned how to do that where I live. Collective meetings of mutual and personal self-criticism. (24–25)

Snyder's Maoist-inspired program of "mutual and personal self-criticism" would indicate that unless Corso was willing to get with the program, he would be excommunicated, or worse. Snyder actually suggests violence to one of the interviewers who is having a hard time understanding one of his friends who has adopted an Eastern viewpoint. "I'd kick the fuck out of him, that's all," Snyder says. And then he says, blandly, "Say, 'Make sense, you son of a bitch.' That's what I do with people" (27). Such truculence, even when presented in a jocular manner, overrides the delicate problem of understanding Corso on his own terms rather than forcing him to make sense on Snyder's terms.

Corso's thinking undoes the Buddhist ecologist's insistence that nature make sense. But does the food chain make sense? Can it be understood? Should Corso be stomped for this? Can Corso be forced to make sense on Snyder's Buddhist ecological grounds, in which Snyder wants to write about nature, without including any of nature's terror, its nightmarish aspect, in which creatures die without dignity in the maws of others? Is it possible to maintain a sacred perspective of a world in which predators race through the jungles, killing things for nutrition? If Snyder was asked (by a group of writers sympathetic to Corso) to make more sense on Corso's terms, he might find it difficult to speak as well.

Corso shares a similar problem with many postmodern philosophers and Gary Snyder: he questions the special place accorded humans in Western philosophy's arrogant relationship to the natural world. But Corso came from a world of gangs, prisons, and hard beatings as he grew up in New York City. He doesn't have the kind of privileged background Gary Snyder or Allen Ginsberg or most other members of the cultural elite took for granted in their childhood, and thus they can perhaps more easily idealize the world. Jacques Derrida, the well-to-do French postmodernist, says in his interview "Eating Well":

> [O]ne must begin to identify with the other, who is to be assimilated, interiorized, understood ideally. . . . The sublime refinement involved in this respect for the other is also a way of "Eating well," in the sense of good eating but also doing well to eat. (115)

This project of "respect for the other" whom we must eat has been left out of Western civilization since Plato said that animals were outside of the realm of Being, unworthy of respect, because they could not speak. Derrida asserts that we ought to at least have respect for the animals we devour and say as much, as if that would somehow matter to them. Corso distrusts all speech and points out that "[e]verything that is said is said by man—I say it is stupid, disgusting, to listen!" (*AE* 143).

In an interview with Jean-Luc Nancy, Derrida, too, questions the artificial boundary between humans and animals. He extends subjectivity as far as the vegetable realm, but my question is, Does this matter, since we are still eating vegetables? Should a vegetable say, "Thanks for the rights, Jacques?" as it is being spread over his steak tartare in thin slices to make a tasty accompaniment?

J-LN: When you decide not to limit a potential "subjectivity" to man, why do you then limit yourself simply to the animal?

JD: Nothing should be excluded. . . . The difference between "animal" and "vegetal" also remains problematic. (106)

Corso sometimes looks halfheartedly to the American Indian for a philosophical answer to the dilemma, but only for laughs. The American Indians considered humans to be members of the same family as animals, making no crucial distinction between them, even though they ate their brothers willingly. Does it matter if we treat animals and vegetables as brothers and sisters as long as we still eat them, or does that just augment the horror? Can we return to that early table the Pilgrims were offered by the Indians and not have any moral compunctions? Gregory Corso describes the collision of cultures in the Massachusetts Bay Colony in his "Spontaneous Requiem for the American Indian": "Pilgrim blunderbuss, buckles, high hat, Dutch, English, pat- / ent leather shoes, Bible, pray . . . o but feast, turkey, corn, pumpkin, sweet confused happy hosty / guests, Iroquois, Mohawk, Oneida, Onondaga, Thanksgiving!" (*EF* 16). Can we make friends with the beings that we eat? After all, their brothers and sisters (termites, worms, and the like) in turn will eat us when we die. Corso opened this question and was aware of its difficulty some years before the major postmodern thinkers began dodging it. In contrast to the easy righteousness of the ecological movement, which shares the apparently common American Indian belief that animals willingly gave up their lives to be food for humans, it is obvious that humans are the narrators in this picture.

How it is that ecological fundamentalists and their Native American counterparts can eat things they consider to be human, or at least on the same level as themselves, is a puzzle. Animals are not saints. They eat whatever they can, without apparent attacks of conscience. Meanwhile, they try to protect their own skins. No human would willingly feed an animal with his or her own body, so it seems rather arrogant to assume that an animal would want to feed us. Even berry bushes have spikes all over them to protect their fruit, so I don't believe that the bushes think of themselves as willingly giving up their fruit.

Corso depicts man as a member of an obscene and comical animal world and presents another aspect of Indians in "Spontaneous Requiem for the American

Indian." At the end of the poem, an Indian on a motorcycle screams into New York to sit at Horn and Hardart's with Western women, and Corso writes, "O, he's an angel there / though sinister sinister in shape of Steel Discipline smoking / a cigarette in a fishy corner in the night . . ." (*EF* 17). Corso doesn't buy the idea of Indians as angels of perfect ecological insight. After all, they too slaughtered the buffalo, as well as each other, before whites came, and when they did come, they burned the white settlers, scalped them, and torched their houses.

> Dust, hordes, tribes, death, death, blonde girls to die, gowns
> of ladies to burn, men of redcoats and bluecoats to
> die, boys to drum and fife and curse and cry and die,
> horses . . . to die, babies . . . to die
>
> (*EF* 16)

in the miserable "battlefield of life" (*M* 265). Corso, always questioning categories, doesn't buy the saintliness of Indians but insists in his poetry on showing their sinister side. They were beaten by superior technology, and Corso is sometimes sentimental about that, but more often he is simply realistic, recognizing that Indian tribes before whites came slaughtered one another and held each other as slaves. Michael André discusses this with Corso in his interview:

André: One of the questions I was going to ask you was about your elegy for the Indians. You were interested in the same thing, that say, Gary Snyder and Allen [Ginsberg] are interested in.

Corso: Yes.

André: But you handle it in a completely different way. You just elegize them and describe them today, rather than attempt to revivify their whole value system.

Corso: Yes. Now there you go. I wrote that Indian thing very early, in 1958. That was not done when the Indians started, you know—the opening up with the Blacks and civil rights. The feeling was the loss and I still feel that today. Of course they didn't build the nation, but the land that they did have and the life they did have is gone. There are the hippies and the new Indians, but it will never be the same, it's changed. I look upon it as a stain . . . There is nothing I could do for the Indians before they went, although there are nine million Indians today, they say, the same as there was when the white man first came to this country.

André: Really?

Corso: Less buffalo, of course, but the same number of Indians. The genocide wasn't exactly genocide. It was the genocide of taking their land. (129–30)

At least in one place in the interview, Corso dismisses the Indian way of life as something as worthy of study as Mediterranean culture:

André: In many ways there is as much left to study in the American Indian civilization as in Greek civilization.

Corso: Oh, not in architecture, anyway, except the pueblo. I would think the

Indians had a better way of life, but . . . The Greeks could have had technology. The Renaissance picked up on that, through the Byzantine; Giotto learned the two dimensional Christ from the Byzantine. (154)

Corso's dismissal of Indians because they had no architecture doesn't take into account that most Native Americans were nomads and thus had no settled domiciles; nor was there a professional category of architect devoted to distinctive housing design within the tribes. Corso's response makes sense, nevertheless, because to look to American Indians for answers to the problems of a settled society whose members do live in cities—especially when those answers are now proposed by anthropologists and nature poets who work in universities within a Western tradition—creates a jumble. Can answers come from other paradigms while being sensitive to the reality of Western culture? The Western world was superior to the Indian world in at least one area—martial ability. Just as the Iroquois Indians were superior to the Delaware and used that advantage to make the Delaware warriors lay down their arms and take the names of women (Parkman 10–17), so the western Europeans destroyed Native American cultures and made them lay down their weapons.

Now the West is about to be conquered by Native American ontology, since many have complained that Western ontology is inadequate. The Western viewpoint saw the world as composed of things, with humans alone as having a soul, whereas the Indians lived in an immanent world where everything, even trees and animals and tools, had subjectivity and thus could not be used without some sense of respect. But how does one eat something respectfully? If someone were to eat me, I wouldn't care if they did it respectfully. What would it matter? If a mosquito were to say a short prayer while taking blood out of my foot, it would just make me more irritated. Thanks to the ecology movement, Western civilization is going back to the notion that everything is imbued with a spirit. But for what good reason?

We invite each other out to dinner, celebrate good times over food, and go happily to the grocery store, but we are rarely conscious that we are eating other beings. Would it be a better thing if we were to realize it? We can recognize and empathize with animals' sufferings, and we can even find some signs of sentience in plants, but our lives are based on their exploitation. As the animal rights movement declares that all living beings are created equal, Corso's poetry will be increasingly relevant to describing and understanding the ethical dilemma that we face.

The spiritual diaspora accepted in the Western tradition beginning in Plato and continuing with the Gnostic theologians, in which man is trapped here in an alien body and on an alien planet, was an initial answer to the question of evil. They concluded that there is evil on this earth because this is *not paradise*. Paradise was in heaven. Early theologians sought to remove the animal aspects of humans in order to recreate heaven on earth and prepare us to go to heaven.

Corso's comic poetry, by bringing the violent animal nature of people back into the center of the *polis,* opens up an ontological conduit that goes both ways. It challenges the dignity of humans. Not only does "humanity" flow into animals but "animality" flows into humanity.

Corso's Western orientation seems at first to be irreligious. He appears to accept only facts, the factual nature of the world, and sees the world like a machine, engineered for comfort. He seems to have much in common with postmodernist Gilles Deleuze, who writes, "What is required is humor, as opposed to the Socratic irony or to the technique of the ascent" (*Logic* 135).

> Deeper than any other ground is the surface and the skin. . . . The tragic and the ironic give way to a new value, that of humor. For if irony is the co-extensiveness of being with the individual, or of the I with representation, humor is the co-extensiveness of sense with nonsense. (*Logic* 141)

Deleuze concludes: "The values of humor are distinguished from those of [Socratic] irony: humor is the art of surfaces and the complex relations between the two surfaces" (248). Corso's humorous writing is ahead of its time in America because it takes up the Nietzschean problem of a world without transcendent values, but he doesn't just stop there and accept it as Gilles Deleuze does.

Without some standard that stands outside the whole system, there is no objective way to judge good and evil and thus no reason to feel guilt, which Nietzsche saw as a leftover of the priestly mentality. From a purely animalistic viewpoint, ethics make no sense. To inform a tiger that he shouldn't have destroyed a deer would be wasted effort. Nietzsche thought the same should go for humans. He writes against morality throughout his work as a tool of the priestly caste who "concentrated their effort on arousing moral and religious responses, and the moral norm was vicariously invoked where by rights a powerful aesthetic magic should have transported the listeners" (*Birth of Tragedy* 134–35). Nietzsche laughs explicitly at the "vegetarian absurdity" that had already swept Europe in his day, a ramification of the growing guilt over the subjectivity of formerly objectified animals (267).

The "face" of man, in Levinas's and Heidegger's sense, is for Corso merely a mask whose sole function is to hide his animal nature from himself. In his deconstruction of human subjectivity, Corso closely parallels recent trends in French postmodern thought, but he goes further. I am arguing for a reevaluation of Corso's poetry within the light of his anticipation and taking of these developments in French postmodernism to their furthest extreme. Aside from a few in-group appreciations from the likes of fellow Beats Ginsberg, Kerouac, and Burroughs, Corso's writing has received scant critical attention. (A summary of some of the more important Corso criticism is found in Stephenson; a more extensive bibliography in available in Skau.) Much of this has been negative, and almost all of it has misunderstood or skimmed over Corso's philosophical intentions.

Until recently, Corso has not fit into any of the reigning critical paradigms. His impiety has gotten him rejected from serious consideration. And yet, at least a decade before Derrida and Deleuze, Corso interrogated all the transcendent economies of being and found the exits blocked. The important puzzle of the ethics of eating has yet to be addressed satisfactorily by either the ecological movement or postmodern philosophy. If we are neighbors and not ontologically superior to the creatures we eat, the idea of ethics goes out the window when we're eating; and we must eat several times a day or die. Corso's paradoxical poetry deals with this notion in a manner more profound and more vivid than anything yet written by Deleuze or Derrida. Corso knocked out the absurdity of an eternal God and universal judgment and impartial ethics years before postmodernism, but what are we left with? Mere cannibalism, without justification!

For Corso it has meant that all of his early hopes for an ethical aesthetic reaction to the natural world were broken; his hopes as a utopian philosopher were dashed at the same time he was reborn as a poet who was no longer ebullient but was tougher and more realistic just the same. Corso's thinking led him to poetry, which is where he remained. And his poetry over the next two volumes would retain many references to Catholicism, but they would do so with apparently more hard-earned effort, as his doubts kicked in some time in the early 1960s and never fully left him.

Nietzsche, the godfather of postmodernism, shows that art takes over where logic and science can go no further. He writes:

> Every noble and gifted man has, before reaching the mid-point of his career, come up against some part of the [scientific] periphery that defied his understanding, quite apart from the fact that we have no way of knowing how the area of the circle is ever to be fully charted. When the inquirer, having pushed to the circumference, realizes how logic in that place curls about itself and bites its own tail, he is struck with a new kind of perception, which requires, to make it tolerable, the remedy of art. (*Birth of Tragedy* 95)

In the aporia between the need for eating and respect for the other, logic "curls about itself and bites its own tail." It is right here that Corso's art is centered. In the heart of immanence lies Corso's crowning curse: if humanity is animal and has no transcendent soul, are ethics, then, just for laughs? Surprisingly, Corso would say no. Because animals do not have imagination, they thus cannot change things. They do not have agency, in Luc Ferry's sense, but humans do, and this gives us the imperative to act ethically. Corso's final response is somewhat similar to Nietzsche's. Nietzsche transformed himself into a deity—Dionysus. Corso transformed himself into yet another deity—a Poet, which in many places he links to the deification that the romantics accorded to the Poet. In order to be personally transcendent and to thus stand apart from the general battleground of life, Nietzsche and Corso both opted for the pose of a magical being. In one of Corso's final poems in *Mindfield*, "Fire Report—No Alarm," he writes:

And that I did not adhere
    to any man's God
neither a comprehensible
    Absolute
nor the inexplicable
    unseen breath
        of Omnipotent power
—that I did indeed feel
    the awesome lack
that in Heirophantic
    ardour
        is awesomely contained
and not fall to
    my knees
    in abject piety
or even for a failing
    moment
give in
    to the warmth
    and secure
of God-embracement
—that I did not adhere
    to arcane trinities
or bow to lettered
    ambiguity
so that my soul
    be stencilled
    in wanton faith
—that I stood
    amongst the brethern
and aided the old
    and poor
as well the young
all for whom I
    did open the door
like an act of Jesus
Such be my metaphor
who with autochthonal
    spirit
stands before the
    universe alone
God-free
    father of my children

             and upon my finger
                 the ring of poetry—

                                                    (*M* 234–35)

This would indicate that Corso was not therefore willing to dispense with beauty, with love, with chivalry, simply because the soul is not necessarily transcendent. Also, he links the poet to Jesus, the strongest metaphor he can summon. Corso retained a Christian conscience. For this reason, Corso was not simply triumphant concerning the white destruction of Indian cultures as Nietzsche would presumably be; Corso considered the destruction of aboriginal peoples to be a stain upon the American conscience. Corso saw that, in the variable scale of things, the Indians might have had some things to offer, but apparently he never studied them the way that Gary Snyder, among others in the Beat movement, did, because he thought the greater beauty was in classical European and Christian culture.

Corso's lineage goes back to the romantic poets. When he was seventeen, he was given a copy of Percy Shelley's verses while in prison; it was one of the most important "books of illumination" that the "angels of Clinton Prison" handed to him (dedication page to *Gasoline*). Corso's role of the poet was probably defined by Shelley, in such poems as "Hymn to Intellectual Beauty," in which Shelley claimed to have pledged allegiance to this spirit.

        I vowed that I would dedicate my powers
            To thee and thine—have I not kept the vow?
        . . . .
            Thus let thy power, which like the truth
            Of nature on my passive youth
        Descended, to my onward life supply
            Its calm, to one who worships thee
            And every form containing thee,
        Who, SPIRIT fair, thy spells did bind
        To fear himself, and love all human kind.
                                        (cited in Perkins 971)

Corso's vocation as a poet was probably formulated in lines such as these, in which Shelley saw the poet as someone who had dedicated himself to the spirit of intellectual beauty, to receiving this message from a Platonic world above and beyond this one, and to relaying this truth to others in an attempt to spread justice and loveliness in contemporary human affairs. Shelley wrote in the preface to "Prometheus Unbound" that morality was a part of poetry:

We owe the great writers of the golden age of our literature to that fervid awakening of the public mind which shook to dust the oldest and most oppressive form of the Christian religion. We owe Milton to the progress and development of the same spirit: the sacred Milton was, let it ever be remembered, a republican, and a bold inquirer into morals and religion. The great writers of our own age are, we have reason to suppose, the companions and forerunners of some unimagined change in our social condition or the opinions that cement it. The cloud of mind is discharging its collected lightning, and the equilibrium between institutions and opinions is now restoring, or is about to be restored. (cited in Perkins 982)

Corso probably took seriously this calling in his youth, this calling to be the one to listen to the divine and translate it into human terms, and yet he often parodied it as well. Shelley, who was an atheist, had discovered in poetry some last vestige of the divine. To this extent, ontological hierarchies are reconstructed in that the poet has a "higher calling" than other humans. In the poem "Sunrise," Corso writes a rather irreverent version of this mission:

> I sat on the toilet of an old forgotten god
> and divined a message thereon
> I bring it to you
>   in cupped hands
>
>   (*HA* 6)

Corso's intentional parody of the messenger-spirit motif comes just after his fresh minting of the image of an eternal relay and recalls Mikhail Bakhtin's work on the comic literature of the Middle Ages.

> Here, as in Rome, the tendency was towards a laughing double for every serious form. We recall the role of medieval clowns, those professional creators of the "second level," who with the doubling effect of their laughter insured the wholeness of the serio-laughing word. We recall all the different kinds of comic intermedia and entr'actes that played a role in the "fourth drama" of Greece and in the cheerful exodium of Rome. (79)

Corso's implicit argument, which wavers but often comes back quite strong, is that we can still have faith in ourselves and in our imaginations. It is our imagination that created God. Therefore, we can act with the magnanimity of Jesus. St. Thomas had accorded to all of nature the role of being an aspect of God's creation. In Eco's *Aesthetics of Thomas Aquinas,* he writes:

> For the medievals, the fact that goodness was a transcendental meant that there could be nothing evil in being—not, that is, in the metaphysical sense. In the same way, defining beauty as a transcendental implied the elimination of the seeming deformities and dissonances in the universe. Such an enterprise involved a kind of ardor and an aesthetic optimism which, on its own theoretical level, reflected the sentiments of St. Francis' *Cantico della creature.* (22)

Similarly, Eco writes of a group of Franciscans:

> The authors of the Summa Fratris Alexandri were like their contemporaries in wanting to show that even monsters were beautiful, in that they are beings, because every being is beautiful and God creates nothing that is not beautiful. (44)

Corso is a long way from seeing everything as beautiful in his later work. Nevertheless, in much of his later "God-free" logic, he seems to come to a new position. If we can imagine a decent thing, then we can do it. Against nature and nature's darkest inclinations, Corso posits the classical humanist spirit of humor and imagination and love. As he turns toward a world of divine powers, his humor is somewhat eclipsed and a very serious and different kind of poet steps forth, but Corso just as often "gooses" this more serious poet. Corso's poetry is based on an exploded Thomism, which retains some of the incredible optimism about the universe of the Catholics, while God, angels, men, and animals fly through his poems with dizzying interchangeability. Corso's comedy, such as it is, is very close to tragedy and leads him toward an extremely powerful and often moving lyricism. He is perhaps the greatest surviving poet of a tradition that began with St. Francis's canticles, St. Thomas's philosophy, and Dante's epic poetry. Corso's work might best be described as that of a doubting Thomist: his doubts and his Thomism intertwine in a stunning vision that is perhaps, thanks to its often comic character, the most unjustly neglected poetry in American literature.

3

Static Thomism or Progressive Romanticism?

In Corso's early poetry, he works Darwinism against a Catholic vision of life, but in the middle period, Corso's most easily seen reference is to surrealism and the surrealist heritage in romanticism while Catholicism takes a back seat. Among the surrealists, God is within the unconscious; they view the deity as a mental faculty that humanity contains within. Surrealism took up romanticism, especially German romanticism. As Jacqueline Chénieux-Gendron writes of the surrealist canon: "All German Romantics receive universal admiration, and are never déclassé" (13). The German romantics and their optimistic metaphysics spread through surrealism and continued their course within the Beat movement, especially within Corso's work. Gottfried Leibniz already in the early eighteenth century believed in an "endless becoming" (Lovejoy 259), and Hegel as early as 1807 saw the world as moving toward an identification of spirit and matter in *The Phenomenology of Spirit*. But it is Friedrich Schelling to whom we owe the romantic idea of an evolutionary theology. Schelling wrote:

> I posit God as the first and the last, as the Alpha and the Omega; but as Alpha he is not what he is as Omega, and in so far as he is only the one— God "in an eminent sense"—he can not be the other God, in the same sense, or, in strictness, be called God. For, in that case, let it be expressly said, the unevolved God *(unentfaltete), deus implicitus,* would already be what, as Omega, the *Deus explicitus* is. (cited in Lovejoy 323)

Schelling's sense of God was, then, that God was not perfect and complete at his first moment but that he is moving toward perfection. This progressivism is mirrored in nature and in humankind's attempts to better itself throughout history. Lovejoy comments:

> On the face of it, the world is, precisely, a system in which the higher habitually grows out of the lower, fuller existence out of emptier. The child

grows into a man, the ignorant become learned; not to mention that nature itself, as we all know who have the requisite acquaintance with the subject, has gradually risen from the production of more meagre and inchoate creatures to the production of more perfect and finely formed ones. (323)

Against the static conception of God offered by the Thomists, Schelling offered a conception of God as an endless *becoming*.

The God of the older theology . . . had been a God eternally complete, "ready-made once for all," as Schelling puts it. But no conception could be more barren and unprofitable than this; for it is really the conception of a "dead God," not of the God that lives and strives in nature and in man. (Lovejoy 324)

In the poem "Man About to Enter Sea," a version of which was published in the *Penguin Modern Poets* series, Corso writes of a man on the beach in Tangiers.

Walking into the summer cold sea
arms folded
trying to keep the waves and frolicy bather
splashings from further chilling him
He moves as if not to—but I know
he'll eventually go with a NOW IN! and
become warm—

(*Penguin* 24)

What Corso writes about here is not only the simpler factual account of a man about to take a swim but an analogical account of the way in which humankind can make a mental saltation, a leap into a different kind of future. In this poem, Corso uses not only Christianity and Darwinism but a third force, the force of romantic poetry, to contest the other two. The imagination is a special attribute of humanity. As Chénieux-Gendron writes, "The meaning of the Romantic revolution (to which surrealism is connected . . .) was to give imagination a *cognitive* function" (4).

Humanity is surely animal in that we share DNA with other species and are very close to certain kinds of chimpanzees, our closest common relatives, splitting off only 1.2 million years ago (Dennett 337). But we are not simply animals. Daniel Dennett, an extreme Darwinian scientist with no belief in God whatsoever, or even in the concept of the soul, argues that nevertheless we need imagination and the ability to sift evidence carefully—features we share with no other animal—in order to be fully human. Because there are no rules to follow, we must instead use the higher faculties of our mind to leap to the right conclusion, "[n]ot by any systematic generalization and testing of Kantian maxims—there are too many to consider" (Dennett 509). Even Dennett concludes that humanity has one special attribute, its mental power. Corso writes of the man, after the leap into the sea:

> That curious warm is all too familiar
> as when frogs from fish kicked
> and fins winged flew
> and whatever it was decided lungs
> and a chance in the change above the sea—
>
> There he wades millions of years that are legs
> back into that biggest and strangest of wombs
> He stands—the sea is up to his belly button
> —He would it nothing more than a holiday's dip
>
> But I feel he's algae for skin
> He who calls the dinosaur his unfortunate brother
> And what with crawling anthropods
> oh they're only bathers on a summer shore
> yet it is possible to drown in a surface of air
> deem the entire earth one NOW IN! and once in
> fated out again—
>
> (Penguin 24)

The poem is evolutionary in its subject matter but revolutionary in its theme. Corso discusses how the man calls the dinosaur his "unfortunate brother," since dinosaurs were wiped out long before humankind arrived, but doesn't mention that in their disappearance they provided a route of growth for mammalian species. Every disappearance leads to another route of growth. When our "brothers" the dinosaurs disappeared, the way for humanity was opened. In Corso's most beatific moments, early on in his poetry, he doesn't really deal with competition between species but wants instead to see all as one, moving toward a utopian future.

At the beginning of life, there was only algae, which the man has "for skin." And yet, is it possible that humankind can all jump back into the oceans and become one again with the fish, in an underground Atlantis, as the poem implies? What then will happen to the fish, and how will humanity deal with sharks? What also of the idea that people should be moving in general toward the stars, toward becoming angelic? Corso goes against this notion, somehow, in a move reminiscent of the surrealist love for the half-woman, half-fish Melusine and Breton's love for the professional mermaid Jacqueline Lambda.

Could humans live in the sea? Daniel Dennett cites the research of several scientists who hypothesize that people may have

> descended from earlier primates via an intermediate species that was aquatic! These aquatic apes purportedly lived on the shores of an island

formed by the flooding of the area that is now in Ethiopia, during the late Miocene, about seven million years ago. Cut off by the flooding from their cousins on the African continent, and challenged by a relative sudden change in their climate and food sources, they developed a taste for shell-fish, and over a period of a million years or so they began the evolution-ary process of returning to the sea that we know was undergone earlier by whales, dolphins, seals, and otters, for instance. (244)

Dennett continues: "There seems to be nothing *inherently* impossible about the idea; other animals have made the plunge, after all. Why couldn't our ances-tors have started back into the ocean and then retreated, bearing some telltale scars of this history?" (244).

Corso's poem seemingly refers to such an event, in order to throw into a greater light the strangeness of humanity's evolutionary past and the possibilities that we can imagine for our future. The surrealist imagination saw a prophetic ten-dency in dreams and in great poetry. If it moves us, it opens a royal road to our destiny. We don't know where we have come from, but in many ways, we are, from a genetic perspective, much like the crabs crawling upon the shore, a com-parison Corso also makes in the poem: "And what with crawling *anthropods* / oh they're only bathers on a summer shore" (emphasis added).

And yet, in important ways, we are different. We have an ethical apprecia-tion of the world. We have imagination. We have the ability to laugh. These ca-pabilities make us uniquely human. Are we therefore the "omega point" that Catholic theologian Pierre Tielhard de Chardin described us as in his celebrated *The Phenomenon of Man*? Dennett would argue that we are not.

He [Chardin] proposed a version of evolution that put humanity at the center of the universe, and discovered Christianity to be an expression of the goal—the "Omega Point"—towards which all evolution is striving. . . . It is fair to say that in the years since his work was published, it has become clear to the point of unanimity among scientists that Tielhard of-fered nothing serious in the way of an alternative to orthodoxy; the ideas that were peculiarly his were confused, and the rest was just bombastic redescription of orthodoxy. (320)

Nevertheless, Corso's description throughout *Long Live Man* of humankind as the "victory of life / And Christ be the victory of man—" (10) would show the parallel Corso developed with Tielhard's thinking, and Catholic thought in gen-eral, in his depiction of humankind as an omega point. In this way, as well, Corso is not very far from the thought of André Breton, the great surrealist thinker whose childhood was steeped in Thomist thought and who, it could be argued, remained a kind of inverted Thomist in his later career. However, Breton, through the German romantics, didn't have a static conception of God; instead, he wanted to posit that God and nature were in a process of *becoming*. Breton felt that God lay in the unconscious and that to open up the unconscious would allow us to reclaim our divinity. As he writes in *Les Vases Communicants:*

> Comme je voudrais qu'une méditation profonde sur les puissances in-conscientes, éternelles que tu recèles soit au pouvoir de tout homme, pour qu'il se garde de reculer et de subir! La résignation n'est pas écrite sur la pierre mouvante du sommeil. L'immense toile sombre qui chaque jour est filée porte en son centre les yeux médusants d'une victoire claire. [I would like to make a profound study of unconscious powers, eternal powers which are at the behest of every man, so that they can stop shrinking away from submitting to them. Resignation is not written in the moving stone of sleep. The immense sober canvas which every day is stretched once again carries in its center the Medusa eyes of a clear victory.] (168)

Although it is clear that humanity is linked to animals and is still susceptible to future transformations—just as different skin colors have developed due to different climactic conditions, with those in the far north, such as Scandinavians, having fair skin and those at the equator having darker skins—it is not certain in which direction humankind is evolving. Do dreams of swimming indicate that we might one day return to the sea? Very slight evolutionary changes indicate that humanity has not ceased to evolve on the genetic level, but Breton claims that in dreams our evolution is given direction, moving toward ever greater liberty. In dreams, we have the ability to fly, to make love with whomever we like, to enjoy beautiful cities, and so on. Is this the direction of evolution? Most importantly, we have evolved greater minds than the other animals, and it is this evolution that will make future leaps possible, as our minds will permit us to build the cities and societies we can first only dream. Whether or not this powerful mind is necessarily a divine bonus, as it is regarded in romanticism and surrealism, is also left open to question. Kenneth Burke writes in *On Symbols and Society* of the difference between man and other animals from a rather non-uto-pian perspective:

> Darwin sees only a difference of degree between man and other animals. But the theologian sees a difference in kind. That is, where Darwin views man as *continuous* with other animals, the theologian would stress the principle of *discontinuity* in this regard. But the theologian's screen also posits a certain kind of *continuity* between man and God that is not as-cribed to the relation between God and other animals.
>
> The logological screen finds itself in a peculiar position here. It holds that, even on the purely secular level, Darwin overstated his case. And as a consequence, in his stress upon the principle of *continuity* between man and the other animals, he unduly slighted the evidence for *discontinuity* here. For he assumed that the principle of discontinuity between man and the animals was necessarily identical with a theological view of man.

Such need not be the case at all. Darwin says astonishingly little about man's special aptitudes as a symbol-user. His terministic screen so stressed the principle of continuity here that he could view the principle of discontinuity only as a case of human self-flattery. Yet, logology would point out: We can distinguish man from other animals without necessarily being overhaughty. For what other animals have yellow journalism, corrupt politics, pornography, stock market manipulators, plans for waging thermonuclear, chemical, and bacteriological war? I think we can consider ourselves different in kind from the other animals, without necessarily being overproud of the distinction. We don't need theology, but merely the evidence of our characteristic sociopolitical disorders, to make it apparent that man, the typically symbol-using animal, is alas! something special. (120)

I cite this in order to foreground Corso's utopian-surrealist orientation. Corso went both ways. In poems like "Bomb," "Many Have Fallen," and "Bombed Train Station, 80 Killed," Corso recognizes the reality of bombs, but for him this is somewhat mitigated by Catholicism, even when he is also suspicious of it in its more orthodox forms. At the end of "Bombed Train Station, 80 Killed," Corso writes:

> Bombs EXPLODE
> and people explode them
> I tell you, hear!
> the bomb is near
> and it'll be too late
> when it reaches your ear
>
> How to stop its approach?
> The poet can only try
> And the Pope believes the path
> to heaven is to die
>
> (*HA* 28)

Corso continued to have a certain romantic faith in humankind. He believed, like many of his generation, that a giant leap would be attained through a change in consciousness. This change has been argued for through the mass use of LSD in the work of Timothy Leary and the early Allen Ginsberg; or through the spread of new sexual practices in the so-called sexual revolution; or through Marxism, which would create equality between races and genders; or other belief systems having to do with surrealism. Corso's reliance on poetry in this regard links him to the millenarian utopianism of the romantic movement and also to the surrealists, who felt that a change of consciousness would herald what the evolutionists call a "saltation," or a leap, that would transform the nature of humankind in one or two brief generations. It is this unlikely idea that ignites some of Corso's most spectacular poetry. It is this heraldry to which his work and life were rather half-seriously dedicated. I say "half-seriously" because Corso had doubts about this mission as well and often appears to be a trickster amidst the more sincere utopian poets of the surrealist and Beat generations of the twentieth century.

Where did this utopian orientation among poets come from? Ernest Lee Tuveson, in his *Avatars of Thrice Great Hermes: An Approach to Romanticism*, makes the case that the romantics had been introduced to a curious Egyptian Gnostic document purporting to be a series of magic letters that indicate how to become an avatar of Hermes through an acceptance of the entire universe, seeing all of it as one cosmic good. Tuveson writes, "What business is there in life higher and more compelling than to know and to absorb the cosmos?" (6). For Hermes Trismegistus, everything in the universe is part of God, from the lowest whores to the diadems on the highest queen. The hermeticists "glorified the physical universe as did no other view of the ancient world" (20).

> [I]t separates this world-view from all those which involve some kind of world-rejection and world-transcendence. The "rebirth" consists, not in escaping from the material creation, but in accepting it, celebrating it, identifying with its whole being. And most important, it is *imagination* that is the final agent for effecting this regeneration. When the Romantics exalt the imagination, they are continuing this kind of tradition. (25)

Tuveson continues:

> It follows that man in his encounter with God confronts a Mind indeed vastly greater than his own, but not radically different in kind. The human being can therefore become literally godlike, even a microcosmic god, if he works to expand his own psyche to imitate the great Mind that beckons to him in all his surroundings. The first step is gnosis—the saving knowledge, simply, that these things are true. (41)

In this worldview, the universal spirit is everywhere, and not only upstairs at the top of a great chain of being. Tuveson writes, "The ancient world was dominated by conceptions of hierarchy: but hermeticism is a doctrine, especially, of the *democracy* of the universe" (45). Because heaven could be seen in a grain of sand, it was not necessary to think of a gradated ontology, in which humankind lived in darkness, overseen by angels and the greater glory of God. According to Tuveson, this rather secretive ideology (which he traces laboriously from its conception in a rather rigorous and painstakingly convincing manner) was the core of the romantic message.

Shelley's spirit of intellectual beauty, according to Tuveson, was simply this hermeticist notion of a spirit in the woods (to paraphrase Wordsworth). Tuveson points out:

> These lines, from Shelley's "Ode to Liberty," for instance, breathe the very spirit of hermeticism:

> One ocean feeds the clouds, and streams, and dew;
> One sun illumines Heaven; one Spirit vast
> With life and love makes chaos ever new,
> As Athens doth the world with thy delight renew.
>
> (163)

Tuveson continues, "Shelley has the feeling, like ancient hermetists ordinarily, of seeing what he called 'this divinest universe' from a great height. But the close view, the sense of divinity in terrestrial scenes, is equally valid, and it is typical of Wordsworth" (163). Tuveson caps his presentation with a reading of Whitman's poem "To a Common Prostitute," which was an integral part of *Leaves of Grass*.

> Be composed—be at ease with me—I am Walt Whitman,
>   liberal and lusty as Nature,
> Not till the sun excludes you do I exclude you,
> Not till the waters refuse to glisten for you and the leaves to
>   rustle for you, do my words refuse to glisten and rustle
>   for you.
> My girl I appoint with you an appointment, and I charge
>   you that you make preparation to be worthy to meet me,
> And I charge you to be patient and perfect till I come.
> Till then I salute you with a significant look that you do
>   not forget me.
>
> (cited in Tuveson 235)

Tuveson comments:

The poem may have been inspired by the story of the woman taken in adultery, related in the eighth chapter of the Gospel of St. John, but the differences strikingly illustrate how radical Whitman's position really was. In the Gospel anecdote, Jesus challenges any one without sin to accuse the woman; when all of her would-be accusers have slunk away, he dismisses her, "Go, and sin no more." The real point is the hubris of human beings presuming to exercise the power of God to accuse and to judge; there is no denial of the reality of the sin. But this is exactly what Whitman does; and, to make the thing far more outrageous, he identifies his self with Nature's, and far from forgiving her, asserts her legitimate place in the great whole. . . . The Masonic institution of "brotherhood" . . . expresses the ideal of an unselfish, completely enlightened association for the liberation of mankind; much of this ideal is in Whitman as well. (235)

This acceptance of all of mankind became a major aspect, through Ginsberg, of the Beat movement, which drew its inspiration from romanticism and surrealism. As Michael Skau writes, "The Romantics are a clearly discernible influence on the themes and concerns of the Beat poets, most of whom (especially

Ginsberg, Kerouac, Corso, and Ferlinghetti) can be seen as urban Romantics of the twentieth century" (6). Skau continues:

> In terms of American literary influences, at times Corso seems to have skipped the first half of the twentieth century, deriving much of his influence from the poets of the nineteenth century (particularly those most likely to be found in a prison library, and Whitman and Dickinson, as unlikely as the pairing of the two seems to be on a formal level). (9)

While Ginsberg self-consciously continued Whitman's tradition of accepting all, however, Corso often parodied it. According to Skau:

> "Lines Written Nov. 22, 23—1963—in Discord," Corso's elegy on the assassination of John F. Kennedy, is a truly unusual hybrid; on the one hand, its references to the captain and his ship clearly call up one of Whitman's elegies on Abraham Lincoln, another slain president; on the other hand, the narrator's adoption of the role of a transhistoric assassin seems to do for assassins what "Bomb" did for bombs—to deny the agents of destruction both credit and responsibility. (131)

I read Corso's embrace of the bomb and of assassins, rather, as sarcastic doubt toward the program of a universal embrace of the cosmos advertised in Whitman and in Ginsberg.

Skau reads Corso's framework differently: where he sees a blundering between two unassimilated worldviews, I often see deliberate, dismayed hilarity on Corso's part. Corso doesn't accept the framework of Beatitude, much as he would like to, and this hesitancy creates a comic tension between the ideal and the real. Unlike Ginsberg, who had a fairly undisturbed sacred attitude towards life, Corso wavered, and his poems depict that wavering.

In Kenneth Burke's *Attitudes Towards History,* he writes of Whitman from a perspective that is similar to Corso's.

> Were some things repellent? He would make himself the universal maw nevertheless, the all-consuming appetite. (And there the limitations of acceptance suggest themselves. If a whole people perfected his ways, building his frame of acceptance into a collective poem as vast as that of the mediaeval church, we can imagine someone saying in effect: "You would digest everything? Very well, here is a diet of sawdust and nails. Try casting that into your belly.") (14–15)

Burke continues to stretch this law of having to include everything as part of a positive poetic program to the point of absurdity. The Italian futurists, Burke writes, such as Tomasino Marinetti, took the program to the point of seeing war and brutality as beautiful.

> Marinetti contrived to attain "yea-saying," at whatever cost. Like a cruel caricature of Whitman, he would be the omnivorous appetite. By a cult

of the picturesque, his project categorically silenced objections. To any who might say, "This modern world is disease," it could answer, "But what a *perfect* example of disease!" . . . Were the streets noisy? It could counter by advocating an uncritical cult of noise. Might there be stench? It would discuss the "beauties" of stench. . . . As a cult of yea, it would say yea to the reigning symbols of authority at all costs. (33)

Corso's project could be linked to Italian futurism as he took the project so far it became hilarious in its grotesque overblown romanticism; it thus warped into laughter. The title of Corso's collection *The Happy Birthday of Death* revels in this kind of acceptance—and not only acceptance but also celebration—of what is most repugnant. On the cover of this volume is a photograph of an atomic explosion. Corso clearly makes the Beat acceptance of all and sundry an absurdity by taking the project to the point that perhaps even Whitman would reconsider. Would Whitman accept nuclear annihilation? In the poem "Last Night I Drove a Car," Corso writes:

> Last night I drove a car
> > not knowing how to drive
> > not owning a car
>
> I drove and knocked down
> > people I loved
> > . . . went 120 through one town.
>
> I stopped at Hedgeville
> > and slept in the back seat
> > . . . excited about my new life.
>
> > > > > (*M* 42)

In this poem, Corso turns himself into an all-accepting deity cum trickster but simultaneously knocks out the idea that any one thing might have more value than another. His own kicks seem therefore to have gotten into the driver's seat, and others, mown down, don't matter. This weird acceptance of everything, part of the romantic program, is still a major aspect of contemporary poetry. German romantic Friedrich von Schlegel wrote, "The abnormal species of literature also have their value—even the eccentric and monstrous" (cited in Lovejoy 306). If the God of creation created every last possible configuration, then individualism ought to be fostered to the point of weirdness. As Lovejoy writes:

> If the world is the better the more variety it contains, the more adequately it manifests the possibilities of differentness in human nature, the duty of the individual, it would seem, was to cherish and intensify his own differentness from other men. (307)

Individualism must be developed, the romantics thought, and "[t]he more personal, local, peculiar, of its own time, a poem is, the nearer it stands to the centre of poetry" (Novalis cited in Lovejoy 307). Corso questions the monstrousness of egoistic individuality by implicitly taking it too far in "Last Night I Drove a Car," showing us where it leads. Should we enjoy the peculiarities of child sex-murderers, simply because they are a little different? How much "difference" can we stand? If someone wants to drive 120 miles an hour through our suburbs, threatening children and pets, shall we give him a medal rather than a speeding ticket?

Darwin's work made us uncomfortably aware of our animal links. It reopened all the metaphysical questions. What kind of a world is this, and how are we supposed to live in it? Corso's work is to reopen the channels of beauty and humor against the dry rationalism of the scientists but to do it via mischievous poetry. Lewis Hyde writes of the trickster figure:

> A trickster does not live near the hearth; he does not live in the halls of justice, the soldier's tent, the shaman's hut, the monastery. He passes through each of these when there is a moment of silence, and he enlivens each with mischief, but he is not their guiding spirit. . . .
>
> Sometimes it happens that the road between heaven and earth is not open, whereupon trickster travels not as a messenger but as a thief, the one who steals from the gods the good things that humans need if they are to survive in this world. (6)

The gods that the trickster has to steal good things back from in this case are the scientists, who have seemingly taken on the role of gods in order to authoritatively point out that we are animals.

Darwin perhaps overstressed our continuity with animals. However, the link between humanity and animals can be questioned without turning necessarily to Christianity, or even turning toward optimism, as cynic Kenneth Burke has cleverly shown. We are animals, but we possess spectacular memories compared to other animals, along with a sense of judgment, an advanced sense of humor, and a belligerent violence that goes beyond any other animal. Not only can we murder others, but we can do so via the atomic bomb. Finally, it is our symbol-using capability, as Burke points out, that separates us from the other animals, but we don't necessarily need to be optimistic about this capacity, as were the romantics and the surrealists.

In order to figure out what created this strange optimism regarding symbol-using ability, we might scroll back and take a longer look at romantic ideology and its belief in the sanctity of nature before we turn again to surrealist thought. Instead of thinking of ourselves as one with other animals, or as transcendent and barely belonging to this earth at all, we might do best to consider ourselves as a species with utopian hopes and dystopian tendencies.

Many thinkers of the German romantic movement allocated divinity to humankind (Schlegel and Fichte noted that the disappearance of God made it an imperative that man fill this vacancy himself). Kimmo Sarje writes that

> Fichte took as a premise for his entire philosophy the conscious self, *das Ich überhaupt,* which developed in Schlegel's aesthetics into the creative subject, the Romantic genius, though with the proviso that the genius must realize his individual qualities in full. The Romantic genius himself thus defined the laws of artistic beauty through himself. (130)

We can see how much one aspect of Corso's conception of the artist's mission belongs within the romantic period. Corso's creation of an original worldview that interrogates the natural sciences and traditional ontological categories owes a great deal to his vast reading in the romantic period, not only in Shelley but also in Hölderlin, who he says in his interview with Gavin Selerie was his single greatest influence (46). From his critique of this reading, he picked up a viewpoint that puts him in the same group as Ginsberg and Kerouac and Burroughs in terms of creating a personal religion. Schlegel wrote, "'Only he who has a religion of his own and an original conception of infinity can be an artist. . . . The artist's center is within himself.' He may not choose a leader other than himself, 'for man cannot be without a living centre'" (Sarje 131). Corso's output can be seen to stem from such a revolutionary calling. Sarje writes:

> According to Schlegel, the "amoral"—in his view a positive attribute—person rejected all intellectual imperatives, for the inner calling was for him the supreme factor controlling human activity: "The first stirring of morality is in opposition to positive legality and conventional justice." (132)

According to Schlegel, then, the artist is like a god, creating a world out of his or her own personality. Fifty years later, Darwin pointed out that man is an animal. Corso was left with this legacy, with humans as both gods, in the romantic sense, and animals, in the Darwinian sense. With these new paradigms in mind, he rarely acted human, and the result was often unattractive. Thinking of himself as having access to animal energy as well as divine powers, Corso's body of poetry—as well as his life—questions the traditional limits of what it means to be human. Confronted with the reality of Corso, the contemporary reader might see that humanity appears to rest on an abyss with nothing above it and the most dubious of creatures below. The creature in between God and animal, if allowed to behave as such, can become something of a terror to other humans, as Corso's biography attests. And yet, Corso wasn't merely an opportunist, or merely a Sophist, because he was always devoted as well to the divine.

Are we now both God and animal, or is there some separate category of humanity that must bow to the sacred and yet rise above animality? Our intelligence is superior to that of animals in that we can think of the future and speak ironically and others can hold us responsible for things we did decades ago. And yet we do not have the omniscience we have traditionally ascribed to God. If God was a fiction all along and was hidden in the unconscious, then the devil must have been hidden there too.

Corso's recognition of his humanity is fleetingly described in his poem "The Poor Bustard," which appears in the middle volume *Elegiac Feelings American.* He writes:

> I am not the King of birds,
> Nor am I the Nuncio of their priests;
> But I am the craftsman who carves the words
> At the mouth of shooting arrows;
> The hammered voice of the drawn bowstring.
>
> (78)

This poem is virtually a definition of what it means to be human. Kenneth Burke, in the chapter "The Human Actor: Definition of Man," writes that several qualities determine mankind. One is that he is "the symbol-using animal" (*On Symbols and Society* 58). Corso writes that he is *not* the "King of birds" but rather the one who "carves the words / At the mouth of shooting arrows." The symbols at the mouth of shooting arrows are not carved by any other creature. Burke writes further that mankind is the "inventor of the negative" (62). Nowhere else does the concept of the negative exist except in the realm of humanity. Man defines himself *against,* Burke writes. Against Whitman and the poets of the mystic acceptance of the universe, humanity is able to be discriminating. Corso writes, seemingly following this, "I am *not* the King of birds, / Nor am I the Nuncio of their priests." *Nuncio* means "messenger" in Italian and is also Corso's middle name. Corso says in this poem that he is *not* the King of birds, which leaves the question of his identity open. He is also not the *messenger* of their priests. He realizes that he does not belong to the animal world. The poem also seems to refer glancingly toward St. Francis's intercession with the emperor on behalf of the birds, but Corso is not Franciscan nor divine enough to be the arbiter of the birds, either, and these first two lines act as a kind of self-reproach.

Gregory Stephenson reads this poem as an indictment of a "bird of prey . . . fated ultimately to be overthrown and destroyed by the lioness and the lion, emblems of a nobler and more elevated level of being" (62). However, a bustard is not thought of as a fierce bird of prey such as an eagle or a hawk but rather is linked to the cranes and plovers and is a fairly common sight in European meadows and on the African savanna. Moreover, the word "bustard" could be linked through Corso's New York street pronunciation with the term "bastard," and in this sense the phrase "the poor bustard" would be a sympathetic appraisal of a fellow human being and, by extension, of the human plight. The poem appears to skirt the line between these two interpretations and is meant to be read on at least two levels. But how could a bird be a "craftsman"? Only a human being can craft arrows. The poem ends:

> I am not the King of birds,
> Nor am I the Nuncio of their priests;
> But I am the skull who fills the hands
> Of the African dwarf; I have nothing to say
> Until the lioness goes away.
>
> (*EF* 79)

The poem's ending brings to mind the image of Hamlet holding poor Yorick's skull and discoursing upon the futility of human life. Corso appears to be doing something similar, although he is simultaneously drawing in sympathy for the animal world, especially for birds, and for the problematic nature of mortality that we share with the animals. If Corso is not the King of birds, then he is human, and he cannot speak until "the lioness goes away." In other words, he cannot speak until the animal leaves him, as speaking somehow links him to what is human as opposed to what is animal. This poem is about what it means to be human, and it marks a turning point in Corso's work between the reflection that humankind is animalistic, which predominates in the early work, and the notion that humankind is divine. It is a rare moment in Corso's work where he reflects briefly on what it means to be human.

In Burke's definition of humankind, he adds a third condition, which is that man is *"[s]eparated from his natural condition by instruments of his own making"* (*On Symbols and Society* 67). Corso writes in a middle section of the poem, "Behold, the midnight of my mockery / Has its voice in the vault of an embassy!" (*EF* 78). These lines show the speaker's separation from his natural condition, in that his voice is in the vault of an embassy, which is the only non-natural image in the poem, aside from the arrows mentioned in the first stanza, and this is seemingly what turns it to mockery, as if it was captured by some outside institution and put to use by it.

Fourth, Burke argues that mankind is hierarchical (69–70). The image of hierarchy can be seen in the wording "I am not the *King* of birds" and in his indication in the second movement of the poem that "kingly birds" are "bowing to me." The poem operates on a fear of "mockery" in the third movement, and "mockery" and "sneers" appear in the fourth movement, indicative of a social hierarchy.

Last, Burke argues that mankind is "rotten with perfection" (70), indicating that he is always shaping the world around him to make an airtight meaning. It is in this sense that the speaker has "nothing to say / Until the lioness goes away." He can speak only when the wilderness leaves him and he remains entirely human and can find a shape for his vision.

This poem has a dreamlike repetition in it, which makes it almost nonsensical until after many readings. However, in understanding Corso's obsession with the distinction between animal, human, and divine worlds, this poem takes on a very clear theme and is a hauntingly lovely evocation of the human condition. It is perhaps Corso's finest achievement at stating the situation of humankind after the romantic philosophers dispensed with God, only to turn human beings (or at least artists) into gods, and after Darwin destroyed the notion of a special status for human beings, which had been defined by Plato as logos. Until the speaker can rid himself of the lioness, he has nothing to say. However, how is he then able to speak, since the lioness is presumably still there?

> My dead self came to me, and said:
> "I am not happy! The specter lion
> Has spotted me; I am pursued
> Within his chasmal aviary!"
>
> (*EF* 79)

In this short stanza, however, it appears that the food chain exists even in the afterworld, such that there is never to be any escape from the fact of nutrition. Corso's humor is always playing with these ideas. The point of the poem seems to be that "the poor bastard" speaking in the poem has lost access to his magical powers and can no longer fly; he has lost his wings. He is not the King of birds. He is grounded, and merely animal, instead of being a majestic figure with otherworldly powers. The poem, at the same time, contradicts itself. Although he claims not to be the King of birds, kingly birds bow to him; although he is not the "Nuncio" of their priests, Corso's middle name is Nuncio. Can anything he says be trusted? How could his dead self come to him and speak? Again, Corso appears to be playing with ontological levels as well as with the reader's mind.

Other poems in *Elegiac Feelings American* link God to the animal world and even bring him down to the animal level, such as in "God Is a Masturbator." And yet, at the same time, this poem seems to celebrate God's sexuality. Ernest Lee Tuveson investigates how in the medieval hermetic tradition, which had inspired the romantic poets Shelley, Wordsworth, and others, sexuality was regarded as a beautiful thing:

> It is a truth to be accepted as sure and evident above all other truths, that by God, the Master of all generative power, has been devised and bestowed upon all creatures this sacrament of eternal reproduction, with all the affection, all the joy and gladness, all the yearning and the heavenly love that are inherent in its being. (14)

Corso, unlike many of the poets in the Beat and surrealist traditions, appears to be laughing at his own tradition and inspecting it with a morose resignation in his middle period, and his mood remains elegiac. The strange, moody poem at the end of this middle volume marks the gloomy aspect of Corso at this time in his life and shows that as he takes stock, he isn't entirely playing about, for once, and has a more serious intention. "Immutable Moods" is a long, slow evocation of Corso's state of mind. The poem is remarkably difficult, dense with image clusters and references to Schelling, Hegel, and Fichte as he thinks of the universe:

> Time geometrics sneaking in and out
> bona fide dimensions

> Enunciating and commencing
> space expansions
> —In extremis, cold April, Fichte
> Schelling, the relay is cumbrous and obscure
> —unconverging infinite, inductile
> stretch, leagues—
> sublimity of distance and proximity
> —Transmutations manifesting
> a metallic apotheosis
> measureless, bountiful,
> and with no volitancy
> —In extremis, Fichte, Hegel,
> Cold April

(*EF* 118)

The strange movements of the poem surpass summarization, as they have already condensed whole worlds of learning, whole philosophies of consciousness, into telegrammatic phrases that come with a worrying and haggard melancholia. The universe exists, but we are without "volitancy" (the ability to fly). The next movement is a letter to "A"—probably Allen Ginsberg—in which he discusses "the kiss of angels, / the humanity of saints—" as something in which he still believes, but perhaps more so when he is speaking with Ginsberg. The rest of the poem shows instead his "elegiac feelings American," which the entire book revolves around. There is genuine heartbreak in "Immutable Moods," as he ends talking about a "grunting Christ" pointing towards an "inhuman heaven" (*EF* 120).

And yet, revealing a trace of hope mixed in with the generally disheveled dismay, he says that he too is a "tree," apparently a reference to the opening poem of the book in which he describes Kerouac as a "rootless flat-bottomed tree" (*EF* 3). Does this mean that he, too, is neither nourishing nor nourished? There is a certain pathos in that Corso is the least regarded of the major Beat writers; perhaps he wishes to call attention to himself in these final lines in saying that "he, too," is a tree. But he is also saying that he, too, is defeated and rootless, like Kerouac, as the volume closes with the ambiguous "Behold behold I too" (*EF* 120).

Corso's strength is in his powerful ability to condense worlds of intellectual history into poems that can be read almost as nursery rhymes. But because of his background as an autodidact, a drug addict, and an ex-convict, he has not yet been taken seriously by more than a handful of scholars. And yet, he has had at least as much education as Shakespeare, and since he had open access to libraries, could sit in on university programs, and argue with some of the finest minds of his time, his education was arguably better. François Villon was also a felon. Coleridge was a drug addict. Corso's achievement is major and addresses the most important question of our time: What is our role in the universe?

After Darwin and the romantic philosophers, what is left that we can call human or sacred? Ezra Pound was obsessed with usury, stuck within a simple

Christian scapegoating of the Jew, which is especially reprehensible in light of his having worked in Mussolini's Italy without remorse and with more self-righteousness than humor. Corso breaks out of this scapegoating system; his themes are larger, more comprehensive, and his questions more volatile. Corso's mysteries are vaster than any short critical book could contain. The greatest mystery lies within Corso's depiction of the universe, which has a long, hermetic pedigree, but he breaks out of this often into a dazzling doubt. It is composed of a number of philosophies, beginning with the early Catholic notion of a hierarchical chain of being, and yet this is challenged by a Darwinian paradigm, and then both of these are challenged by a hermetic philosophy that Corso apparently gleaned from the romantic poets in which the poet is capable of posing himself as a god, ready to vie in strength and magical abilities with the universe itself, as a trickster might. It is the question of how to tap these abilities that remains. At the same time, Corso retains a progressivist program that is equally a legacy of the romantic and the surrealist movements. Corso's poetry is a record of his attempt to integrate these philosophies at the same time as it is a critique of them.

Corso's earliest poetic role was that of a Franciscan clown, and he always retained some of the trickster's attributes, even as he explored the traditional role of the poet as messenger of the divine in his later work. More than most poets, Corso's origins are obscure, because his parents had abandoned him in his infancy. Creating a lineage, therefore, was of primary importance. It is necessary to reflect on what Corso's inspiration drew, or rather, what it was drawn toward. Unlike Gary Snyder, Corso was not drawn to the sententious version of the American Indian but rather to the trickster, and not to hierarchical Buddhism but to the Crazy Wisdom school or to Japanese Zen. Unlike Allen Ginsberg, Corso was not deeply absorbed in William Blake or in various and more serious Indian and Tibetan religions. Unlike William Burroughs, Corso did not see the framework of an out in science fiction or in Count Alfred Korzybski's linguistic theories. Unlike Jack Kerouac, Corso's poetry is not primarily one of the road, where Kerouac drew inspiration from the unlettered *fellahin,* bouncing back and forth across the North American continent in search of kicks. In fact, unlike all of these writers, who were busy with Eastern religions or linguistic science, Corso's investigation was focused on classical Western art and myth. His art is in reference to older Mediterranean art, and his poetry is a recuperation of various human communities from ancient Greece to the founding days of America, but he most often has a comical attitude toward this tradition.

Corso does not look to nature, or to nomadism, for a source of poetry, nor does he look away from Western civilization but into enduring institutions in the West, and yet more often than not he furthers the destruction of this lineage. His moods vary, and thus his picture of the universe is unstable, and many different frameworks collide within a poem, causing humor when he is conscious of it and causing incoherence when he is not. Usually, he seems to be aware of the different frameworks that work against each other in his poetry, but even this is not clear.

Corso celebrates assassination, or confused rebellion, but does so ironically. When he looks instead at enduring civilizations, such as the Egyptian (as did many of the romantics), in one of his longest poems, "Geometric Poem," he also appears to do so ironically, or at least without a conclusive affirmation of any kind. "Geometric Poem" is a meditation on the eternal forms of triangle, square, and circle. In the poem "Elegiac Feelings American," he muses over the death of the American vision just as he previously mused over the death of the Egyptian vision, but this latter poem is also a look at the death of Jack Kerouac, who represents this vision, to some extent. As usual, it is only the humorous parts of his work that function well; when he gets serious, he seems most awkward and tentative. Doubt is never very far from his usual mental state, and it is his characteristic feature.

Against nature, Corso looks at what human beings have built. His poetry is an investigation of things that have outlasted one generation and become an institutional force based on myth, but the results are difficult to summarize, because he rarely achieves stasis. One could see that this is his greatest strength, but it is also his greatest problem.

A sense of continuity over generations provides stability. Corso's Italian American roots are most apparent in his early poems. Many in his second volume of poems, *Gasoline,* point to his ethnicity. He seems to have begun his search for continuity and stability there. "Italian Extravaganza," "Birthplace Revisited," "The Last Gangster," and poems to Italian painters such as "Uccello," and "Botticelli" are mixed with poems that indicate his restless wandering from these roots. Mexico, Holland, and Paris are equally treated in this early volume, but in these other places he is clearly a visitor exploiting local curiosities, while in New York he is at home, as much as Corso could ever feel at home. Finally, as much as place figures in Corso's poems, it is not a place itself as much as it is the dream that arises from a place that Corso is after and with which he seeks to secure an alliance.

Critic Gregory Stephenson writes:

> The "Geometric Poem" is much more than a re-statement of Egyptian mythology; it is a re-interpretation of it. The poem is Corso's response to the disorder of our age, its lack of cohesion, of unity, of a centre. Through his selective emphasis on particular figures and events from Egyptian myth, Corso expresses the fundamental concept of Egyptian civilization: *ma'at,* an idea that embraces all order in life, including natural and social order, justice and truth. The ancient Egyptians recognized no distinction between the divine realm and the world, all was a unity: the cosmos, nature, mankind. It is this essential mythos, this sacramental vision, that Corso wishes to revivify, to restore to the life of the world. . . . This triumph is to be achieved by means of geometry, which for Corso is a metaphor for the

essential, transcendental laws of the universe, the eternal patterns and di-vine archetypes (analogous to the Platonic Idea) that constitute the prin-ciples from which the material world (imperfectly) derives. (65–66)

It is vision, Stephenson writes, that brings a culture together, that allows gen-erations to succeed one another, but vision is hard to come by. One can wander a long time in the desert before hearing a voice from God. In an early poem from his first collection, *The Vestal Lady on Brattle,* Corso is advised by a Boston ac-quaintance to walk along Brattle Street, as Herman Melville once did, in order to get a vision like the one Melville once got in order to write *Moby Dick.* Corso walks this street, but has no visions:

> Tired of walking,
> Tired of seeing nothing,
> I look out from a window
>> belonging to someone
>> nice enough to let me look.
>
> And from a window Cambridge is not all that bad.
> It is a great feeling to know
>> that from a window
> I can go to books to cans of beers to past loves.
> And from these gather enough dream
>> to sneak out a back door.
>> (from "Cambridge, First Impressions," *M* 17)

It is frequently this tension between inspiration and escapism that provides a source of beauty in Corso's work. Corso's lineage, like the other Beat writers, is based on beauty, but that is not the full scope of his lineage. Unlike Pound, who appears to have been a workaholic, Corso and the Beats were decadents who alternated intense periods of work with even more intense periods of vagabond-age. Corso was lazy, squandering his talent, only rarely putting out books of poetry, preferring to gamble, chase women, and get bombed on drugs and alco-hol. In the poem above, Corso indicates this indolent quality in himself, which kept him from founding a great myth but also made him human and charming. Corso's poetry was consecrated to surrealist hilarity, with the beauty of Mediter-ranean culture seen through American eyes, but how far did he get, and did he posit something as a founding structure as Pound posited the scapegoating of the Jews?

It is true that at the beginning of his work, there are two hymns of praise to American jazz and frequent references to jazz scattered throughout several of the other early poems. But the two strictly jazz-oriented poems, "Requiem for Bird Parker" and "For Miles," are among Corso's worst: sentimental to a degree un-usual for Corso, they almost seem to wax nostalgic over a music that Corso felt compelled to praise. Fortunately, he dropped that line quickly before they permanently marred his work. Corso's work, when it turns to the panegyric, gets carried away with high emotions, and the street-level sarcasm vanishes into an overwhelming wave of alliteration and syllabic beauty that comes at the expense of sharply nuanced thought. When Corso merely affirms, in the Whitmanic tradition, he loses contact with his own reality and his own inner music. Corso's strength as a poet needs this music, but when he lets the idealism take over, he sometimes dissolves into schmaltz. What Corso seeks in his early poetry is a vital myth that will create a poem that can endure. To do this, it must have rhythm, beauty, and a moral structure. In addition, it must be a poem that people will willingly recite and pass on to their children. It must be in some way good for the species, within realistic as well as idealistic parameters.

Corso's emphasis in building this vision is through the romantic conception of the artist as magician and prophet, but at this point, early on, he was also still guided by Catholic theology and its vision of reason and hope. As an accompaniment to these early poems, Corso provided his own line drawings. He had a brilliant eye, and when he concentrated on sketching a vision, he could be dazzling.

It is for this reason that we can look at Corso's love of Western painting, as most of these poems work successfully, such as the poem to Uccello and the wonderful poem of uncertain date (but that seems, on account of its subject matter and style, to belong to the early period) on Vermeer, which appears at the end of *Mindfield:*

> **Vermeer**
> See him stand beside a tiny gate
> Around him lazy dogs congregate
> In bright windows above his head
> girls with porcelain jugs pour milk
> while lonely men with heavy knives slice bread
> and older wives in secret feel their silk.

> (*M* 216)

Corso animates a still-life with the verbs "stand," "congregate," "pour," "slice," and "feel." The verbs set in motion the painting until one can sense the feeling beneath the stilled depiction of events. The poem portrays a good life in a real city, with lonely men compensating their anguish with bread and secretive older women compensating their aging bodies with the touch of silk. The rhymes and similar line lengths provide a feeling of serenity, rare in Corso's work.

European classical paintings are a strong source of identification and power for Corso as he seeks a legacy, an arc of humanity, that will outlast his own life. This is what the postmodern poet must do: sing the song, not of the tribe, or the nation, or the individual, but of the species. It seems that Corso went back to Europe in order to discover an identity from which to begin, but by this period of the mid-1960s, he was already heavily involved in drugs and his vision was getting more skewed. Corso says in his interview with Michael André:

I was in Paris in 1965, and in a beautiful room on Monsieur le Prince, where Rimbaud lived; it's really nice, a nice little hotel room. All winter, I'd only go out to get my food and my junk, my dope, and back into that room. I had a big book on hieroglyphics and I studied geometry; I had a compass. I put the two together because ancient Egypt was very geometrical. (135)

The poem that resulted from this, "Geometric Poem," published in *Elegiac Feelings American* (37–68), is hard to make out in terms of any kind of finished art. It is a result of Corso's scribbles, with his versions of hieroglyphics in the borders, where he often takes different hieroglyphs and humorously grafts them on to each other to make words like "love-death," as he often grafted together different words in English to make a new word. But the result is unfinished in terms of a vision. As Corso himself says, "As you can see they are mostly just work papers. I never thought to put it into any kind of form as a poem" (André 135). "Geometric Poem" was exceeded by even deeper research into Western civilization—Corso went back as far as ancient Sumeria, the only non-Semitic nation in the Middle East. At Naropa Institute, in the summer of 1977, the *Epic of Gilgamesh* was on Corso's teaching syllabus. Corso was constantly referring to Gilgamesh and Enkidu as proto-Kerouac and proto-Cassady, two friends in search of the mystery of everlasting life. His work was to go back and pick up on what had been lost and draw parallels. He says:

So I did my studies pretty well, as I say. The geometry thing, not through school, I only went to the sixth grade. In that sense, I never went to study geometry or trigonometry or algebra and the other shot of languages. Now I can speak French, Italian, Greek when I'm there and put up to it. What I can do is that Egyptian. Cuneiforms don't move me. The Sumerians wrote the first books, before the Egyptians; Gilgamesh was the first thing written down. You know why it's important to me? Because I like to go back to the sources. (André 137)

On the page next to this statement is a drawing Corso made of a shaman dressed as a deer. The drawing is a copy of one made thirty thousand years ago, found on a cave wall; it is a copy of the first known drawing, as Corso puts it, made by a human being. It is always the visual that attracts Corso and is why cuneiforms, perhaps, exercised no such powerful appeal while geometry and painting did. Corso's work is profoundly and vividly visual, while music, dance, and the other fine arts are modes through which he was less able to build a memorable icon.

What we can see in Corso is a long and varied lineage. Reflections on Thomism, Darwinism, and romanticism are in nearly every poem. Is there any one thread holding it all together? Gregory Stephenson writes that Corso's is an "essential surrealist aesthetic" (25). Is Corso strictly within the surrealist mode? Although he references other cultures, it is the surrealists, and particularly the surrealist love of humor, that can be seen as the strongest aspect of Corso's later project. Corso's particular relay of surrealism was passed to him very early. "André Breton; I dug him when I was 14 years old" (Knight and Knight 184). As with the surrealists, the visual arts are Corso's most important ally, separating him from Kerouac, who found such a strong source of inspiration in jazz, or Ginsberg, who often sang his poems in public.

This emphasis on the visual linked Corso to the tastes of surrealist leader André Breton. There were no surrealist musicians, as Breton didn't particularly like music. Mark Polizzotti, Breton's biographer, wrote that Breton "couldn't distinguish Stravinsky from Satchmo" and that he was "[u]nable to 'hear the difference between two sounds,' as he once confessed" (298). Breton, on the other hand, did appreciate the visual arts, and his close friends constituted a who's who of twentieth-century art—from Pablo Picasso to Max Ernst to Meret Oppenheim to Marcel Duchamp. Corso tried to go back to the origins of Western civilization to rediscover a vision for the West, but his work has a surrealist visual quality to it. The surrealists, like the Beat writers, tried to explode rationality in order to let in the primitive emotions, the sense of humans as animals. At the same time, they sought out the divine, which they would then contrast against the madness of capitalism.

In "Suburbia Mad Song," Corso writes of the desperation of a 1950s marriage with a kind of surrealist hilarity:

> Gathered against the ants
> A husband and wife calculate their worth;
> they freeze tight on their chairs
> troubled by the table
> —He screams: "Housewife! Housewife!"
> She screams: "Rinso white! Rinso bright!"
> And when the child comes
> he'll swoon unrelative to the dire of Elm Street.
>
> (*LL* 11)

This nightmare on Elm Street was written long before Freddy Krueger reached the screen, but it shares a sense of alienation, of a society that has lost its communal vision and become a troubling caricature of a decent life. She is haunted by detergent powder, and he is "unrelative" or can't relate to the dire situation. How to negate the harmful effects of a commercial civilization and render it into a holy civilization? It was through mysticism that Breton and his later adherents would attempt to revivify Western civilization, but Corso, unlike Ginsberg, seems to be too realistic, too canny, to go along with mysticism.

Darwinism's bleak truth does not recognize the soul of a human, or even the idea of community. Surrealism does but lacks the institutional resources of Christianity. Christianity, and Corso's early Catholicism, offers a millennial tradition, with orphanages, schools, cemeteries, incredible churches with stained glass windows, and communal singing. Darwinism offers rational truths, which is not exactly uplifting. What can Darwinism, or even surrealism, offer that can top a church full of like-minded souls united in song? Breton rejected music (Polizzotti writes that he forbade surrealists from attending concerts or musicals unless they were written by Offenbach, because he appreciated the witty lyrics [298–99]). By doing so, he neglected to cultivate one of the most potent art forms.

Breton's work was meant especially to open up the divine unconscious, which he felt was where God lay hidden. Once opened through a close attention to dreams, the royal road to our divine destiny would be revealed. Breton's faith in the unconscious as the new god, or rather, where God had been hidden all along, can be seen as Thomism in reverse. All that has been repressed is divine, and all that has been repressive is Satanic. Thus, women had secrets that had been forgotten, as did primitive peoples, children, criminals, and madmen. Breton championed these downtrodden groups. In a surrealist society, imagination would be opened and out would come the marvelous: leisure-time games, erotic love, all manner of fun, which would then be arrayed against the quotidian. Breton's inverted Thomism especially sought in women and primitive peoples the answers to the repressive and devilish white civilization. In *Arcane 17,* one of his later books (1945), he writes:

C'est à l'artiste, en particulier, qu'il appartient, ne serait-ce qu'en protestation contre ce scandaleux état de choses, de faire prédominer au maximum tout ce qui ressortit au système féminin du monde par opposition au système masculin, de faire fonds exclusivement sur les facultés de la femme, d'exalter, mieux même, de s'approprier jusqu'à le faire jalousement sien tout ce qui la distingue de l'homme sous le rapport des modes d'appréciation et de volition. [It is to the artist, in particular, that it belongs, in protestation against the scandalous state of things, to make predominate all that springs from the feminine system in opposition to the masculine, to found his work on the feminine faculties, to exalt, even better, to appropriate to the point of jealously making his all that which distinguishes her from man in terms of will and modes of appreciation.] (58)

Breton assiduously studied the arts of primitive peoples for clues to humankind's destiny, visited American Indians and Haitian natives, and collected the art of Oceania. He wrote in regard to the American Indians, "Today, it's above all the visual art of the red man that lets us accede to a new system of knowledge" (cited in Polizzotti 505). Breton further stated,

Surrealism is allied with people of color . . . on the one hand, because it has always been on their side against every form of white imperialism and banditry . . . ; on the other hand, because there are very deep affinities between so-called "primitive" thought and Surrealist thought: both want to overthrow the hegemony of consciousness and daily life. (cited in Polizzotti 531)

The royal road was not open to animals. Breton was furious with Leon Trotsky when the two met in Mexico, because the Russian figure celebrated animals.

> Breton was outraged when Trotsky . . . referred to a favorite dog as his "friend" and asked Breton whether he didn't think the animal had a "human look." Shocked by Trotsky's animism, Breton retorted that calling a dog "friendly" was just as senseless as saying a mosquito was "cruel" or a crayfish "reactionary" . . . on his return to Paris he fumed to Luis Bunuel, "A dog doesn't have a human look! A dog has a dog's look!" (Polizzotti 460).

At the same time, Breton loved the beauty and mystery of nature, as he amply showed in his book-length prose poem *Arcane 17,* which casts the Canadian island of Rocher Percé as a sacred place, a church of nature that will last thirteen thousand years, reconciling our world with the cosmos via love and poetry, a kind of Notre Dame of Paris, out in the Atlantic Ocean, that would replace Paris, which at the time Breton was writing was in the process of being liberated by the Allies.

> Dans sa profundeur on a plus que le temps de voir naître et mourir une ville comme Paris où des coups de feu retentissent en ce moment jusqu'à l'intérieur de Notre-Dame, dont la grande rosace se retourne. [In its profundity we will have more than enough time to see a city like Paris be born and die again where gun shots are taking place at this moment in Notre-Dame, whose rose window turns.] (48–49)

Breton, in a sense, was trying to do what Corso tried to do as well—negotiate a compromise between nature and the Thomist tradition of his youth (Breton also grew up Catholic) but within a progressivist, romantic conception. Breton's work is conceptually overly optimistic, however, when placed next to Corso's, because Corso goes much further, finally questioning the surrealist conception that imagination will become the new god and make life into a rosy romantic-Thomistic conception of convulsive love and beauty forever.

What makes Corso's work so strong is that he attempts to mobilize Christian thought and feeling within a surrealist aesthetic but with a strange sense of humor, which undercuts the package to the point that even unbelievers can get interested in it and yet see the danger in it. What the church doesn't offer is irreverence, or personal thinking, and this is where surrealism, and especially Corso's surrealism, triumphs. If Thomism was in a sense reversed by surrealism, surrealist thought was still Thomistic, and therefore dualistic, placing above the immediate realm of necessities another realm of the divine. Where Thomism placed God above our world, surrealism found the realm of God in the imagination, especially in the unconscious, and declared, "All power to the imagination!"

The most immediate weapon of surrealism was the realm of fine art. Corso picked up on surrealism very early, long before most American youth of his time would have heard of it. In 1944, when Corso was fourteen, many of the major French surrealists, including Breton, were living in New York City as exiles from Europe during World War II, and their exhibitions would have been outrageous enough to have been talked about on the street and reviewed in the daily papers. Humor ended up being Corso's inspiration from this, as many surrealist precursors were humorists (Alfred Jarry, Charles Cros, Rabelais, Jonathan Swift), and some of the surrealists concentrated on blasphemous hilarity—Benjamin Péret, Georges Bataille, Raymond Queneau, Philippe Soupault, Marcel Duchamp, and Salvador Dali, to name a few—as Freud and other psychiatrists had noted the humorists' link with the insane, with imagination, and with the liberation of the unconscious. Allen Ginsberg himself had been heavily influenced by surrealism, as were many other members of the Beat generation. As John Tytell writes:

> Surrealism suggested the state of mind that proved liberating enough for Ginsberg to see the political realities of his day with passionate clarity. . . . Surrealism was very much a part of the *Zeitgeist* surrounding Ginsberg in his youth. During the war, a number of the key Surrealist painters had settled in America, and by 1942 Ernst, Masson, and Tanguy were living in New York City, as well as André Breton, one of the theoreticians of the movement. Breton's belief that subconscious irrationality could provide the basis for a positive social program separated the Surrealists from the Dadaists, their more nihilistic forebears. Breton's manifestoes contain arguments that anticipate the inner flow of experience Ginsberg was to express so powerfully in his poetry. (171–72)

Humor was a great part of this program, as it emphasized the bursting of logical foundations.

The sweet humor of Corso's great early period shifts in the middle period toward a doubt concerning the role of humor, and his poetry begins to lose its utopian cast—and also much of its power. Corso seems to move from clowns and clowning, the role model of the early poetry, toward a more grave model, with tricksterish humor deemphasized, in the poetry that comes in the mid-1960s and onward, and he starts to appear dispirited. We still get poems that have a superficially humorous intention (but with a deeper agony awaiting a deeper reading), which we can link to "Marriage" or the early poems in *Gasoline,* such as "Last Night I Drove a Car," but they are more and more scarce. Corso's attempt to listen to the critics may have slowed his production, but it may also have been Corso's belief that St. Francis, Bretonian surrealism, and good humor were only part of the story of our food chain and that optimism was no longer justified. It is at this point that Corso's work nearly stops and never recovers its zest, instead opting for a kind of haggard inquisition of the universe. Some of Corso's critics applaud this change.

In Michael Skau's 1999 study of Corso, *A Clown in a Grave,* he discusses the humorous aspects of Corso's poetry in a rather scolding tone. After explaining

Corso's "play theory of art" (99), Skau writes that in the middle part of his career, Corso

> even seems to realize that some of his early work may be vulnerable to charges of comedic posturing and that maturity (a quality seldom applied to Corso by his critics) has taught him the need to make his humor pointed:
>
> > I don't act silly any more.
> > And because of it I have to hear from so-called friends:
> > "You've changed. You used to be so crazy so great."
> > They are not comfortable with me when I'm serious.
> > Let them go to the Radio City Music Hall.
> >
> > ("Writ on the Eve," *LL* 92)
>
> Clearly, Corso believes that his humor has outgrown mere entertainment and must have a point to satisfy his poetic goals. (Skau 99)

The prejudice against humor in poetry comes through very powerfully here, keeping critics from taking Corso's early work seriously and haunting his later work until today. While comic novelists such as Kurt Vonnegut, Laurence Sterne, Rabelais, Jane Austen, William Gaddis, Tom Robbins, and so on are taken seriously, the comic poet is felt to be immature, as if something is wrong with him or her. Perhaps something is wrong with a writer who is always having fun and can't see the more troubling aspects of the world, but this has never been held against comic novelists. Comedy is postmodern in that it challenges given frameworks, dismantles old perceptions, and creates new concepts. I would reverse the social stigma attributed to the comic poet with the idea that the comic poet is the mature one and the wheedling bathos of much romanticism is immature and puerile, unable to be written or appreciated by fully developed adults. Comedy is also more mature than the "just the facts, ma'am" mode we usually attribute to adult consciousness, where objectivity is so highly prized.

Kenneth Burke writes:

> The comic frame, as a *method of study* (man as eternal journeyman) is a better personal possession, in this respect, than the somewhat empty accumulation of facts such as people greedily cultivate when attempting to qualify in "Ask Me Another" questionnaires, where they are invited to admire themselves for knowing the middle name of Robert Louis Stevenson's favorite nephew (if he had one). Mastery of this sort (where, if "Knowledge is power," people "get power" vicariously by gaining possession of its "insignia," accumulated facts) may somewhat patch up a wounded psyche; but a more adventurous equipment is required, if one is to have a private possession marked by mature social efficacy. (*Attitudes* 170–71)

Corso's best work reads as comedy, and he falls apart when he tries to work in other modes, performing at his best when he smashes many modes together, in order to toss them all into the blender. Comedy needn't necessarily be all sweetness and light; it can take on serious problems such as death and acne without going into a pout. Comedy, as Bakhtin has shown, can mix levity with gravity and high and low vocabularies. In this sense, Corso's revival of antiquated diction takes on a comic air. Michael Skau, again, takes exception to this mode in Corso's work. In one of Skau's best chapters in his book on Corso, "The Poesy That Cannot Be Destroyed," he tracks the myriad tackings about that one can find in Corso's poetry: misspellings, antiquated diction, chopped and artificial meter, and changes of direction in meaning from one version of a poem to another. Skau performs a detailed archaeology of the many drafts of poems that have appeared in different guises over the decades, but his sense of Corso's constant changes is pejorative, and he makes a good case for Corso's carelessness.

Skau writes:

> Unfortunately, too often Corso seems to use the apostrophe as a mere decoration, to sprinkle it haphazardly on his poems without recognizing its effect, apparently simply inserting it on occasion to give a poetic appearance. Thus, when a single line describes "Ox-flushings, scour'd malady, suffused sulphur" . . . or when a pair of lines states, "Soft-voiced Velveteer! with buttons snow-pronounc'd / When your wings closed" . . . a reader is likely to assume either that "suffused" is intended to be a three-syllable word and that "voiced" and "closed" are each to be pronounced as two-syllable words or that Corso is not applying his typographical indicators according to any meaningful pattern. (102)

This is good, close criticism of the kind that Corso's work has sorely missed out on over the decades. However, it is possible to read Corso's strange punctuation and reversals of syntax, among his other small crimes, as a burlesque routine, parodying traditional poetry and its silly conventions at the same time it refers to them, making the reader highly conscious of their comic effect. Kenneth Burke comments in a different context that "[the comic frame] cherishes the lore of so-called 'error' as a *genuine aspect of the truth,* with emphases valuable for the correcting of present emphases" (*Attitudes* 172).

In a similar vein, Corso parodies the traditional poetic sense of a longing for eternity and replaces it with a weird comic vitality, as in his early "In the Morgue," where one of two gangsters narrates a poem in which he sees himself and another dead gangster lying on the morgue table. He is still alive and able to feel, even though his body doesn't move. His soul is living. Unlike a dead young girl or a noble prince, are we supposed to care about a dead gangster? Throughout Corso's work are references to the afterlife, and they become stronger as his career moves along, but they are almost invariably comic as Corso seeks to shift this traditional poetic frame and undermine its bathos. At Kerouac's funeral, Corso wanted to pick up the body and throw it across the room so that people could see that they were worshiping only a dead body, but he somehow managed to restrain himself. This is the sort of impiety and cracking of convention that Corso felt compelled to act upon throughout his career.

With the poetic interest in eternity comes a counter-questioning of laughter and whether or not laughter is divine. Corso writes of laughter at a middle point in his career:

> To Die Laughing (?)
> I came into the world
> and laughed at what I saw
> Indeed today is laughable
> but beware such laughter
>
> It can fill you with sorrow
> It were best to contradict
> Laugh at tomorrow
> but keep today strict
>
> Yet if I leave this world
> and weep that I must leave
> then indeed I am laughable
> and nothing to believe
>
> (*LL* 58)

Corso's serious interrogation of laughter is circular in that he wishes to find that which is permanent and stable, which laughter, it seems, isn't. Corso came to see himself as part god, but even this was presented in a ridiculous light. At Naropa Institute, he was constantly saying that he was "three-fourths god, but it is the fucking human part that's dragging me down." In his research on ancient Egypt, this sense of immortality inspired him to write some of his only finished lines in the collection of work papers published as "Geometric Poem":

> This the wheel of Egypt, the blending flow
> of all things endlessly wheeling,
> embodiment in which time is without
> consequence; the creation infinitely
> reasserted; in which death is nothing real,
> And the next life a triumphant
>   continuation of this life—
>
> (*EF* 48)

The lines don't sound like Corso but rather like some generic romantic poet. It seems that he was practicing the attainment of a certain poetic tone. When we think of ancient Egypt, it is not humor that springs to mind; when we think of the *Epic of Gilgamesh*, again it is not P. G. Wodehouse. The ancient cave drawings are not of clowns dancing about a fire; they are serene and mysterious, seemingly pointing, like the points at the top of the pyramids, to something beyond this world. Humor appears to be a more recent invention, not permissible in the depictions inside the pyramids. A cave painter would probably not have thought of making silliness his forte, in order to crack up generations to come. The older frames of consciousness posited seriousness because they could more easily be controlled. Humor is wild and uncontrollable and not welcome in the pyramids for precisely that reason. Corso, in investigating the fascistic roots of Western civilization, may have felt that he was becoming classical, but what he was becoming was a mummy. Fortunately, he recovers slightly and begins to answer his critics in the next volume.

In the poem "Ancestry," from the late collection *Herald of the Autochthonic Spirit* (1981), he references the elephant god Ganesha as well as Hermes. In these figures, Corso appears to have collapsed the two roles of messenger-spirit, or divinity, and clown into one role in order to create a new role, that of a clownish messenger of the gods, which would thus be acceptable both to himself and to tradition. Both of these gods were messengers and, it is significant to note, were carriers of news, but the most recurrent of messengers in Corso's poetry is Hermes, a prankster. In the poem "Destiny," in the same collection, Corso writes:

> It does not knock
> or ring the bell
> or telephone
> When the Messenger-Spirit
> comes to your door
> though locked
> It'll enter like an electric midwife
> and deliver the message
>
> There is no tell
> throughout the ages
> that a Messenger-Spirit
> ever stumbled into darkness

(HA 46)

More important than the priest, then, is a vast relay of semi-divine persons of which the poet is the latest messenger-spirit to deliver funny inspiration from a dark source of some kind, which is eternal. As part of that spirit, the poet is also eternal, employed by the spirit on a conditional basis, bringing humorous news to the universe. In his "Columbia U Poesy Reading," Corso is quite adamant about his being a member of an elect race of spirits:

> . . . born of ourselves,
> ours was a history with a future
> And from our Petroniusian view of society

> a subterranean poesy of the streets
> enhanced by the big butcher: humor,
> did climb the towers of the Big Lie
> and boot the ivory apple-cart of tyrannical values
> into illusory oblivion
> without spilling a drop of blood
> . . . blessed be the Revolutionaries of the Spirit!
>
> (*HA* 2)

But the messenger gods Ganesha, Thoth, and Hermes interrogate Corso as to whether he serves dope or whether he serves poetry.

> "I ask you: Do you favor heroin more than you do me?"
> The three each held a bloody needle
> each needle a familiarity
> "Was I with you when heroin was with you?"
> . . . .
> "You have butchered your spirit!" roared Ganesha
> "Your pen is bloodied!" cawed the scribe Thoth
> "You have failed to deliver the Message!" admonished
>   Hermes
> With tearful eyes I gazed into Her eyes and cried:
> "I swear to you there is in me yet time
> to run back through life and expiate
> all that's been sadly done . . . and neglected. . . ."
>
> Seated on a cold park bench
> I heard Her moan: "O Gregorio, Gregorio
> you'll fail me, I know"
>
> Walking away
> a little old lady behind me
> was singing: "True! True!"
> "Not so!" rang the spirit, "Not so!"
>
> (*HA* 5)

Corso's job, as he saw it fleetingly in his life, was to bring the Message, the Message of the Comic Muse, to the planet. Exactly what this message is, however, is not clear to Corso, nor to the readers of his poems. Was he a revolutionary? In pretending to be so early on, he helped to kick off a youth revolution, but soon after that he turned to heroin, neglected his mission, and concentrated instead on solitary asocial pleasures such as drug abuse and promiscuity. It is unclear how seriously Corso took his poetic vocation. The romantic poets took their vocation too seriously and mostly died young as a result of the strain their idealism placed upon them. One thinks of Shelley, Keats, and even Byron (who died fighting in Greece) as overly idealistic and pious in their dedication to poetry. Corso, on the other hand, seems to be impious and to waver in his dedication. It is hard to think of him as joining an insurgent army in their fight for freedom, as Byron joined the Greek cause. In Corso's own description of the Beat generation's poetry, he says that he climbed "the towers of the Big Lie" with "humor." How is it that a poet who claims a lineage in Shelley could be so devoted to humor? It is probably thanks to the surrealist legacy, which he had known even before Shelley. Shelley's unwholesome sententiousness slowly drained Corso's natural surrealistic vitality and put a strain on his personality.

The movement between seriousness and cheerful idiocy marks Corso's work and his attempt to find a role as a poet. Whether he writes as a clown or as a messenger-spirit, it is still poetry that he is writing, using these two heads, emblems of a long distant past, a poetry that goes back at least to Rome and Petronius, a two-headed poetry of tragedy and comedy, traceable to the origins of decadence. Early on, Corso believed intensely in this destiny, especially in the collection *Long Live Man.* Moreover, his message there is that the spirit is immortal. In his latest poems, he continually returns to this motif of a spirit that is beyond place and time and is eternal, but he does so in a mocking voice, the voice of the half-serious comedian, moving in and out of high and low languages, mixing them together so that each voice can question the reality of the other. In one of his last poems in *Mindfield,* Corso again touches on this theme:

> To believe that life dies with the body
> is to be spirit-sick
> This is the great danger
> to body-think the spirit an ephemeral thing
> The cancer victim of healthy spirit
> is nothing terminal
> whereby the body of health
> dim of spirit, is—
> As the fish is animalized water
> so are we humanized spirit
> fish come and go   humans also
> the death of the fish
> is not the death of the water
> likewise the death of yr body
> is not the death of life
> . . . .
> And don't let a dead body in a grave
> marked Gregory Corso
> make you laugh "har har,"
> "and he said he'd never die,
> looka the schmuck buried dead"

> Just know that there'll be a sky
> above that grave there
>
> . . . .
>
> remember that people are
> quite often unreliable,
> and it's them, tell you, you gotta die;
> be seeing you on the rebound
>
> (from "Field Report," *M* 226–27)

Thus Corso sees tragedy and comedy as two aspects of the same human spirit. They are both paradoxical. Tragedy is of the body, in that it appears that if the body dies, we have died; comedy is of the spirit, in that if the body dies, it lives on. Together, they form the two faces of humanity, and it is this elemental dualism that forms a third in Corso's poetry, a human being: one who suffers but also laughs and believes in his or her own eternal return.

From the original paintings on the cave walls until now, art has served as a form of communication that brings us together, but it has also served as something that sets us apart and causes strife. Against the general postmodern trend in which institutions are disparaged and nothing is worthy of retention, Corso has looked back at great schools of thought, from Sumerian to Egyptian, and forward to surrealism and sought to build a poetry within the Beat movement that would endure. However, one would have to conclude that Corso, in searching for something stable, has found nothing at all to believe in. Instead, he has created a legacy of compassion and humor against the animalistic tendencies celebrated by the utter zealots, who formulate a program and then kill everybody who doesn't believe it. Corso is religious but in a comic sense, like the ancient Gnostic heresiarchs who lived in Alexandria in the second century A.D. and whose leader was an esoteric Jesus, whom Corso perhaps refers to in a few lines in his "Geometric Poem":

> In walks of emma wheat and rye
> far from the mills
> in voyant eye
> What creature, entranced in orange,
> appears, neither far off nor near?
>
> (*EF* 53)

This fragment is indicative of Corso's baffling poetry, where he himself cannot seem to focus, cannot seem to fix for himself a definite vision of life, but constantly hops between different visions, unstable, aggravating, and for some reason unable to give a strong foundation to his own life or poetry, and yet it is illuminated by humor. It is only in humor that he can manage to create a full poem, somehow feeling that the older mode has been played out. He can question, but he cannot affirm; he can move between different modes, but he cannot take a stand. I believe this is healthy, as he keeps his options open, playing one option off another, juggling paradigms: the Thomist, the surrealist, the Darwinian, the classical, and others. He jumps between very light, positive visions and very dark, negative visions, sometimes without any transition in between, as if he was some kind of two-headed creature composed of Bishop Berkeley on the one side and the Marquis de Sade on the other. This leaping figure is a harlequin, or trickster, and his song, at its best, is deeply and richly comic. Corso never comes across with a program but instead plays one program off the other. Unlike a more totalitarian thinker, who has one paradigm and insists you swallow it or die, Corso has many paradigms and negotiates between them, moving between human and divine and back again. He borrows a great deal from Thomism and its later upside-down variant, surrealism, but he suffuses both with comedy and refuses to turn either one into his ideology. As Corso got older, he opened up his thinking instead of closing it down, developing a kind of crazy wisdom in the process, a juggling act that is ecological in the sense that it balances many different varieties of mental life while retaining Thomism and its belief in the afterlife as home base.

4

Corso's "Perspective Through Incongruity"

Because he doesn't have any one paradigm that he privileges over others, Corso is capable of creating a certain "perspective through incongruity," to borrow a phrase from Kenneth Burke (*Attitudes* 308). Nevertheless, it seems pertinent to question whether Corso's perspective moves toward utter doubt, as in Gnosticism, which influenced several of the Beat writers, especially Ginsberg and Burroughs. What does it mean to be a mental explorer?

This is what Corso describes as the poet's job. "Someone must Christopher Columbus the mind, the great expanse of consciousness, and this the poet does" (*Some of My Beginnings* 173). Corso never actually practiced any religion as an adult, because he preferred to operate as a maverick rather than belong to a given congregation. In the interview with Michael André, Corso briefly discusses his interest in Gnosticism.

André: Allen [Ginsberg] talked a bit about the Gnostic tradition. Rather than the Christian tradition, would you say you are in the Gnostic tradition[?]

Corso: I don't know. The thing that makes sense to me is the "reflection." Sophia, the counterpart of Yahweh, the master worker, the female component, is wisdom, reflects wisdom and light at once, to see itself, light, you know, so it's reflective. Everything in that reflection then comes into being like Yahweh or the gods that be till today, all part of a reflection. They're not even real, they're just part of a reflection of Sophia. Made an awful lot of sense to me. That all this would be literally reflected from something else.

The Gnostics had something going there all right. And they were always hoping for change. (143)

In this short speech, Corso's ambivalence makes clear that he shares a similar suspicion about knowledge with the ancient Gnostics. The Gnostics felt that humankind was imprisoned on earth, which was a prison planet. Many of Corso's prison poems could be seen in this light, in which pure spirits are trapped within a brutal system and an angelic humanity is brutalized by a fallen humanity. The dedication on the front page of *Gasoline* makes this clear: "I dedicate this book to the angels of Clinton Prison who, in my 17th year, handed me, from all the cells surrounding me, books of illumination." He never depicts prisoners as barbaric monsters but rather as misunderstood angels, a point that Gregory Stephenson makes throughout his study *Exiled Angel: A Study of the Work of Gregory Corso.* The Gnostics viewed all of humanity in this light and would have seen wardens and jailers as simply not being awake enough to realize that they were in the wrong.

Allen Ginsberg discusses Gnosticism as a distant ancestor to his own poetic practice in his essay "When the Mode of the Music Changes, the Walls of the City Shake," where he writes:

> I thought and still think that the bulwark of libertarian-anarchist-sexualized individual poems and prose created from that era to this day—under so much middle-class critical attack—were the mental bombs that would still explode in new kid generations even if censorship and authoritarian (moral majority) fundamentalist militarily-hierarchical "New Order" neoconservative fascistoid creep Reaganomics-type philistinism ever took over the nation. Which it nearly has. Thus the title—Poetics and Politics, out of Plato out of Pythagoras—continuation of gnostic—secret and politically suppressed—liberty of consciousness and art—old bohemian—tradition—thru the existence of exquisite paperbacks too many in print to be burned. The clock could never be turned back. (*Deliberate Prose* 253–54)

The Gnostics saw the Bible as the manual of the prison God and read it backwards in order to figure out how to free themselves. They saw the Ten Commandments in particular as a mode of entrapment. The King James Version has the injunction "Thou shalt not make unto thee any graven image, or any likeness of any thing that is in heaven above, or that is in the earth beneath, or that is in the water under the earth" (Exodus 20:4). This strange admonition, which prohibits images of absolutely any kind, would seemingly outlaw aesthetics. Gnostics would undo this bizarre prohibition, as well as the nine other commandments, in claiming that it was only in the breach of these commandments that one could attain heaven. The licentious Gnostics, known as the Carpocratians, went so far as to endorse murder, adultery, and other crimes in order to disgust the archon, or jailer, so that the soul could return to heaven. This is an insistent theme in contemporary counterculture. As Jules Monnerot notes, "The comparison between Surrealists and so-called licentious Gnostics (Carpocratians, Nicolites, etc.) is self-evident" (cited in Chénieux-Gendron 25). Is this theme one simply to open new possibilities for thought or new options for irresponsibility in the name of theology? It raises many questions still today, just as it did at the time of its conception.

Ancient Gnosticism flourished in two sites. The physical site was the second-century city of Alexandria, Egypt. Here, the great influences of East and West rivaled one another for preeminence. The textual site was the Book of Genesis. Why did these two sites create Gnosticism?

Alexandria, wrote Victorian theosophist G. R. S. Mead, was "the city where Egypt and Africa, Rome and Greece, Syria and Arabia met together," and it is where "some of the greatest Gnostic doctors lived" (120). Alexandria was the New York City of its day. It numbered among its inhabitants, Mead writes in his rather archaic and sometimes unintentionally offensive style, "never . . . less than 40,000 Hebrews," as well as "the better class Egyptians and Greeks, most extremely refined, haughty and effeminate" (100). In addition, there was a small bureaucratic class from Rome. The local Arabic population was supplemented by "[t]housands of Ethiopians and Negroes . . . in the brightest possible colors. . . . Phoenicians and Carthaginian sailor-folk in numbers, and traders from far more distant ports" lined the wharves, as well as "a few tall golden-haired people, Goths and Teutons perchance, extremely contemptuous of the rest, whom they regard as an effeminate crowd—big, tall, strong, rough fellows. A few Persians also, and more distant Orientals" (101). In this heterogeneous population, a degree of intellectual give-and-take could be expected.

Elaine Pagels writes that "Gnostics regarded conformity, whether in doctrine or discipline, as something that only beginners needed to take seriously" (72). But, she adds, there is one commonality: "Gnostic Christians, who disagreed with one another on almost everything else, agreed that this naive story [Adam and Eve in the Book of Genesis] hid profound truths" (xxiv). Ioan Couliano comments that "it remains a mystery why our Platonists [Gnostics] were so keen on commenting on the Book of Genesis instead of anything else" (135).

There is a central problem in Gnosticism, Sade, Darwin, and more extreme varieties of surrealism (Bataille, Artaud). Is this world worth living in or not? If earth is a prison planet populated by robotic prisoners, trapped in bodies that prevent them from knowing their own spirits, then it is hell. If this world is some kind of extension of heaven, however, or if it is actually consubstantial with heaven, as the neo-Platonist philosopher Plotinus claimed (see Barnstone 725), then it is good, and beauty can exist within it. The Gnostics in general, as far as I have been able to determine, did not have a theory of aesthetics, nor did they have a significant tradition of art. If this world was ugly, why bother to beautify it? Can beauty exist in a planet that was invented by a demonic agent?

Bishop Irenaeus of Lyon, one of the first patristic chroniclers to crusade against Gnosticism, writes that "like the Lernaean hydra, a manheaded beast has been generated from the school of Valentinus" (112). Irenaeus describes over and over again a system of double-paternity proposed by various Gnostics. The basic format is that there is a perfect God who is beyond knowing, surrounded by a Pleroma of nearly perfect beings, composed of between four and thirty Aeons. One of these Aeons, Sophia, got restless and decided to create something on her own: Ialdabaoth, who is "like an abortion" (112). Ialdabaoth, in turn, believes there is no one above him and boasts that he is the author of all things. Ialdabaoth, whose name means "Son of Chaos" in Hebrew (Jonas 305), is given positive identification by the Gnostics as being the very same God of the Old Testament, Yahweh, who makes such a baffling entrance in the Book of Genesis. As Irenaeus writes, "On her [Sophia's] departing, he imagined he was the only being in existence; and on this account declared, 'I am a jealous God, and besides me there is no one'" (103). What does he have to be jealous of, if there are no others? Exploiting some discrepancies in Genesis, the Gnostic heresiarchs launch their revelations at Ialdabaoth. If God is all-knowing, as he claims to be, why is it that he has to ask Adam, ashamed and in hiding after eating the forbidden fruit, where Adam is when he is walking in the Garden of Eden? How is it that we can all come from Adam and Eve if we are supposed to be against incest? The Gnostics describe horrific lists of generation that parody those in Genesis, in which Adam and Eve and Cain and others beget each other in sinful combinations. But it is not just the Book of Genesis they seek to critique, and this is my central point: they perceive the fall into time as essentially an abomination.

If this world is a prison planet, therefore, the idea of an aesthetics based upon Gnostic thought is rather paradoxical. How can anything be considered beautiful if we can't even trust our senses? If what we see before us is a world of illusions and madness, what is left?

One way to read Corso's laughter is to see it as a reflection from Sophia, wisdom, a reflection of the increate light of the Godhead. What is real in us is eternal and is consubstantial with the uncreated; it is, in fact, part of the increate light that lies beyond time and space in the unspeakable. When the Aeon Sophia remembers her true father, she laughs because she realizes this world is an error (Couliano 78). Laughter is what brings us to a true understanding of our plight. Throughout the patristic writers' texts, they revile the Gnostics not only for their individual heresies and bold innovations but also for their spirit of hilarity. Thus, Ioan Couliano sees part of the Pistis Sophia text as an "impressive parody of Plato" (104); elsewhere, the Savior (Christ) laughs at the thought that a mere wooden cross could kill him (Couliano 135); and Irenaeus says that the light of our world came from Sophia's smile (18). In order to demonstrate the comedy in the Gnostic method of exegesis, Bishop Irenaeus often resorts to lengthy satire:

> Iu, Iu! Pheu! Pheu!—for well may we utter these tragic exclamations at such
> a pitch of audacity in the coining of names as he has displayed without a
> blush, in devising a nomenclature for his system of falsehood. . . . It is most
> manifest that he confesses the things which have been said to be his own
> invention, and that he himself has given names to his scheme of things,
> which had never been previously suggested by any other . . . nothing hin-
> ders any other, in dealing with the same subject, to affix names after such
> a fashion as the following: There is a certain Proarche, royal surpassing all
> thought, a power existing before every other substance, and extended into

space in every direction. But along with it there exists a power which I term a Gourd; and along with this Gourd there exists a power which again I term Utter-Emptiness. This Gourd and Emptiness, since they are one, produced (and yet did not simply produce, so as to be apart from themselves) a fruit, everywhere visible, eatable, and delicious, which fruit language calls a Cucumber. Along with this Cucumber exists a power of the same essence, which again I call a Melon. These powers, the Gourd, Utter-Emptiness, the Cucumber, and the Melon, brought forth the remaining multitude of the delirious melons of Valentinus. (47–48)

Although this is meant to mock the Gnostic heresiarchs for their lack of rigor, it is closer to the Gnostic spirit of hilarious and irresponsible parody than Irenaeus knew. To think about Corso in these terms, however, is possible.

A parody mocks its model in seeking to demonstrate the inferiority of the original; at the same time, it tries to not take itself very seriously. In contrast, a satire seeks to demonstrate its mastery over the model. Gnostic thought acknowledges that we are in a crazy-house, but its reaction to this is a spirit of levity rather than Shelleyan melancholia. Parody mocks the notion of genesis in making fun of the very idea of an original. Corso's mockery is playful, rarely superior in its intentions. When he knocks over an idol, he does so playfully rather than with the bitter zealotry that would characterize a believer in some other system that, he would believe, represented some better tradition.

The cruelty of a ferocious Gnostic like Sade as he is presented in Pierre Klossowski's *Sade, My Neighbor,* however, doesn't really fit into Corso's countervalent tendency, which is toward life, sweetness, and a certain pleasure in natural biology, as is evidenced in "Giant Turtle," which details a turtle laying eggs in a Walt Disney film (*M* 73), or in "Active Night," the poem set in a Malaysian rain forest. One has the feeling throughout the poems that even though the beauty of this world is offset by death and life is food, which is some kind of basic design in nature, life is still worth it. Gnosticism and orthodox Christianity bear a similarity—a concern with a transcendent afterlife at the expense of a concern for this world—but Gnosticism goes much further. For those who reject the belief that this world is just a pile of dead garbage from which our souls must transcend, they must also reject Gnosticism of any variety. Corso has dozens of variations on this theme, see-sawing between love for the world and then depicting the form of life given to us as being itself a sacrilege. He shows us as more closely related to the tyrannosaurus than to God in "Poem Jottings in the Early Morn":

> Walks Tyrannosaurus like a man
> in the monster night
> To this beastkind am I related
> —closer to it than the god
> from whom we're created—
>
> (*HA* 56)

The Book of Genesis is about sex—the beginning of man and the inauguration of procreation. The Gnostics saw this as the beginning of their imprisonment in imperfection. Corso's artistic activity is expressed through a parodic theophany: the signs he makes on paper are deliberate contradictions and as such are stereotypes and, therefore, laughable. He thus lets himself feel free to err, making deliberate mistakes. In creating error, he mimics Ialdabaoth, parodying his efforts at creation, for only the increate is perfect, and the errors of comedy are a crucial aspect of Corso's aesthetic: in doubling the error in following his errancy, he doubles into laughter. It is this same impious hilarity that Irenaeus found so questionable at the very heart of the Gnostic system. Only in exhausting the seemingly inexhaustible can we break the vicious circle of reincarnation and return to the heavenly light; only by rendering the ridiculous things he has done ridiculous, or the things he has made us want to do, can we return to the one true increate Source, outside of time and space and with which we are consubstantial.

The Beat writers have often been charged with bad taste, as they bring in elements of life that more careful, academic writers would like to leave out. Corso used words—like "shit," "cunt," "fuck"—that don't appear in most poetry before the 1950s. In Ginsberg's nomination of Corso to the American Academy and Institute of Arts and Letters, he quotes Corso as saying, "I have better taste than life" (quoted in *Deliberate Prose* 392).

Corso doubts everything, but his faith is surely in life, even if what he finds most distasteful about life is death. This is why he denies death, which gives him better taste than life.

> **Thought**
> Death is but is not lasting.
> To pass a dead bird,
> the notice of it is,
> Yet walking on
> Is gone.
> The thought remains
> And thought is all I know of death.
>
> (*LL* 46)

Corso's work often undoes itself in this way, so that the reader is almost forced to think against the speech of the poet. Although Corso implies that nothing is real, and therefore everything can be altered and changed—which is very similar to the Gnostic viewpoint—we know better. Death is real, and it is permanent, and our bodies are animalistic and have a growth and death, just as animal bodies do. Is this ugly or is it beautiful? This is the world that has been given to us. We are made to feel lustful instincts by our bodies. Post-Darwin, it is difficult to argue that we are not a species of animal, and yet, a truly ingenious demonic god might have placed other animals here to make us think, analogically, that we are a member of the animal kingdom, since we share with them DNA and certain patterns of eating and defecation. Another unlikely possibility, too, is that some people have descended from an angelic nature while others are purely animal, as is stated in the Gnostic Book of Enoch. In this section, the Lord asks the head of a band of unruly angels:

> Why did you leave lofty, holy Heaven to sleep with women, to defile your-selves with the daughters of men and take them as your wives, and like the children of the earth to beget sons . . . ? Though you were holy and spiri-tual, living the eternal life, you defiled yourself with the blood of women, you begot children with the blood of flesh, and like the others you have lusted after flesh and blood as do those who die and perish. Because they perish I gave them wives so they might impregnate them, have children, and nothing be lacking on the earth. But you were spiritual and immortal for all generations of the world. (cited in Barnstone 487)

Corso changes this depiction of angels copulating with human women and conflates it with the act of the creation of poetry, as it is the intermingling of the divine with the earthly.

> Now as of old
> the Sons of God shall come down
> and make it with the Daughters of Men
> now as of old
> with their load of megagalactic semen
>
> Let go O pen thy ink!
> and lo! the page did fill
> Spring came to the true side of April
> I hailed "Here is your Spring Son!"
> She cried "Well done . . . well done"
>
> Of poesy and children have I sung
> Father of both
> . . . .
> (from "Return," *HA* 9)

Nature has provided us with incommunicable desires. These desires are the basis of dirty jokes, which bind us together in laughter, and the basis of porno-graphic imagery, which permits us to glimpse our banished instincts. For Corso, virtue is a matter of disseminating beauty, through the media, concerning these instincts, so that our commonality can be revealed to one another and so that the great pleasure of animality can thus be revealed. We are like gods in that we have the power to create and become fathers. Corso is not against generation in the poem above but is rather proud of it and proud of his ability to participate in it. However, Corso wavers in uncertainty, at one point seeing us as more closely related to the tyrannosaurus—who walked upright. But Corso's "Poem Jottings in the Early Morn" also questions that conclusion of the animality of humanity, inconclusively, with these lines:

> Man is mystical
> Woman magical
>
>   a free spirit
>   is a divine
>   fuck-up
>
>   (*HA* 56)

Corso's references to pagan mystery religions proliferate throughout his poetry and seem to posit Faustus as a central figure, who in turn was derived from the ancient Gnostic figure Simon Magus. Willis Barnstone writes:

> In Latin Simon was referred to as *Faustus* (the favored one). So Marlowe and Goethe, who elaborated the figure of an irreverent scholar and magician, envisioning Helen of Troy as his consort, were using as their source the very old Gnostic Samaritan, Simon Magus. (606)

Corso himself could be seen as playing out this myth in his life, as well as in his art, with his innumerable references to Hermes, Hermes Trismegistus, alchemy, and other heresies. Although he calls himself a "mental explorer, un-Faustian" (cited in Parker 237), I believe he means that he is a white magician, as opposed to a black one, but a magician nonetheless. This is the image he plays with, one that provides him with a persona throughout his middle poetry, but it is primarily as a white magician blessed with a sense of humor that he would like to be seen, an image he seems to have wholly invented for himself based on Gnosticism, the Western tradition of magic, and various pagan mythologies. The sense of humor, which is the most active element in this hodgepodge, however, is something that Corso struggled with, not certain if it was dignified enough for the role of prophet and magician. Corso asks in the poem "The American Way,"

> Could grammar school youth seriously look upon
>   a picture of George Washington and "Herman Borst"
>   the famous night club comedian together at Valley
> Forge?
>
>   (*EF* 73)

Corso was constantly trying to put dignified faces together with the less dignified personae of the entertainment industry, sometimes doubting whether they belonged together, but sometimes thinking they did belong. To this extent, Corso was akin to the ancient Gnostics, who believed in a kind of trickster Jesus, who was similar to the Christian presentation of Simon Magus. The Jesus of the Gnostics often held a Manichean view of light and dark, in which light was associated with laughter and heaven, and darkness was associated with the world of matter. The Gnostics, in order to create this dichotomy, had to argue that this world was a dark and difficult one, composed by a devilish archon, who sought to destroy all knowledge and all ethics.

Plotinus attacked the Gnostics for having no theory of virtue.

> First we should acknowledge that Plotinus vehemently rejected Gnostic pessimism, that acosmic view that considered human beings as alienated creatures in a hostile world created by an evil Creator God. For him the world was good and beautiful. He espoused optimism. (Barnstone 724–25)

Plotinus was a key figure for the romantics and surrealists.

> If we are to speak of a "key" to early Romanticism, it is to be found in one of the thinkers of antiquity, Plotinus. For this Neoplatonic philosopher not only inspired the entire system of Novalis, scattered throughout innumerable fragments, and many of the ideas of Schelling in his middle period; his arm reached farther: through Novalis and Schelling he exercised an influence, though an indirect one, upon both the Schlegels. (P. Rieff cited in Lovejoy 298)

Similarly, Jacqueline Chénieux-Gendron writes:

> Within esotericism, Surrealism tends to find affinities in Gnostic traditions, once it has freed them from their dated imagery, their basic dualism, and their metaphysical foundations. In Plotinus and his followers it finds a thematic of unity, as opposed to plurality, central to Surrealist reflection on the individual. (24–25)

Plotinus doesn't separate the world into good and bad but maintains gradations for fear that this world down below will be treated with contempt. Plotinus's worry is a worry today, too, as a new generation of doubters critique everything, including marriage, decency, and kindness, and think that every human institution is just a prison of the big lie. We can enjoy Gnosticism for its cleverness and its logical rigor, but where does it lead? Plotinus warned:

> Their doctrine, even more audacious than that of Epicurus (who only denied providence), by blaming the Lord of providence and providence itself, holds in contempt all the laws down here and virtue which has risen among men from the beginning of time, and puts temperance to ridicule, so that nothing good may be discovered in this world. (quoted in Jonas 266)

An optimistic view of the cosmos is important, even paramount, to the mental life of the individual or of a nation, but is it possible in light of the fact of death and the fact that everything on earth is food for everything else? Is morality possible in such a cosmos?

Corso often seems more interested in brushing questions of morality aside (within a parodic theological framework) in order to legitimate comic probing, a trait I see as his driving motivation. However, as Corso's thought matures, his thinking goes one notch further, toward the indication that immoral images are precisely moral images, a countervailing argument I saw just as often in him when I was a student at Naropa Institute as I see now in rereading his poetry. Sometimes he would make an appalling joke about the nature of the world (he would say, for instance, that people were just "hairy bags of water"), and I would laugh too hard, in order to worry him that I had uncritically accepted his assessment; he would then cease abruptly. Then he would back off and say something like, "Be careful of what you approve in laughter; not everything that's funny is wholesome."

Skau writes that the phrase "human beings are just hairy bags of water" was originally from William Burroughs, although Ginsberg attributes the phrase to Corso himself in a book published after Skau's (*Deliberate Prose* 362). Skau writes, "Corso demurs: 'But myself, I question the idea that I'm just a bag of water. My body may be, but I'm not yet convinced that I am" (85). In this instance, Corso was struggling to balance his early Catholic religious system with the cynicism of his friend William Burroughs, or else he was again questioning his own cynicism and tempering it with idealism. Corso's work is seemingly balanced on a tightrope walk over a precipice between doubt and acceptance of the cosmos, between optimism and pessimism, and he can totter either way very quickly, into the darkest pessimism or the highest optimism.

At the end of reading his poems, one is forced to say, with him, "I cannot totally comprehend / what it all meant . . . if it meant anything at all" ("Youthful Religious Experiences," *HA* 23).

In the poem "The Leaky Lifeboat Boys," Corso discusses the cosmic beliefs of the two other major surviving Beats. Kerouac had been dead for some time, but Ginsberg and Burroughs were still alive:

> They view the prophets of lift-off with
> understandable envy
> "Just looka Elijah! Muhammed! the others!
>   they made the out-of-here alive!"
>
> Of the three leaky lifeboat boys
> one is of a considerate nature
> . . . wondering how the planet as well
>   can get out alive
>
>   (*HA* 16)

Elijah, according to tradition, is one of only two men who went to heaven without dying first. "Enoch, who lived 365 years, is one of two men who were taken up bodily into the presence of God without dying. (The prophet Elijah . . . is the other)" (Barnstone 485). Corso, in the above fragment, who I am assuming is the one with "a considerate nature," as he often has this half-comic braggadocio as part of his persona, indicates that he is wondering how the entire planet could be taken to heaven. In this sense, he is "un-Faustian" in that he doesn't want to use his magic purely for personal gain but rather to help the whole planet. Corso disagrees with the idea of death, because it doesn't accord with his personal optimism:

> They don't trust death
> "It's a gimmick" they say
> fobbed on them
> by that most unreliable of species, humankind
> Humans unanimously agree
> in time we all must die—
> They disagree,
> To them death's the oldest gossip in planet town
>
> (*HA* 15)

It would be easy to stuff Corso into a Gnostic framework—one who knows that all he can know is humor—and to posit this Gnosticism as a possible escape route from the prison of his early youth, which became a metaphor to him of the entirety of human society. It is only in humor that he glimpsed once more the increate light of peace. "I am in love with the laughing sickness" ("Zizi's Lament," *G* 47)

It is only in this moment that he was able to bend back the reflections of Ialdabaoth and see as in a fun-house mirror the utter stupidity of reason, the god of positivism, which all of his poems work to circumvent. Corso is the poet upside down, the shaman with pants on his head, the man speaking from his asshole, and in this guise is an explosively pleasant alternative to the older canon, to which Corso will never belong, just as the work of the Gnostic libertines could never be included in the Bible. Corso worshiped another god, as well as the Catholic God, one who has many names but who is finally antinomian, beyond culture, one based in humor, whose name within Gnosticism was Sophia.

This is a God of the natural body function, of eating, shitting, and living within a contradictory world. In another earlier poem, Corso describes his fealty to this God.

> **God? She's Black**
> Gases and liquids Her nature
> spewing stars like eggs
> from Her All-Central Womb. . . .
>
> (*LL* 44)

Corso's god here is laughter herself, a reflection of Sophia, unknowably wise as well as lamentably stupid, and in almost every poem in this middle period he pays homage to her and to the spirit of obscenity she bequeathed as the only reminder of our immortality. Corso's relentless attacks on the Biblical God, as in "God Is a Masturbator" and "God? She's Black," could be seen in the light of Gnosticism, as could the ending to the poem "Ah . . . Well," which reads,

> Pain, Death
> The Big Lie of Life
> The apothecarian earth blooms the poppy
> at best

(HA 40)

Corso's work shares with Gnosticism a preoccupation with the next world, but he also sees this world as eminently worthy of living in and is, in many of his poems, afraid to die. Corso is difficult to evaluate, difficult to put into any framework of religion or philosophy, because he so often contradicts himself, having no program whatsoever, except, seemingly, to keep his options open and to expand vision. The one thing that Corso continually refers to is poetry, which he wrote at rapid speed, as an iconoclast might, breaking every image, playing with thoughts as if they were meaningless toys.

In Kerouac's *Desolation Angels* is an image of Corso writing: "Now Raphael [Corso] begins to write a poem, suddenly he's stopped talking as Irwin [Ginsberg] lit a candle and as we all sit relaxing in low tones you can hear the scratchey-scratch of Raphael's pen racing over the page" (cited in McClanahan 119). This image of Corso's breakneck speed is quite different from the slow, thoughtful contemplation one usually thinks of as a poet's composition practice and indicates Corso's headlong manner in general and his lack of reverence, but I often spent time with Corso in the summer of 1977, and he told me that he would usually work on a poem for ten years or more in his head before he wrote it down. The speed of composition that the Kerouac quote implies needn't necessarily imply carelessness. If Corso had piety toward anything, it was toward his art. He would write many drafts of the same poem as his ambivalence drove him from one perspective to another.

Iconoclastic agnostic in the middle period, Corso veers between visions, never holding to any particular one for long and never managing to build an enduring vision but rather leaving behind a record of a poet given to vicissitudes, whimsies, sudden turns, and capricious exploration. To ask whether his vision is ultimately positive or not is again to miscalculate. There is an ecological balance between two different paradigms in Corso, one positive and the other negative, and it is this incessant balancing act that marks, in Burke's phrase, his "perspective through incongruity" and that is reiterated in Corso's famous phrase at Naropa in which he gave the advice, "When in doubt—choose both!"

5

Toward a Psychiatric Evaluation of Corso

Some of Corso's best poems take off in directions that seemingly have no moral compass whatsoever and leave one feeling lost. How does one evaluate such a poem as the following?

I Dream in the Daytime
I dream in daytime
    much too somber
   to greet the angels
      at my velvet-shredded door

They enter salt
   they pour my milk
      they sprinkle white flies on the floor

I cringe my sink
   I gloom my stove

They leave me pink
   I dip my glove

(*EF* 111)

It has complexity and coherence in its rhyme scheme with extremely subtle internal rhymes in a few places, such as "pour" and "floor" and "door," and traditional rhymes like "sink" and pink"; "dream" and "time" almost rhyme. It also scans, and there is parallelism in the syntax, and assonance, but the logic of it goes completely contrary to any sense one might draw from it, and it ends on a brilliant near-rhyme that indicates a certain aesthetic reaction. But what does it add up to? How can one begin to evaluate such a nonsensical sequence? To my knowledge, no critic has ever tried, and yet this poem represents a high point in

Corso's art. A structural mood analysis of the poem would show us that the first stanza presents the narrator as unwilling to greet his guests at the door, but they come in anyway and commit mischievous deeds concerning things white, since they are angels. They enter salt, they pour his milk, they sprinkle white flies on his floor. The narrator is alarmed and "cringes" his sink and "glooms" his stove, rather odd verbs that indicate that the narrator is bent out of shape, but in the last couplet, things seem to have changed for the better. Inspiration appears to have arrived, as they leave him pink, and he dips his glove, as if to try for himself what they have wrought.

The poem appears to be a kind of celebration of inspiration in the way it sneaks up on Corso, like one of those mischievous gentlemen in Damon Runyan's New York stories of the 1940s who sticks matches in the shoes of newspaper readers, lights them, and then laughs at the hot foot that results when the match burns down. The poem can be seen as well from the viewpoint of Gnosticism—the angels who come to the door arrive in spite of his somber feeling, entering his "dark room," which could be a metaphor for his body, and bring him news of his sense of humor, which leaves him feeling healthier, "pink."

In alchemical terms, the poem takes us through the three mental levels the alchemists depicted. The poem opens in a black mood, which corresponds with *nigredo,* which, as Stanislas Klossowski de Rola writes in his book *Alchemy,* is the beginning.

> Thus death, which is a separation, is followed by a long process of decay which lasts until all is petrified and the opposites dissolved in the liquid *nigredo.* This darkness darker than darkness, this "black of blacks," is the first sure sign that one is on the right path; hence the alchemical aphorism: "No generation without corruption." . . . The end of the second work comes with the appearance of the Whiteness, *albedo.* Once the whiteness is reached, our subject is said to have acquired sufficient strength to resist the ardours of the fire, and it is only one more step until the Red King or Sulphur of the Wise appears. (11–12)

Thus Corso's color scheme nearly rhymes with the rising color scheme of the alchemists, from black to white to red. Is his poem a description of the change in mood that the alchemists depicted through the metaphorical process of changing a leaden mood to a golden one, using the mind as a kind of Athanor, or philosophical furnace?

It is always possible to see a double level in Corso's productions. One is a reference to his magical fixations; the other is with the actual realities of his own life, which he searchingly and often playfully documents. Corso's inspiration for his clowning comes perhaps from his early childhood in New York. He was born in the period that Damon Runyan's stories describe; they recall the vivacious Sicilian heritage of many of the characters of that day, their weird feuds over women, and bizarre sense of humor.

Corso comes from a world different from the other Beat writers and has to be appreciated as such. Untrained in formal schools, his school was the rough, hard hilarity of 1930s New York City. Is Gregory Corso a member of the Beat group by anything other than physical proximity? Whereas Ginsberg defined a generation of activists by his stances against the nuclear bomb, the heterosexual family, and white business culture, Corso wrote one of his most famous poems in praise of the bomb, was married several times and had several children, and, in some of his earliest poems, praised or are at least remained neutral toward the Mafia, perhaps the quintessence of corporate culture and the most cutthroat aspects of that culture. While William Burroughs had a paranoid political reading of American corporate culture, in which he posited a sinister group of Dr. Benways who were out to exploit everyone and everything, defined himself against that group of exploiters, and tried to find ways to free himself from the strangler's grip of addictive needs, which he considered part of a strategy of domination, Corso believed in no such thing and in his fiction and poetry makes fun of paranoid conspiracy theories and even of the very idea of knowledge. In one of the rare interviews between Corso and Burroughs, it is characteristic that Corso poses the questions and Burroughs answers even the strangest and most puzzling of them with speedy aplomb:

Corso: What is death?
Burroughs: A gimmick. It's the time birth death gimmick. Can't go on too much longer, too many people are wising up. (Corso and Ginsberg 79)

Burroughs then goes on to describe how to get wise to the death gimmick by rearranging words on a page, by breaking up the control of words, by going into silence. He then breaks up a bunch of sentences, words having to do with political conflicts, consciousness, monopoly, and control. Corso immediately responds, "Reading that it seems you end up where you began, with politics and its nomenclature: conflict, attain, solution, monopoly, control—so what kind of help is that?" (79).

Allen Ginsberg then joins the conversation, and Burroughs and Ginsberg go on to talk about advice they would give to young people regarding evading control and the marijuana policy in Cuba. As the two major Beats figure out how to live in the world and pass on their wisdom, Corso, like Harpo Marx, is silenced, but that doesn't mean the wheels stop turning. Corso's major impulse is not to affirm but rather to contradict. In the prose self-reflection entitled "Variations on a Generation," Corso questions the moniker of "Beat" as it is applied to himself.

—What do you think about the Beat Generation?—
—I don't think it is anything. I don't think it exists. There's no such thing as the Beat Generation.—
—You don't consider yourself Beat?—
—Hell no! I don't consider myself beat, or beatified.—

—What are you if not beat?—
—An individual, nothing.—
—They say to be beat is to be nothing.—
—I don't care what they say, there's no Beat Generation. (90–91)

Corso's work is not about becoming a master thinker or creating the paranoid conditions that would unify one generation against another. The paranoid world that Burroughs and Ginsberg build up of sinister, powerful men, compared with sweet, innocent angels of youth, is not at all Corso's vision of the world. In Burroughs's works, such as *The Job,* he outlines long and specific answers to world problems in terms of a program. Ginsberg does the same thing in much of his prose collected in *Deliberate Prose.* In this sense, Corso is not a Beat, in that he is not certain of his view of the world. His vision of the world is nonsensical. While major philosophy from the beginning has been an attempt to build ideas that are adequate to an understanding of the world, from Plato to Hegel, from Marx to Louis Althusser, there has also existed a minoritarian philosophy, which I would characterize as running from Diogenes, whose philosophy consisted of making fun of Plato's remarks, to Edward Lear, whose work consists of making fun of the preoccupations of the nineteenth-century aesthetic philosophies of Hegel and Kant and parodying Tennyson, on to Harpo Marx, who I would contrast with Groucho Marx. In short, it is always those who think they know something and shoot off their mouths against those who know they know nothing. This latter group is the one preferred in postmodern philosophy as it is defined by Gilles Deleuze and Jean-François Lyotard. Corso falls into that latter group, perhaps more so than any other Beat. As such, Corso is the anti-Beat, the Beat who didn't believe in Beatitude and questioned the ex cathedra thinking of the other Beats, driving them somewhat crazy in the process.

Corso doesn't know what he is talking about. He doesn't think that anybody else does, either. In this sense, he is a lot like Socrates, at least the Socrates who suddenly admitted (just before his death) that the only thing he knew is that he didn't know anything. Corso writes jokingly that he knows everything necessary, laughing at the idea of knowledge as being something that one can master:

> . . . wisdom is a lean thing
> for regard that head on his deathbed
> hemlocking: "All I know is I know nothing"
> You at least claimed to know everything
>   but yourself
> I claim to know all there is to know
> because there ain't that much to know
>   (from "Dear Villon," *M* 181)

As André Glucksmann writes in his book *The Master Thinkers,* "From Socrates to the G.I. deserter, the sharing of inscientia and the deliberate fraternization of ignorances constitutes an experiment in democracy, the only one known" (86).

In a related poem, "Wisdom," Corso denies his own intelligence:

> I feel there is an inherent ignorance in me
> deep in my being
> to the very core
> I know its presence
> by an unforgettable smell
>   first experienced in childhood:
> a nose clogged with blood
>   mixed with the odor of an old man's belongings
>
>   (HA 12)

Burroughs and Ginsberg, therefore, are participating in a pompous and undemocratic session during the interview previously quoted. They pretend to belong to the society of knowledge holders who build a hierarchy of knowledge in order to charge others admission. Corso wants to tear this society down and poke holes in it. Master thinkers such as Karl Marx have ideas that they think are ultimately adequate to the world. Their game is to impress others with what they know. What we should know, at least by now, is that their knowledge, if played out in the actual world, always leads to misery. Huge theoretical constructs are prisons in which millions of people die because the system works only by killing off those who question the system. Thus, the Gulag Archipelago was filled not with bourgeois infidels who ran factories but rather with intellectuals and interrogators and iconoclasts. A master thinker cannot stand rivals and must extinguish them or put them in work camps.

Corso, on the other hand, is one of those who doesn't know, and so he can stand rivals, or friends, because he is not in competition with them to know more. Perhaps he is only in competition with them to see if he can know less. While Corso never made any public policy statements on nuclear power or abortion or any other issue, Ginsberg had himself photographed at the head of various political demonstrations and had an opinion on seemingly everything. Burroughs met people like Susan Sontag regularly and wanted to meet other great master thinkers in order to consolidate their power and come to agreements. Ginsberg and Burroughs at least never developed the final megalomania of the master thinker, which consists in believing that one is God, as Mao or Stalin did, and that his decisions and policies were beyond question, but they did try to come up with strong visions that would help to orient others. Corso seemingly gave up this game of wisdom collection and dispensation and went in the other direction, into anonymity, living in caves in Greece for long periods, keeping a ferret that regularly bit his fingers, and sleeping with beautiful young women who had no intellectual interests or pretensions.

Corso writes in another poem in this late collection:

What the Child Sees
The child sees

the foolishness of age
in a lazy wiseman—
the knowing depth of the child's eyes
innocently contemptuous of the sight
. . . .
the spiritus not present
and suffers the proximity
of the nullified moment

(*HA* 12)

Corso is unknown because we cannot place him alongside Burroughs or Ginsberg or Snyder as a master thinker. Corso doesn't pretend to such mastery. Therefore, what does he have to teach others? How can Corso be taught in a college course if he himself doesn't pretend to have any mastery? What I believe he teaches is thinking itself, thinking as playful interrogation. Thinking as unthinking. The college system must offer mastery to its students. Therefore, only poets who offer mastery themselves are taught. Ezra Pound, Charles Olson, Allen Ginsberg, William Burroughs, yes; Edward Lear and minor nonsensical surrealists such as Philippe Soupault and Gregory Corso, no. Corso's poetry doesn't offer us a role model toward which we can be reverent.

Donald Stauffer writes, "With Ginsberg and Kerouac, Corso was part of a kind of Beat triumvirate, each encouraging and supporting the other and his work. If Kerouac was the father-figure and Ginsberg the rabbi-figure, Corso was the child-figure and the clown" (178). Corso's persona is more complex than Stauffer allows, but he is right to the extent that Corso saves us the embarrassment of cheap identification with gurus and other wisdom figures; however, he seems to offer nothing much in its place.

In his poems "Marriage," "Bomb," "Hair," "Army," "Power," and others with one-word titles, he deconstructs the ideas that surround these cultural focus points and sends them in different directions—without, however, providing a new, grounded meaning. As critic Jim Philip writes about Corso, "There is no easy acceptance, either in personal or wider generational terms, of the role of 'Daddy'" (63).

What he bequeaths to us instead is the legacy of the clown, as shaman, as midget tumbler before conquerors, as saint of laughter, friend of unicorns. Corso's disruptive, manic, and often bitter personae are an implicit criticism of the poetic personae of serious hidden knowledge. As I've already cited, critic Charles Altieri writes, "If we want to understand a general situation that contemporary poets might share, we need to construct a hero, however provisional a one, as our emblem for cultural pressures manifesting themselves in individual choices" (*Self and Sensibility* 1–2). Corso is in the process of deconstructing his own anti-hero, a project that has much to do with the project enunciated by Gilles Deleuze. Deleuze writes in *Difference and Repetition,* "The ego is a mask for other masks, a disguise under other disguises. Indistinguishable from its own clowns, it walks with a limp on one green and one red leg" (110).

Corso's suspicion is that all the humanistic faces that we offer to one another, all the heroic poses that we strike for one another, amount to nothing. Against the calm contemplation of the eternal forms in the philosophy of Plato, Corso advises what he called in his classes "risked and fevered thinking." This is a new kind of thought, born at the moment of expression in a world of implicated intensities. In short, Corso trashes all the old ideals:

> The men of politics I love are but youth's fantasy:
> The fine profile of Washington on coins stamps & tobacco
> wraps
> The handsomeness and death-in-the-snow of Hamilton.
> The eyeglasses shoe-buckles kites & keys of Ben Franklin.
> The sweet melancholy of Lincoln.
> (from "America Politica Historia, in Spontaneity," *M* 154)

In contrast to these fantasies of youth, Corso presents the American he knew:

> He is moonfaced cunning well-meaning & righteously mean.
> He is Madison Avenue, handsome, in-the-know, and
> superstitious.
>
> (*M* 154)

Marilyn Schwartz's penetrating article on Corso, which appears in *The Beats: Literary Bohemians in Postwar America,* develops an extremely subtle and nuanced way of thinking about Corso, worth dealing with at length, even if it is ultimately too optimistic. Schwartz writes:

> Far from nihilistic, Corso's early images of desolation and death point to a developing theme of renewal through catastrophe: violently conjoined opposites such as cold and hot, death and life produce a condition of *undifferentiation,* a creative matrix in which conventional distinctions among meanings and values emerge. (122)

It is by mixing together things that don't belong that Corso creates explosions, which result in new ideas and new values. Schwartz writes that "Corso uses humorous paradoxes and reversals of expectations to create a state of undifferentiation in which he discovers new values" (127). She continues, "Corso's is the power of poetry to transform and renew by the technique of contradiction" (128). These contradictions are precisely what cannot be dealt with in the educational system, which is based on passing on truths. Corso's system is not one of passing on truths but rather of blowing them up and creating something new out of the fragments. This is a process that cannot be put into any dogmatic—or even teachable—format.

Schwartz does claim, however, that in one sequence of poems in *Long Live Man,* she can discern a utopian element, particularly in the poem "I Where I Stand," apparently written while Corso was staying with his friend Alan Ansen in Venice.

[I]n at least one work from the collection his best poetic instincts carry him closer to a vision of the celestial city. "I Where I Stand," commemorating a visit to Venice, affirms the necessity of building the poet's image of perfection on the ground of actual experience. (133)

Schwartz's tantalizing interpretation is perhaps the only sustained attempt at reading one of Corso's more difficult poems from start to finish. Corso's poems are easy to abstract from but difficult to read in their entirety because they contradict themselves and because their very nature is so uniquely framed—and it is necessary to let go of known frameworks and follow him in a vision that can be paranoid and megalomaniacal in one line and naively charming in the next. Even Allen Ginsberg, his best friend for many years, chose to look the other way in terms of Corso's meaning. "But what is he *saying?* Who cares?!" (introduction to *Gasoline* 7).

Because I intend to discuss "I Where I Stand" at length, I am reproducing it here in its entirety for those who are unfamiliar with it. The poem is not generally considered to be one of Corso's most important, but its riches are complex and mysterious, and it deserves a close reading.

> I where I stand   Venice
> Aging my modern vision on winged lions
> Impossible dreamer of cloaks and masks
> Counting passion madrigals variegated figs
> Where I stand   Venice   aging   counting
>
> Peepholes in my Ducal Palace stay
> I simply saw the proudest Doge
> Superior favorable come to steal
> Some wandering look from my eyes
> I   where I stand
>
> Blind as hags
> Sometimes approaching black totality
>   Knowledge of the dreamed city   lead the way
> Although I am the very spot on which I stand
>
> If when the infection of many years gone
> Returns to me at death
> I should see in final vision my ragged childhood
> Leaning against bright alabaster walls
> Munching strips of Euganean wheat
> I will remain where I stand
> And become timorous

> Oh I should see it is fitting so
> The might Doge   The winged lion
> Princes and patriarchs   It is possible!
> They while their carrion deeds in dream of me
> I where I stand   Venice
> The outskirts of a dreamed map

(41)

In the poem, Schwartz tries to find a sense of utopian idealization based on the phrase "Knowledge of the dreamed city." This is a common framework to put the Beat writers into, as it places them in the romantic tradition that stems from William Blake, Percy Shelley, and Walt Whitman, who were clear precursors. For Corso, however, the framework doesn't explain his dark despair over the fact of living in a Darwinian food chain, in which competition dispenses with the infantile notion of utopia, making a utopian reading irrelevant in Corso's case. The ideal of utopia, dear to those who lived in the 1960s, marked a climax in the long sequence of unrealistic dreams that would yield a state bureaucracy as one big milk bottle for the baby boomers and the entire population a contented baby sucking at the silky nipple.

To characterize the hippie generation as immature daydreamers seems too easy, and yet one could at least say that their dreams were often bigger than economics would easily permit. Having had a fairly easy time in the prosperity after World War II, many of the 1960s' dreamers never had to face hunger or ask how their parents got the money to buy the Volkswagen in which they went off to university, and their fuzzy antimaterialism in the midst of plenty has provided sitcom fodder for subsequent generations. Corso never had the luxuries of the baby boomers. He knew hunger and had to fend for himself. I will argue that Corso is not creating a utopian vision in this poem but rather interrogating the utopian vision and upsetting it. Taken as a whole, Corso's volume *Long Live Man* is fraught with ambiguity, paradox, and sly humor.

The title of the poem "I Where I Stand" recalls Martin Luther's reputed phrase "Here I stand," which he apparently uttered in response to his interrogation and the request for a complete recantation before the Diet of Worms during his heresy trial (Bainton 185–86). To stretch the Lutheran connection, one could see Corso's poem as a continuation of Luther's doctrine of the two kingdoms, as it is outlined in contemporary theologian Robert Benne's *Paradoxical Vision* and Per Frostin's *Luther's Two Kingdoms Doctrine*. In this doctrine, the city of God is irremediably separate from our own mundane cities, and at best a ray of light may occasionally fall from that sacred place and illuminate our way. Schwartz's study, however, claims that Corso is trying to articulate "the poet's image of perfection" (133), whereas Luther argued that Christ was the sole revealer. In the Lutheran doctrine, there is no way for a mere human to make this world better by contemplating heaven, as we are so fraught with sin that even our glimpse of heaven is contaminated. Schwartz, on the other hand, presents Corso as an active agent of the celestial kingdom, a heresy in Lutheran eyes as it gives the poet the role of Jesus Christ. Corso's positioning of himself as divine may allow us to see what he imagined as his role as a herald between kingdoms, and the monstrous hubris this would imply might do much to explain his megalomania. However, to the extent that he dealt with two kingdoms, perhaps he did not see himself as Christ as much as he saw himself in a magical role as the stealer of fire along the lines of Prometheus in Shelley's poem. Corso may indeed be fusing the romantic and Christian systems in order to provide the poet with a positive value. Corso's sense of the poet as a member of a relay may be seen in this poem, but it is complicated by the roles of the romantic poet and by his own difficult and often hilarious personality, in which the role he plays is not altogether serious and is always hard to pin down. His sense of the gospel is always mixed together with his own earth-bound humanity, his own vision, which is not the omniscient one that belongs to God alone.

In "Upon My Refusal to Herald Cuba," which appears in *Long Live Man*, he writes, "Best to tease all sides with awakening vibrations; / Cheerful remedies, calm or drastic solutions" (57). When he offers a cheerful remedy, or a drastic solution, then, is he not teasing? When he uses the phrase "the dreamed city," should we not be wary of jest? In order to make her case, Schwartz has to ignore an awful lot.

What does Schwartz make, for instance, of the "hags" who appear in the middle of the poem: "Blind as hags / Sometimes approaching black totality"? Who are the hags? Are they the Beat writers? Is it Corso having schizophrened into a Deleuzian becoming of hags? Are they collective guilt over the cultural memory of the Salem witch trials?

What about the previous section where Corso accuses a Doge of trying to steal "[s]ome wandering look from my eyes"? Corso characterizes the Doge as the "proudest" Doge. So proud that he had to steal a "wandering look" from the narrator's eyes? Doesn't this, then, make the narrator in possession of something even more worthy of pride than the possessions of the wealthy Doge? The narrator, in this case not very far from Corso's own persona, is described in the opening stanza as an "impossible dreamer," a phrase that recalls the narrator's self-characterization in "Marriage," published in the previous collection *The Happy Birthday of Death*, in which the word "impossible" is used to contrast the narrator's extravagant persona with normalcy. If he is an "impossible dreamer," he is not one along Marxist lines but one rather along the lines of a maniac with an unpredictable personality disorder, which leads him to be either riotously funny or seriously disturbing, and sometimes both.

When we read Corso, it is important to remember that we are not dealing with a normal individual. He is impossible and extravagant. To evaluate him, we have to not only evaluate his writings but also attempt a psychiatric evaluation that must deal with both Corso's megalomania and his persecution complex.

To assess Corso's personality from a psychiatric perspective, we have to move from a philosophical consideration of Corso's poetry to a personal consideration, or, in other words, from a macro-perspective to a micro-perspective. One case study by the empirical British psychiatrist Charles Rycroft, whose report on "an unsuccessful actress living an insecure and Bohemian existence" appears in his book *Psychoanalysis and Beyond* (233), closely parallels Corso. According to Rycroft, this actress was an astonishingly gifted individual with a weird mental framework and strange clothing style and pattern of speech, which is reminiscent of Corso's character.

> Her clothes were either untidy to the point of sluttishness—my receptionist nicknamed her the Gypsy—or exotic to the point of being bizarre. She was intensely interested in her effect on other people, but made no attempt to appear either smart or fashionable. (238)

Corso's clothes were similar in their bizarreness—often dirty, and usually weird—such as shirts with puffed sleeves that looked like the shirts of aristocratic fencing duelists from just before the French revolution. He often wore bandannas around his head. On some days he would appear dressed entirely in white, with white shoes and hat and sunglasses. One day he would look utterly disheveled, and the next he would look full of fun and resplendent humor and radiance. But the weirdest thing about Corso was his speech.

Rycroft describes the actress's peculiarities of speech, which resemble Corso's own.

> (a) She made her own choice of prefixes and suffixes, always, for instance, saying 'comatic,' not 'comatose.' (b) She gave words private meanings that were remote from and yet obviously somehow related to their accepted meaning. 'Comatic,' for instance, meant lethargic, intellectually lazy, unawakened. (c) She had a number of favorite words which she used in unusual or old-fashioned senses. One of these was 'reactionary,' which meant sensitive or responsive. (d) She had invented new words and appropriated a number of already existing words to signify various intrapsychic phenomena she had encountered during her self-analysis and for which she had had no words in her pre-breakdown vocabulary. The most striking example of this was the word *effigy* to describe an internal object. (238–39)

Rycroft determined that the actress's problem was that she had difficulty with mother figures. Her own had died early on, and her businessman father was too overwhelmed to comfort the five children. Left alone, the actress had invented a private world that had only a tangential relation to the common world in which there are parental figures who care about children and offer them a sense of reliable human kindness. The similarity to Corso's situation is obvious, here, in that Corso's mother abandoned him at less than one year of age and was long thought to have returned to Italy (in fact, she lived in New Jersey [Ashby 4]), leaving him to a succession of foster homes. Who was there to reliably comfort him? There were substitute mothers, but Corso doesn't cite loyalty to any of them. Corso's father didn't return to retrieve him until he was eleven. Like the actress, Corso developed his own private, internal, emotional language, a language that is quite striking. Rycroft comments:

> Although I became in time familiar with the idiosyncrasies of her speech and knew, for instance, that "reactionary men have no sense of structure," had nothing to do with politics but meant that sensitive men are incapable of lasting personal relationships, I deliberately refrained from making more than the minimum amount of accommodation to them for fear of becoming involved in a linguistic folie à deux which might make it harder for her to work through her hostility to the uncomprehending mother-image. (239–40)

To comprehend Corso's work, it is necessary to turn at least briefly from the history of literature and the avowed goals of the Beat movement and investigate Corso's psychological profile. Anyone familiar with Corso's work will instantly see that the problem of suffixes and prefixes in his poetry is similar to the problem of the actress's unusual endings.

Michael Skau has a wonderful list of unusual Corso suffixes in his study, in which "-ian" is used to formulate "pyramidian," "voidian," "flowerian," "cosmosian," and "glyphian"; "-ic" is used to create "vegetic," "zombic," "spectric," "catacombic," "tattooic," and "wolfic"; "-ry" is used to create "minstrely"; and "-y" is used to create "cheruby," "atomy," and others (115). In addition, there are optional forms, such as "'voidical,' and 'voidian,' 'chasmic,' and 'chasmal,'" (115). Corso's odd diction is not merely a leftover from his self-educated upbringing but is somehow very close to his own personality, as is the unorthodox way in which he uses many words, using nouns as verbs and verbs as nouns. I've never been able to figure out precisely what he means by certain terms such as "haycocking," a frequently used verb with little apparent relationship to its dictionary meaning. What he means by "Frankensteined" is easier to guess but still impossible to make exact, as the symbol of the mad doctor has been so heavily discussed and commented upon as to make it mean almost anything.

Corso was, to put it mildly, a promiscuous man who used his immense charm in order to sleep with dozens, if not hundreds, or even thousands, of women, if the summer at Naropa was in any way typical. Corso was about fifteen years younger than the actress of Rycroft's study, and so we could see that his sexuality fit into the upheaval of the 1960s, but perhaps it would have taken place whether he lived in that period or not. Rycroft's actress was from a slightly earlier period—she was about thirty-five years of age in 1950—and her sexuality resembled Corso's.

Is it crucial that they share a sexual typology? Rycroft comments:

> She would not have used the word *promiscuous* about herself, but it would be hard to find another word to describe the bewilderingly rapid series of

transient encounters that made up her sexual life. In her view it was a search for an ideal partner with whom she could experience complete sexual harmony uncontaminated by either love or sensuality. Occasionally, or so she said, her search was successful, when she found a "reactionary" man, but then, alas, they always proved to have no "sense of structure." The others always proved "comatic." Rather inconsistently, I thought, she referred to her sexual partners as lovers. (241)

To continue this parallel typology, Corso had a bizarre way of referring to his girlfriends as "cunts" but without, seemingly, anything pejorative attached to this term. He was not a misogynist, in other words, but used the term affectionately, giving to it, as to so many others, his own distinctive meaning. He liked the smell of women, he liked to have sex with women, but he attached no sentiment to his relationships and didn't seem to care if the relationships had a "structure." Corso often saw women as generic, as he does in his interview with Robert King. "Mainly, I sleep with my cats and the female. I love female. I've been with this one female now for a year. I like living with female. I keep close to her and all that; I don't bother much with the outside" (160). According to Rycroft, this lack of individual attachment is created through an inability to relate to the "mother-image." Because the sense of abandonment by the mother is so profound—there had been no one to comfort the child after her departure—those emotions that create the ability for shared attachment either do not exist or are not trusted, and so they are not a substantial part of the emotional life. Corso ran away in order to establish his independence at the age of eleven. The actress whom Rycroft describes ran away at the age of fourteen to join the circus.

Rycroft describes the actress's speech in more detail.

Her neologisms were amusing, but quite unintentionally so. A lowerarchy was a hierarchy viewed from above—those of us who are not at the top of course usually view hierarchies from below. She once, again quite seriously, said: "Annoyed? I was paranoid." (240)

The parallel with Corso's strange vocabulary is clear. Corso once asked a group of us at Naropa if we had any "fire," by which he meant matches. When taking on Corso's poetry, readers have to acclimatize themselves to a rather extensive personal vocabulary and mental framework that only remotely resembles that of most other persons.

Another similarity between Corso and the actress was that both had a great affection for animals that they didn't have for humans. The actress loved cats, Rycroft writes; she could emotionally accept only animals (242). Corso's many affectionate poems about cats, donkeys, birds, and other animals maintain this parallel.

How did Rycroft diagnose the actress, and could we use the same diagnosis for Corso?

In describing Miss Y.'s character I have already used the terms *counterpho-bic, paranoid,* and *manic,* and the question arises, I think, whether she was, *psychiatrically* speaking, psychotic. She certainly displayed incongruity of affect. This was well described by one of her lovers who once remarked to her: "It's the glorious irrelevance of you. You look at the sugar-bowl with intense hatred and talk of the weather with an expression of ecstasy." (243)

Rycroft decided she was not mad, but he writes:

Since Miss Y. often behaved and spoke in a way that in everyday life one might be inclined to dismiss as pretentious, absurd, and bizarre, I must mention explicitly that very early on I decided that she was in fact a very gifted, though profoundly disturbed, person, and, in particular, that she had an unerring aesthetic sense. (243)

The actress created imaginary lovers based on real people who lived far enough away that they could do nothing to disillusion her. Corso's projection of ideal women, as in the poem "Marriage," were all shot down, one after another, leaving only the character "She," a woman not only impossible but so thoroughly fictional that she could never be reached. In this sense, too, could we see Corso's "dreamed city" in "I Where I Stand" not as a utopian projection but as a safe ideal that could not be besmirched by daily reality? Something safe that could never leave?

Corso is not describing utopia but rather his extremely complicated mental state. The title repeats the word "I" insistently. The opening line repeats it again. Venice is a stage for this narrator, as he introduces himself in the third line, "Impossible dreamer of cloaks and masks." It is the pageantry of Venice that draws him. The next line indicates his activity: "Counting passion madrigals variegated figs." In other words, he is inventorying his delights, which are to be carried out "masked" and "cloaked," without him having to reveal his sensitivity. All around, his pleasures await him like bizarre fruits.

In the next stanza, the narrator's megalomania is announced yet once more. Corso's narrator relates an assumption of the power to mix with the high and mighty and to have special powers.

> Peepholes in my Ducal Palace stay
> I simply saw the proudest Doge
> Superior favorable come to steal
> Some wandering look from my eyes
> I   where I stand.
>
>   (*LL* 41)

Did the narrator really stay in a duke's palace? And were there peepholes? And what do peepholes represent if not suspicion and paranoia? The narrator then claims to have "simply" seen the "proudest Doge." Like a child who lies, he adds the word "simply" to try to make the lie seem more authentic. After this, the Doge, who was the chief magistrate of the Old Republic of Venice with no real power, has come to steal the narrator's "wandering look." This proud and rather empty figure of the Doge is obsessed with stealing the narrator's vision? It seems that here the poet is contrasting his antiquated "poetic" powers with the powers of a position that even in antiquity held no power and is now merely titular, and yet he finds his own superior. Is this megalomania or self-confidence or merely a very weird kind of joking? The recurrent line "I where I stand" is meant to nail the empty boast, as if to say, as sure as I stand here, this is the truth.

The next stanza links again to the stealing of vision:

> Blind as hags
> Sometimes approaching black totality
>   Knowledge of the dreamed city   lead the way
> Although I am the very spot on which I stand
>
>   (*LL* 41)

The narrator has seemingly left out some narrative links in this passage, indicated by the space gaps left inside of the third line in this stanza. What he seems to be arguing is that we tumble blindly toward an ideal city, which we haven't seen in reality, because we are in fact "blind as hags." What hags? Are hags in fact blind, or do they not have the gift of foresight, as they do in *Macbeth*?

At best, Corso's poem appears ambiguous, torn between "knowledge of the dreamed city," or the world of magic, and the verifiable concrete self who is in a given spot. "I am the very spot on which I stand." Is not the given spot meant to reify the magic by swearing that the narrator is real, and therefore his seemingly hallucinatory experiences are real?

The fourth stanza contains a clear reference to a famous romantic poem, Shelley's "Lines Written Among the Euganean Hills." It is a poem of praise to Venice, as a shelter from the stormy life Shelley was leading at the time. Corso's line reads "Munching strips of Euganean wheat." How is Corso using Shelley's poem? Isn't "munching" a somewhat comical thing to do?

> If when the infection of many years gone
> Returns to me at death
> I should see in final vision my ragged childhood
> Leaning against bright alabaster walls
> Munching strips of Euganean wheat
> I will remain where I stand
> And become timorous
>
>   (*LL* 41)

These lines show us that the poem is not about attaining a utopian city but rather about Corso's emotional identification with romanticism, on the one hand, and his countervalent struggle with a nearly overwhelming paranoia and megalomania, which one could see throughout his work, and his fear that he will be afraid, in the final analysis, rather than romantic and heroic when finally confronted with death. The macho posturing of "I Where I Stand," and Corso's constant reiteration of the word "stand," as in "to take a stand," or to be brave, is suddenly comically undercut, however, by his avowal of timorousness at the final moment of death. Corso's poem is an undercutting of romantic heroics. Each stanza begins with romantic bluster and ends in an undercutting of the previous emotion. Is the poem a self-analysis, or is it an intertextual poem based on the history of English literary reception of the city of Venice?

In Shelley's "Lines Written Among the Euganean Hills," there is a link between the personal states of affection and distrust and the state of Venice and whether or not it is a place of liberty or death. Is the same true for Corso's poem? More context is needed in order to decide. Is Corso's poem personal, or literary and historical, or some kind of combination?

Ginsberg said in a class I took at Naropa Institute in 1977 that Corso went to Venice because he had been arguing too much with Orlovsky and Ginsberg in Egypt, and they wanted to get rid of him. They sold a leather coat to get him to Venice, where he could stay with the wealthy Venice resident and American expatriate poet Alan Ansen. It is easy to see why Ginsberg and Orlovsky needed a break from Corso. At Naropa, Corso veered between two personalities: one was harsh and interrogative and unyielding in its coldness, the other could have charmed Stalin in his worst mood, and the two personalities alternated at random, like sudden changes in the weather.

Compare the personality of the actress described by Rycroft:

In one character she was hard, aggressive, querulous, and argumentative, and usually sluttishly dressed. In another she was transfigured and radiant, absolutely confident in her ability to charm everyone she encountered. In such moods everyone in the street stared at her appreciatively as she passed and complete strangers came up and talked to her. (242–43)

With close friends, of which the actress had very few, she was constantly making tests of loyalty. Rycroft writes:

Just because I was the person she had put into a position in which I could prove myself trustworthy and make her aware of her need for love I became the person it was most necessary to prove hateful, insensitive, and ununderstanding. Furthermore, she had to test out that I could continue to be benevolent, however venomous she might be. (247)

In this regard, Corso had a special relationship to Ginsberg, one of the few "nurturing figures" whom he could trust in his life. He needed Ginsberg, but because Ginsberg was one of Corso's few points of certainty, Corso could push his hardness to the maximum and know that he would not be abandoned. I don't know if Ginsberg was a masochist or just a kindly person, but he would become extremely mild in contrast to Corso's rage, almost seeming to delight in Corso's behavior. The Rycroft description could easily fit with my understanding of Corso, down to his fear of death, which, like Corso, the actress denied as a physical reality, as she claimed that it was something that people did emotionally, to hurt each other, rather than any actual physical failing. Corso had a similar denial of death. Rycroft comments on the actress:

> It did not, of course, require much imagination on my part to appreciate that someone who had lost three mothers in her childhood and who as an adult had had to fabricate theories denying the inevitability of death needed endorsement of her threatened insight when confronted with the fact of her father's death. (255)

Corso's own fabrication of theories with which to confront death varied from running into a movie theater to going into outer space with the whole planet intact. As Michael Skau writes, "[H]e is reluctant to see it [death] as more than an even odds bet against him," and in fact, he sees himself "as a symbol of life in a moribund world. . . . As the generator of life-giving qualities, the poet is a fitting antagonist for the forces of death" (80). Skau continues, "Corso's impudence in the face of mortality stems from a belief that denies the finality of Death. . . . Corso repeatedly rejects the finality of death" (82–83).

Corso's work cannot simply be placed within the history of literature as an unfolding of various utopian political tendencies. He denies the obvious reality of his own eventual death, which thus becomes a source of lyric tension for him, as he whistles in the dark. This doesn't mean he is crazy. Millions of Catholics deny the reality of death. For nonbelievers alone this reality is strange, but Corso goes further than most Catholics, into the realm of the obsessed.

Skau mentions how prevalent the strangeness of Corso's attitude toward death is in the various criticisms of the poet. "Citing Corso's denigration of death, Rosanne Benedetto asks, 'Is this attitude his approach to life or is it false bravado in the face of mortality?'" (83).

After his Catholicism had somewhat waned, his attitude toward death remained the same.

> Corso's more contemporary response to the possibility of death is often unmistakably escapist. In a 1974 interview, he reveals this blatantly: "Now would you get scared if you felt your heart was feeling pattering and suddenly you turned pale? And you might just have a heart attack and drop dead there? I think I'd go to a movie theater. I would. If I felt that was happening I'd run into a movie house. . . . I thought I'd just get my mind off it or something." (Skau 83)

Is all of this something that Corso put together as some kind of literary joke for the amusement of his audience, or is it his own serious defense mechanism, or is it just Christianity?

Corso's mother ran out on him when he was less than a year old. This has to be crucial, somehow, in terms of understanding him on a micro-level, even if on a macro-level we can see his mother's position as that of a poor immigrant, a teenager, trapped within an Italian cultural framework that didn't allow her gender the ability to earn much of a living at such an age, nor to gain much freedom after having had a child. Her disappearance is mysterious, and as far as I know, no one has tracked this woman down or gotten her story. She would, at the time of this writing, be about eighty-eight years old.

Corso's mother left the situation, taking much of Corso's eventual capacity for normal mental health with her. Rycroft, elsewhere in his book *Psychoanalysis and Beyond,* comments that "[c]hildren have a 'germinal capacity for mourning' by the age of 16 months, in as much as they have constructed and can retain an image of the absent mother" (154). Since Corso's mother left the family when he was only about eight months of age, and since the father, too, had disappeared, Corso's capacity for mourning was perhaps entirely absent.

In this respect, it is possible to understand Corso's bizarre fantasy at the funeral of Jack Kerouac. He wanted to pick up the dead body and throw it across the room.

> When I saw Jack in the funeral parlor, where everybody was paying a last visit to him, I had this idea of picking up his body and throwing it across the room. I thought it might have been a Zen thing that he would have dug. Because he wasn't there, this was the body. So: *plunk!* I don't know what they would have done to me, maybe put me in the looney bin or something, 'cause you don't do things like that. You *don't.*
>
> I'm glad I didn't do it. I'm not that impulsive, but it was a thought that went through my head, to break it.
>
> "Break this, Gregory. Break this bullshit hypocrisy of funerals and all that. People mourning something that ain't there." (Gifford and Lee 315)

Is this humor, or perhaps an indication of a deeper inability to mourn, an inability to see oneself in relationship, within a tradition of continuity, which must be both celebrated and mourned, as it is one of the most central aspects of life? Corso may have seen himself as essentially alone, with others as objects to which he had little or no relation. In his poem "Elegiac Feelings American," in which he does mourn Kerouac, he writes, "you stood upon America like a rootless / flat-bottomed tree" (*EF* 3). Is this a description of Kerouac, though, or of himself? Kerouac had a father and mother and a tormented but deep relationship with them. Corso's own relationship with his parents suffered from a lack of roots. What he did have, instead, were his relationships with women, which were quite shallow, and with Ginsberg, which was his only real relationship at the time the poem was written, as far as I can make out.

Nevertheless, on a long trip to the Mediterranean, where Ginsberg could get no rest from Corso's tirades, even Ginsberg's legendary patience seems to have given out. Shelley's "Lines Written among the Euganean Hills" seems to praise old friends who are willing to give us shelter in a storm. These friends are like islands of verdure in the sea of anguish.

> Ay, many flowering islands lie
> In the waters of wide Agony:
> To such a one this morn was led,
> My bark by soft winds piloted

The poem continues with a description of Venice:

> Underneath Day's azure eyes
> Ocean's nursling, Venice lies

And then there is a strange description of Venice as a kind of cauldron, bubbling with spirit:

> Lo! the sun upsprings behind,
> Broad, red, radiant, half-reclined
> On the level quivering line
> Of the waters crystalline;
> And before that chasm of light,
> As within a furnace bright,
> Column, tower, and dome, and spire,
> Shine like obelisks of fire,
> Pointing with inconstant motion
> From the altar of dark ocean
> To the sapphire-tinted skies;
> As the flames of sacrifice
> From the marble shrines did rise,
> As to pierce the dome of gold
> Where Apollo spoke of old

(cited in Perkins 973)

In these lines of Shelley's, we again get the sense of an Athanor, or philosopher's cauldron, but this time Venice itself is a kind of "furnace bright," which yields the changeover from "the altar of dark ocean" to "the sapphire-tinted skies" that would "pierce the dome of gold." This movement from *nigredo* to rosy-colored is the pattern of this passage, repeated throughout the poem, in which liberty comes out of darkness, until the closure:

> And the love which heals all strife
> Circling, like the breath of life,
> All things in that sweet abode
> With its own mild brotherhood:
> They, not it, would change; and soon
> Every sprite beneath the moon

Would repent its envy vain,
And the earth grow young again

(cited in Perkins 976)

The cauldron of Venice is meant to heal the ailing poet with its vision of a profound spirit, much like intellectual beauty, which has once again found him.

As I mentioned above, Corso's poem "I Where I Stand" clearly has a reference to Shelley's poem: "Munching strips of Euganean wheat." However, is it about an ideal city or about munching; about an ideal vision or about eating? In Shelley's poem, the Euganean hills are suffused with an intellectual spirit. In Corso's poem, he is casually "munching" this spirit. Isn't this another reference to the way in which Corso knocks out the spiritual impulse and grounds it in the monstrous caloric needs of the human animal?

In the lines Schwartz cites from Corso's poem, she abstracts some lines that fit her utopian thesis, but she doesn't deal with the strangest line of all, which occurs in the last stanza. Corso writes of the mighty Doge, the winged lion, and the princes and patriarchs that, "It is possible! / They while their carrion deeds in dream of me." This strange line in nearly perfect iambic pentameter refers to the food chain and to the princes and patriarchs not as leaders of a beautiful city but rather as monstrous carrion eaters, or those who traffic in death and sadism. I do not see the "outlines of a 'dreamed city' of which Venice is but a temporal version" (Schwartz 133) in these lines but rather an ambiguous vision of a city that is rotten to the core, with the outlines of a "dreamed city" perhaps hovering mockingly in the background. The line is exceedingly difficult to unpack, and Schwartz skips over it. Skau has agreed with me that Schwartz's criticism of Corso is "the best around" (personal letter, October 9, 1999), but here, it seems, even Schwartz is reduced to jumping over checker pieces she hasn't earned fairly and removing them from the board, a common practice in Corso criticism because Corso's poetry is so difficult to read. What does Corso mean by the line "They while their carrion deeds in dreams of me"?

If we think of the word "while" as in "to cause to pass pleasantly," then we could read the first part of the line as something like, "In their dreams these people (Doges, princes, patriarchs) lazily perform their lethal transactions" and the second part as "using me as their inspiration." Suddenly the poem is not so easy to read, with this glaringly megalomaniacal line inserted into the end. The narrator speculates that the whole city, or at least its most powerful members, are enacting lethal transactions, using him as their inspiration. The paranoia of this statement staggers the imagination as we try to grasp its megalomania. The short sentence just before this line reads "It is possible!" and I read the line as linking with the next one. It is possible, in other words, that the high and mighty dream of him when they commit their lethal felonies. As sure as he stands there, this is possible. Is it impossible to read Corso in this way? A lot depends on the preposition "in." What does Corso mean by it—does he mean that they act badly in his dreams, or that they dream of him, in order to act badly?

Corso's hilarious megalomania, far from being an unusual instance in this poem, is typical. Michael Skau cites a similar instance of Corso's megalomania combined with a persecution complex on the first page of his book, where Corso speaks to one of the heads of the Tibetan religion, Choygam Trungpa, during the latter's conference at one of his packed lectures at Naropa Institute in 1975:

> There's too much killing. You want to kill ego too. You want to say that I peaked and killed culture and I made it in America. You dumb ass. You're one of the best foreigners that came here when this country was gone sick. . . . Trungpa, sufi, you picked on me that night when I read poetry. You're doing things with my head. Look, look around. (Skau 1)

This strange paranoia of Corso's is that the world is obsessed with him, mocking his best efforts.

Schwartz's sense that "I Where I Stand" is one poem that avoids her generally penetrating reading of contradiction and paradox is itself contradicted by the lines of the poem she cites. Corso's poem contradicts itself. It clearly contains a reference to Shelley's poem, which is a poem of beauty alternating between depression and high hopes, but Shelley manages to ring in the wonder of beauty at the end. Corso doesn't, and yet Schwartz writes, "Corso's vision thus remains focused long enough to discern the outlines of a perfect 'dreamed city' of which Venice is but a temporal version" (133). I don't see the whole poem as able to sustain Schwartz's utopian claims. When Corso writes, "Oh I should see it is fitting so / The mighty Doge   The winged lion / Princes and patriarchs   It is possible!" So far, "It" might be "utopia," but the next line reads, "They while their carrion deeds in dream of me," which clearly undercuts this utopian reading of the poem. Corso is not having any of this. The poem is, rather, a vision of mock terror, in which the narrator is surrounded by masks and pageantry that are ultimately sadistic. The "it" which is "possible" is more likely that the whole city is obsessed with stealing his vision, frightening him with death, and undercutting his poetic stance. It is the strangeness of this statement of Corso's that makes it necessary for him to repeat that right here, in Venice, "where I stand," this is happening.

To return to Rycroft and his actress, he writes:

> Similarly her conviction that almost everyone other than herself was sadistic was as much a contradiction of her need for love as a projection of her own sadism. This was shown by the fact that it was just those classes of persons whose occupation it is to care for others and whose care she needed that were in her view most sadistic. She considered all doctors, especially women doctors and psychiatrists, to be sadists. In principle psychoanalysts were not, though during the first year of analysis most of my interpretations were considered to be deliberate sadistic attacks. (242)

Compare Corso's attacks on the medical profession and the healing profession in his poem "But I Do Not Need Kindness" (treated more fully in the next chapter). In this poem, Corso indicts on grounds of secret sadism "the fat pontiffs of kindness," and specifically

> the little old grey-haired lady,
> the neighborhood priest,
> the famous poet,
> the mother . . .

$$(M\ 32)$$

The history of our reception of Venice in English literature could be cited as background for "I Where I Stand." Christine Froula writes of Ezra Pound's "Canto XVII," which discusses Venice as a utopian city:

> The canto's imagery evokes . . . Venice. . . . Venice, as the scene of the literal metamorphosis of marble, formed of organic matter by time and pressure, represents art's power to transform the vital, natural world into permanence and formal beauty. But the beautiful city is also a scene of disaster, as the canto's last images recall. (153)

Pound's fascism, which Froula skips over, is also part of this poem, in that Pound is clearly trying to resurrect a feudal past of noble aristocrats who loved art, when in fact most of them were merely mercenaries who "whiled their carrion deeds" while dreaming of their own pleasures. Venice has its sinister past of imperial domination, which must be registered in Corso's intertextual engagement with earlier poets' work, especially that of Shelley and Keats, which he had certainly read, but also that of Pound, whose work of reconstructing fascist Catholic Mediterranean civilizations provides a dark parallel to Corso's own career. Ginsberg knew Pound personally and had no doubt communicated something of this knowledge to Corso in their long friendship, but Corso must have also had firsthand experience of Pound's work, as he was extremely well read. Corso's particular and very quirky personality must also be considered, making a totalizing reading of the poem very tricky.

Part of what makes Corso's writing so difficult is the private nature of much of the language. "I Where I Stand" is not about utopia but about Corso's megalomania, his sense that the whole world is out to get him. Given the context, that it is written to a friend who clearly knew better, the poem is also a very good joke at Corso's own expense, which undercuts his megalomania, revealing Corso's magnificent self-awareness, which at least at times made him into an important artist rather than just a difficult friend. At his best, Corso could see himself as others saw him and do this with startling clarity.

Corso invented his own world, apparently assuming that any meaningful communication with others was at best a one in a million shot, but his language and the imagery are not so far from the conventional practice that we cannot open them, poem by poem, and see how they do in fact relate to the world. Did he deliberately wish to be unreadable, and therefore might we imply that he felt he was above the common herd? With the friends he had, who didn't listen to him, and with his parents who left, and with his choice in lovers, which tended toward unintellectual beauties, his chance of developing mutual, democratic relationships seems unlikely.

Corso is not merely narcissistic or aware mostly of himself, as the actress Rycroft describes appears to be, but he is also intensely aware of the Western tradition, portions of which he mastered, being able to name poets, painters, and precise works with encyclopedic certainty. When he refers to these works, however, as he does with the Shelley reference above, it is not clear what he means; Corso's reading of earlier poetry is always idiosyncratic as well as ironic and often has only the most tangential relationship to more conventional readings. However, taken within Corso's general framework in which he seeks to place spirituality within the terror of the food chain, the line "They while their carrion deeds in dream of me" makes perfect sense.

Like Ezra Pound's, the work of Gregory Corso interrogates the humanist ideals of classical modernism, and although it is intensely responsive to Renaissance painting and music, it works toward warping and undermining that tradition and ushering in a world of paradoxes that cannot be straightened into any kind of logic. It is hard to separate how much this is Corso's own emotionally disastrous life being wreaked in vengeance upon a hallowed tradition and how much it is a thought-out variety of postmodernism. Corso's work denies Beatitude, as much as it wants to celebrate it, and he never arrives at any point of stable harmony. The poem "Uccello" is a description of a man who is paralyzed within an aesthetic masterpiece and finds it almost impossible to communicate with others in a martial and sadistic situation, which is nevertheless permanent. For Corso to celebrate it is ironic. The poem ends: "a silver man on a black horse with red standard and / striped lance   never to die but to be endless / a golden prince of pictorial war" (*G* 29).

Among many of the most brilliant scholars who study modern poetry, not so much as a line on Gregory Corso thus far exists. Charles Altieri is looking for poets who offer a model of reverence. "With nothing to revere the humanities have very little to teach" (*Canons* 6). Corso seemingly has only irreverence to teach. In the place of heroes, who he thinks are idiots, Corso offers the clown, or the clownish members of the god family—Ganesha, Hermes, Loki, tricksters. A hero is someone who offers to liberate a neighborhood, a gender, a nation, or a species from domination by others. Corso can see no such liberation in the offing. What is liberation? Liberation, for Corso, is the liberation from the idea of liberation. The idea that once and for all we can be free implies reverence. For this reason, he is not interested in heroes but rather in clowns. In Corso's second-longest poem, "Clown," he celebrates the clown's ability to shake free all the meta-narratives of heroism. The idea of utopia evokes a world as a kind of loving mother always bending over us with tremendous concern, and this vision is simply not found in Corso's work. He didn't have the mother in the first place and so never experienced this situation. What we have in Corso, instead, is the trembling realism of a man on the run using comedy, irony, and sarcasm as means of investigating and undermining the intentions of others, which Corso assumes to be sadistic even when proven otherwise.

Corso has no family, in the sense of an emotionally and genetically related group who watch out for one another and provide a mutual support network. On the other hand, within the literary realm, Corso is a hardheaded survivor with roots in romanticism and its contemporary incarnations in the surrealist and Beat movements. However, he offers something that goes beyond these movements. He realizes he is on his own. "I Where I Stand" is about himself, surrounded by romanticism and cloaks, masks and pleasures—and also by the "carrion deeds" of those we too often romanticize. If the poem is sobering, it is because Corso stands between the two visions—the utopian vision of humans as citizens of heaven, and the other vision of them as inhabitants of an inscrutable jungle. Corso's poem is meant as comedy, in the best sense. As Kenneth Burke writes, "In sum, the comic frame should enable people to be *observers of themselves, while acting.* Its ultimate would not be *passiveness,* but *maximum consciousness*" (*Attitudes* 171).

Corso's early poetry is marked by a close attention to the outside. The later poetry, after 1963, is increasingly marked by a close attention to finding a means of evaluation that would negotiate between inside and outside. The outside has been subjected to an axiological examination, and Corso's relation to the outside becomes more disturbing, even if it remains comical. Corso has traded his belief in a divine exterior orientation for the role of a disturbed disturber. Thus, we have the beginning of a completely disorienting poet who is rather alarming to read but who has captured an audience without once kowtowing to their prejudices or discussing a common topic of interest, such as ecology or gay rights or any kind of rights, or playing any kind of pious wisdom figure for them but rather presenting himself as an iconoclastic interrogator, who in his finest moments manages to tear down all the false sense of security we have built for ourselves. His poems to the bomb, to the inability to build a marriage, are testaments to his incapacity for continuation. Corso's writings have a Dionysian energy and not much Apollonian.

Ginsberg was Corso's strongest link, his one source of continuity outside of himself. How did Ginsberg do it? Ginsberg comments in an interview that dealing with the insanity of his mother helped him gain tolerance for similar individuals, presumably including those such as Corso:

> I developed a tremendous tolerance for chaos; other people's illness, irrationality and contradictory behavior. I tend to throw it off like water off a duck's back. . . . Quite often there's a tragedy happening and somebody's

sinking right in front of me, but I don't see it. On the other hand I have a lot of tolerance for people who use drugs or are half-mad. (Ginsberg, "Interview")

If Corso's poetry is to outlast that of his other friends, I would argue that this would be so not on account of what he has to say but on account of his comic intensity. This is a new value, developed by Nietzsche and the surrealists as a counter-claim to the Apollonian schema of the philosophy or morality of a poet being most important. Can one be a hateful, personally difficult, paranoid mega-lomaniac and yet find enough moments of sanity and mental equilibrium to nevertheless be one of the finest poets America has ever produced?

In addition to the task of placing Corso psychiatrically, there remains the task of placing his work within the Beat school or the New York school or the romantic tradition stemming from Shelley. To some extent, he belongs to all of these schools, and yet he is also such a strange loner that, except for the case that Rycroft builds around the actress, I would say that Corso is one of a kind. And, unlike Rycroft's actress, Corso was a very hard worker. This is the testament of most who have known him well, even though many who have admired him from afar have assumed quite the opposite. I have often met the assumption on the part of literati that the Beat writers as well as the New York school of poets were know-nothings who spent their lives in the street and at parties. I spent two summers with these poets and writers at Naropa Institute and would like to correct this impression.

For instance, at one time I lived next door to William S. Burroughs, and his industriousness drove me crazy. Burroughs woke at seven A.M. and began to work with an old typewriter, clattering away at the keys with rapid, nervous bursts with only rare pauses. He typically wrote for at least four hours before lunch, then worked for another four to seven hours, making my apartment uninhabitable due to his clacking typewriter. His apartment walls were lined with hundreds of books, although he was in Boulder only for the summer to teach and see his friends. He often complained that too few of the students had a "professional" attitude towards literature. He himself carried a briefcase, could talk of his sales figures with acuity, and was keenly interested in literature as an export commodity. Burroughs was sixty-eight years old at the time, an age at which most professors have retired. He had a full two decades of work yet before him.

Allen Ginsberg, the son of a well-known poet, was a quiet scholar who had been to an Ivy League school and taught for many years in higher education. He spoke French fluently (he put out his pinkies when he did so) and worked on Blake and Whitman long past what many practicing academic specialists have done. His short but brilliant exposition of Blake in *Your Reason and Blake's System,* as well as essays on Whitman such as "A Walk Through *Leaves of Grass,*" leave no doubt as to the clarity and profundity with which he could read those works, which indicated arduous application and excellent summarization. His recent book *Deliberate Prose* reveals what a strategic mastermind he could be in terms of thinking about how to deal with the media from *Time* magazine on down to the smallest literary periodical.

Jack Kerouac, who had self-destructed from overwork and drink long before I met these writers, could quote long passages from Shakespeare and had read most of the classic writers in English and French, according to what I picked up from Ginsberg and Corso. He had favorite passages from a wide arsenal of writers, including Conrad and Celine, which he used as touchstones by which to judge his own work.

The New York school of poets had an equally solid work ethic, combined with high standards of taste. They had met at Harvard and were all familiar with the entire tradition of the French avant-garde as well as most American literature. I visited Kenward Elmslie's three-story townhouse in Greenwich Village, and each floor was packed with as many as forty thousand books, on everything from dance costumes of the 1920s to Nietzsche to French surrealism. One can only assume the same was true for the other New York school poets as well, from Kenneth Koch to John Ashbery, as they were all friends and thus would have had to have about the same level of culture in order to accept one another. Marjorie Perloff, in her masterpiece on Frank O'Hara, writes of him that "[s]urely he was one of the best read and most learned poets of his time" (33). As O'Hara loved Corso's work and considered him a close friend, he must have also accepted Corso's erudition as commensurate, as O'Hara tended to look down on unsophisticated individuals.

Corso's underprivileged background belies the tremendous effort he had put into educating himself. He had been to Harvard, where he became a close friend of Frank O'Hara and where he had audited classes. Corso is the only individual I've ever known who had read his way through the dictionary. He had also read his way completely to the bottom of many poets. He taught a course on Shelley at the University of Buffalo. He knew his own poems by heart and could cite them effortlessly; he often did so during his classes, even while dead drunk and full of manic hilarity. Corso was familiar with English and American canonical literature and could cite Chaucer, Shakespeare, Shelley, Dickinson, and more minor poets, such as John Cleveland and John Suckling. He had thought about these writers and what had made some of their work better than others, and he was keenly interested in ranking different poets, as well as their compositions, and in understanding the criteria for doing so. With student poems, he invariably picked out the best ones with great ease.

Corso was intensely familiar as well with jazz, of which he had an encyclopedic knowledge, and had put together various anthologies of jazz recordings in the Naropa library. He was also keenly interested in the history of Western painting. He spent one evening in a bar with me talking about Leonardo da Vinci's *The Last Supper* and Andy Warhol's mimicry of it and the importance of geometry, in general, in art.

Corso was not forgiving of lapses in others' educations. One poetry reading ended with Corso's fury when no one in the audience appeared to be familiar with the work of Adrien von Ostade, a minor Dutch painter who had been a student of Franz Hals. Corso screamed that this was not his audience and left the podium, throwing his papers in the air in frustration.

Critics often contrast the Beat poets with the New York school of poets, seeing the former group as vulgarians and the latter as an elite group. However, they were friends and accepted one another. The New York school was interested in the art crowd as their primary audience, but the Beat group was also interested in the art world. John Ashbery, Kenneth Koch, Frank O'Hara, James Schuyler, Kenward Elmslie, Barbara Guest, and others were also democratic, left-leaning, and concerned with seeing the "marvelous" aspects of the crowd, as is evidenced in O'Hara's *Lunch Poems*.

Allen Ginsberg is known for his Whitmanesque interest in the "common man," but he was also capable of citing Jean Cocteau, by heart, in the original French. Ginsberg must have spent thousands of hours in protest marches, sit-ins, and other non-literary efforts to help the "common man." This squares with Walt Whitman, who, after gaining a sinecure at the end of his life in Washington during the Civil War, didn't simply concentrate on making his name.

> Instead of retiring to his desk to write poems, however, he spent his days and nights in the military hospitals, visiting more than 100,000 wounded soldiers: talking with them, comforting them, writing their letters home. To finance the gifts of food, drink, and books that he brought them, he raised funds in Boston and New York, writing letters to any and all who might help him. (Logan 82)

One could imagine Allen Ginsberg or Peter Orlovsky performing similar services, but Frank O'Hara and Kenward Elmslie, who were more tuned in to a French aesthetic, a Baudelairean attitude toward literature, or an attitude of art for art's sake, also spent a lot of time with less fortunate artists, keeping their courage up through phone calls, letters, and general kindness, as well as gifts of money.

Corso needed to drink to be in public, and drinking had an unfortunate effect on him. His paranoia mounted, his understanding of others disappeared, and his rage flew in every direction at once. But he had quieter moments where he was keenly interested in others and could even be kind to children. Corso had a general common sense that deserted him only when he was blind with drinking, which he too often was. What I was most impressed with was his way of condensing a very sophisticated critique of a person or a poem into a phrase or two, even when blind drunk.

What Corso captured in his poetry was a combination of the best of the American imagist tradition with the best of French surrealism. In this way, Corso's work was very close to O'Hara's, in that O'Hara, too, had seemingly learned to fuse French surrealism with William Carlos Williams's idiomatic variable foot, written in conversational language. Marjorie Perloff writes of O'Hara that "not until O'Hara learned to fuse these two modes—to adopt Surrealist images and forms to an American idiom—was he able to write the poems that we think of as his central achievements" (38). Corso worked at the Poet's Theatre in Cambridge where O'Hara had worked as a young man (Corso had a play produced but also worked as the janitor, according to an article on the Poet's Theatre by Nora Sayre). Corso was as intensely appreciated by O'Hara as he was by Ginsberg. O'Hara and Corso must have performed together in at least one play, because O'Hara writes in his poem "To Hell With It" of his memories of "Bunny and Gregory and me in / costume" (cited in Perloff 21). O'Hara wrote one critical article on Corso, collected in *Standing Still and Walking in New York,* and also made numerous references to Corso in his poetry, including one entire three-page work in his *Collected Poems.* "Gregory Corso: *Gasoline*" appears to be a review in poetry form of Corso's early collection and partially ends,

> What Corso is doing
> > is surrounding the world with
> the positive question
> > of his own value
>
> > > (317)

Where Corso differs from O'Hara is that Corso had a much greater grasp of philosophy. He especially understood the Thomist tradition. This is the clue to his work. Almost every piece is a critical response to this ontological system. O'Hara's work is more personal and has less of an overall philosophical unity in terms of its thematics. For Corso, the questions of what is nature, what is human, and what is divine are an incessant theme.

Does Corso fit better into the Beat school or into the New York school? Gary Lenhart writes of Whitman's attitude, "He hankers for a literature that addresses itself not to a particular 'coterie,' but to every individual" (134). This would be quite characteristic of Allen Ginsberg's work as well. But Corso is not so easy to read. His diction requires the dictionary, and his philosophical interests require a broad framework to understand what he is getting at. I don't think any of the poets in his milieu had this understanding, and so they overlooked and underestimated him, but he has a better sense of form than any of the poets in either school, even though this grasp is rarely obvious. His use of language very rarely lapses into cliché, and he is always saying something impressive.

Corso's critics have tended to lump him with those who have been more easily digested within academic discourse. Thus Neeli Chernovsky has placed Corso with the Whitmanic Beats, even though his chapter on Corso describes Corso's classical interests, and Gregory Stephenson and Michael Skau have lumped Corso with the surrealists. Stephenson and Skau are more accurate. Although Ginsberg was clearly influenced by Mark van Doren, who was a big champion of Whitman and taught at Columbia, there is very little trace of Whitman's influence on Corso's poetry. O'Hara and the so-called New York school had leaned toward French surrealism, often translating these writers. There is a much greater knowledge of surrealism in Corso's work than there is of Whitman, even if it is not surrealism per se that Corso is interested in but rather a critique of the Thomist ontological tradition from within a surrealist orientation. In this sense, Corso was alone, a solitary figure working on a language of his own inside two large overlapping groups, none of whom saw Corso from within his own framework. Corso was not a surrealist in the sense of being an automatic writer. Unlike the surrealists, he was a conscious artist, shaping his poetry and reshaping it, often reworking a poem over the decades until he felt he had it right. This accounts for the many versions of his poems that appeared throughout his lifetime (and which Skau traces in his bibliography).

The Beat and New York school poets' major point of connection was O'Hara, who must have known thousands of people. Before O'Hara, there was a mutual interest in the work of Ezra Pound, William Carlos Williams, and the surrealists. Perloff notes that O'Hara knew and was influenced by Pound's work as early as 1951 (61).

There is a general critical consensus emerging that Ginsberg, O'Hara, and Ashbery were precursors of postmodern thought. In this sense, Corso, too, could be considered a postmodernist in that he challenges the ontological framework that kept the old ideology together. He goes further than the others and ends in a predicament in which he can no longer tell which way is up, he so thoroughly deconstructs his own philosophical origins.

Another way to think about Corso is to separate the Beat writers and the New York school by class. All of the major New York school poets were quite wealthy or had good jobs and could afford to buy modern art and stay in good hotels. The Beat writers, including William Burroughs, had very modest incomes; they had come from poorer backgrounds and had to work as merchant marines and collaborate with mass media vehicles in order to make a living. Kerouac, Burroughs, Ginsberg, and Corso all wrote for pornographic journals at one time or another, something the New York school didn't have to consider; they preferred to write art criticism, which pays very little, even if it is more prestigious. When Kerouac traveled, he slept in a car, as did Ginsberg and Corso, while Burroughs, with a small inheritance, could afford to stay in cheap motels.

To separate the two groups, therefore, we ought to remember not only the individual qualities of the artists but also the class backgrounds from which they emerged, as it helps place their target audience and to understand their own perspective of themselves. It is impossible to imagine Corso or Ginsberg or Orlovsky writing the classist line of O'Hara's, "I want to be / at least as alive as the *vulgar*" (emphasis added, cited in Perloff 21).

I don't want to devolve into Marxist self-righteousness. The New York school had financially solvent families who came from older money and wiser stock, and they had considerable emotional adhesiveness that required generations to put together. The Beat writers, on the other hand, suffered from exploded family situations and crazy, difficult relatives and were under a lot of strain—from Corso's runaway parents to Kerouac's angry parents to Ginsberg's insane mother to Burroughs's depressing family of predatory arriviste capitalists. This does say a lot about the work in the two schools and the intentions of the two groups. The Beat writers were much more revolutionary, as they were not satisfied with their upbringing and wanted changes, while the New York school was much more comfortable.

Finally, Perloff writes, "'schools' or movements always recede into the background as the permanently interesting artists emerge from their ranks" (xxxiii). There were many other artists with the background of the New York school or the Beat writers who have disappeared due to lack of talent or lack of application. Those writers who survive do so because they have taken a tradition and contributed permanently interesting work to it. To do this, they first had to master a tradition. All of the major writers of the Beat school and the New York school had attained this mastery, and they didn't do it by going to parties—even though the parties may have helped them exchange information, keep up morale, and mix aesthetic ideas.

Corso, mixed up in both schools—having gone to Harvard and yet living most of his life in New York and San Francisco in close proximity with the Beats—was nevertheless a loner. He was crazy in the same way as Rycroft's actress, but what is important is that he was also an important artist with a strong sense of discipline, knowing thoroughly the form and the history of the tradition in which he was working.

6

Monstrous Aesthetics

Against a backdrop of the sensible asceticism of Marx in which exploitation is morally opprobrious, Corso's poetics consist of paradoxical exploitation of one thing by another: the more monstrous, the more lovely. In "Don't Shoot the Warthog," he writes:

A child came to me
swinging an ocean on a stick.
He told me his sister was dead,
I pulled down his pants
and gave him a kick.
I drove him down the streets
down the night of my generation
I screamed his name, his cursed name,
down the streets of my generation,
and children lept in joy to the name
and running came.
Mothers and fathers bent their heads to hear;
I screamed the name.

The child trembled, fell,
and staggered up again,
I screamed his name!
And a fury of mothers and fathers
sank their teeth into his brain.
I called to the angels of my generation
on the rooftops, in the alleyways,
beneath the garbage and the stones,
I screamed the name! and they came
and gnawed the child's bones.

> I screamed the name: Beauty
> *Beauty Beauty Beauty*
>
> (*G* 35)

In this poem we see a figure of innocence being unfairly chased through the streets, murdered, and eaten, as if the entire society wishes to taste the child, to incorporate him into their own bodies. While Allen Ginsberg, in his infamous poem "Howl," sees the unfairness of society as belonging to Moloch while his own generation and friends are innocent, Corso implicates the narrator in his poem in the line "I pulled down his pants and gave him a kick."

Much of Ginsberg's anguish is often traced by critics back to his mother's madness. For instance, Diana Trilling writes of Ginsberg:

> His mother was in a mental institution, and she had been there, off and on, for a long time. This was the central and utterly persuasive fact of the young man's life. . . . Here was a boy on whom an outrageous unfairness had been perpetrated: his mother had fled from him into madness and now whoever crossed his path became somehow responsible, caught in the impossibility of rectifying what she had done. (58)

It doesn't seem quite sensible, as it does to Trilling, to hold Ginsberg's mother responsible for her madness (or to indicate that she had fled from *him* specifically), as the very definition of madness precludes rationality and therefore responsibility, but it is possible to hold Corso's parents responsible for having chosen to abandon him. Imagine Corso's anguish and inability to comprehend a society that left him without parents. Imagine also his attempt at comprehension, which this poem represents. And imagine his analysis: the child is the poet, himself, marginalized to being one of society's victims and yet feeling that he was himself beauty. Beauty is also in the warthog. Don't shoot it. Inside Corso's vision of beauty is, finally, a vision of morality, closely intertwined. But it isn't a morality he trusts. And his distrust is meant to undermine our own. There is nothing for him to trust. Morality is a fable, whereas eating is the dark and hidden reality as the "angels" of his generation "gnawed the child's bones." In the poem "But I Do Not Need Kindness," he discusses kindness in his usual rollicking manner, breaking one more icon with his doubt.

> I have known the fat pontiffs of Kindness,
> the little old grey-haired lady,
> the neighborhood priest,
> the famous poet,
> the mother,
> I have known them all!
> I have watched them, at night, dark and sad,
> pasting posters of mercy
> on the stark posts of despair.
> We spoke of nothing unkind,

but one night I was tormented by those strange nurses,
those fat pontiffs
The little old lady rode a spiked car over my head!
. . . .
The famous poet picked me up
and threw me out of the window!
The mother abandoned me!
I ran to Kindness, broke into Her chamber,
and profaned!
with an unnameable knife I gave Her a thousand wounds,
and inflicted them with filth!
I carried Her away, on my back, like a ghoul!
down the cobble-stoned night!
Dogs howled! Cats fled! All windows closed!
I carried Her ten flights of stairs!
Dropped Her on the floor of my small room,
and kneeling beside Her, I wept. I wept.

(*M* 32–33)

In this poem Corso discusses a primal scene in which he has lost his faith in kindness and killed it in himself. This terrible murder haunts his poetry and is also powerfully linked to his aesthetics, which almost seem to plead for him to ransack all the books of history and all the stories of religion for some redeeming value, some trace of what he had never had, or never reliably had. Corso's world is one in which nothing is to be trusted, and anything decent that comes has to be thrown out quickly for fear of being burned by it. His money, his wives, his friends, his publishers, all have been burned before they burned him. It is probably thanks to Ginsberg's experience with his mother that Corso's poetry exists, because Ginsberg alone was able to put up with him and give him some sense of stability and trust. And it is thanks to Corso's poetry that Corso was able to exorcise and understand some of his beginnings and develop the strength needed to get up. His is indeed a "giant art," as Richard Howard has called it. What does Corso's poetry offer? It's something like the strength to persevere in and even enjoy a world that makes no sense without the reliable kindness of our fellows, that is purely contradictory, and whose only measurement is sheer intensity to the minds of surrealists and other aesthetic solitaries, such as murderers and the clinically insane. Corso struggles with this aesthetic and tries to develop a sense of a worthwhile culture, but the only person he feels he can depend on is himself.

In Corso's poetry, there is also always clearly present a sense that life is profoundly worth living, which one doesn't always get in the surrealist avant-garde, which can tend toward nihilism. The Catholic theologian Karl-Josef Kuschel writes in the introduction to his *Laughter: A Theological Reflection:*

So this book is an attempt to provide a critical theology of laughter. It claims its legitimation from an indelible memory. Christians will never forget that in the bitterest hour of his life, their Master from Nazareth was one of those who were laughed at and mocked. So it will regard that kind of laughter once and for all with mistrust, hostility, indeed resistance. A critical theology of laughter will have to begin here, and each time ask in what spirit their laughter is. So an objection will be raised here to the tendentiously destructive and nihilistic character of a certain kind of laughter. . . . It will be an objection to mocking laughter from above downwards: laughter at the defenceless and marginalized, when comedy merely follows the line of the power relationships which already prevail. It will be an objection to cynical laughter: the proverbial laughter of hell, which stems from the denial of truth and ethics and which feeds on Mephistophelian anti-faith: "So it would be better if nothing came into being." (xx–xxi)

Corso, like theologian Kuschel, rarely lets such laughter into his work. Even in the above poems, which are fairly devastating, he titles one "Don't Shoot the Warthog," which returns the reader to his or her moral senses, and in "But I Do Not Need Kindness," the implication is that he clearly does. There is a life-affirming stance in Corso's writing that surely arises from his Catholic origins and separates him from the suicidal surrealists who litter the twentieth century, from the early friend of André Breton, Jacques Vaché, who killed himself for no apparent reason shortly after World War I, or Urmuz, the Romanian shooting star who inspired Tristan Tzara, who killed himself for a joke just to show that it could be done. There is none of this nihilism in Corso.

Corso writes in his poem "They":

> They, that unnamed "they,"
> they've knocked me down
>   but I got up
> I always get up—
> And I swear when I went down
>   quite often I took the fall;
> nothing moves a mountain but itself—
> They, I've long ago named them me.

(*LL* 83)

In this poem, we have not only a poetics but also a treatise on life. After one reads Corso's poems for so long and with such intense appreciation, much of this ability to get up to answer the bell transfers to the reader. His strength is based on his ability to handle contradictions. It's a poetic logic that he developed for himself but which is unique; it is the logic of one who has faith to rely upon—not a common condition in the surrealist universe.

Corso's poetry is an homage to religious faith as well as to obscenity. Unlike the traditional wisdom, which says that one can serve only one master, Corso has chosen two equally contradictory masters and serves them up to each other. On the one hand he is Christian, believing that everything is God-like, and on the other hand he is Darwinian, believing that everything is animalistic. Corso, therefore, seems split in two, or possibly three, directions. In one direction, Corso seeks to reevaluate earthly life, with its charming animal population and human classics, and study ancient civilizations to discover what made them tick. In another direction, he seeks to investigate the modes of the afterlife, based in spirit, and sees in Gnosticism a partial understanding of spirit as being trapped in animal nature. In yet another direction, he sees animal life as being all there is, and once the human being dies, there is nothing more. The spiritual position provides him with hope, while the animal position is funny but causes anguish. Corso relentlessly investigates these different paradigms throughout his career, and it is these different tendencies that provide a variety of moods in his writing. One can partially see that they were present even in his earliest thinking as a child on the streets of Little Italy in New York City, and humor was the only way he could reconcile these split systems.

Corso's poetry is an anxious investigation. Although there is imagination and idealism here, thanks to his split worldview, there is also realism and sudden despair.

> **In the Fleeting Hand of Time**
> Time takes me by the hand
> born March 26 1930 I am led 100 mph o'er the vast
> market of choice
> what to choose? what to choose?
> Oh—and I leave my orange room of myth
> no chance to lock away my toys of Zeus
> I choose the room of Bleecker Street
> A baby mother stuffs my mouth with a pale Milanese breast
> I suck I struggle I cry O Olympian mother
>
> . . . .
>
> Led 100 mph over these all too real Mafia streets
> profanely I shed my Hermean wings
>
> (G 15–16)

Corso's account of his birth emphasizes his divine origins as Hermes, but he is born "profanely" into a real situation of "Mafia streets." This situation is mediated by Corso's Catholicism, which is his first religious reference system. In the poem "Youthful Religious Experiences," Corso runs his finger over a strange incident in his childhood concerning a dead cat in the street:

> When I was six
> I saw a dead cat

I put a cross on it
and said a little prayer
When I told the Sunday school teacher
what I had done
she pulled my ears
and ordered me to go immediately
back to the dead cat
and take the cross off it
I love cats I've always loved cats
"But don't cats go to heaven?" I cried
"Thou shalt not worship false idols!" she replied—
I went back to the dead cat
it was gone
the cross remained
Fittingly so . . . that day the earth had died

(*HA* 22–23)

What Corso means here is that within his early religious system, the earth was a "false idol" with only the human spirit being treasured upon it. The cross was now on the earth itself, rather than just the cat, indicating that the earth was mortal. Corso doubts this early Christian reference system throughout his works, but it is something that he also continually comes back to, as it is home base. Is life apart from the spirit worthwhile? In this respect, Corso interrogates all the known reference systems of value and evaluates them, often rather harshly.

It is this relentless spirit of investigation that characterizes his poetry, as well as his mind. He never settles with any given truth but continually moves on over the vast marketplace of choice, choosing to put two or more things together into a single choice, making it surrealistic. With a love for bombs, various wives, nature, and spirit, he combines things and puts them into brackets together. It is as if Corso is smuggling things into shopping bags and walking out of the store with them, things that don't belong together but he wants to take anyway. Logic wouldn't let him get away with it, but it is for this reason that he dispenses with logic and turns toward surrealist aesthetics. It is feeling that Corso wants to create in his poetry: not a shared, communal feeling but rather a bizarre, solitary one. He looks straight into the heart of his own madness and transcribes what he sees.

To understand Corso's aesthetic, it is necessary to look again at how he uses his Christian past in order to create a kind of Gnosticism based not on "knowing" or on "insight" but rather on Dionysian catharsis, on an outpouring of emotional voluptuousness that is meant to get the repressed sensations to work again. To do this, Corso often uses outlawed images, breaks icons, and welcomes every kind of impoliteness as long as it is authentic on the emotional register, thus providing us with a key insight into the aesthetic practices of a group of iconoclastic individuals who begin with a distrust in humanity, perhaps based on an unreliable upbringing.

It is possible to see that across the board, surrealists in general denied reality, because reality didn't comfort them. They therefore created an alternative reality, along with a long list of precursors, all of whom were in some way indisposed to the simple domestic happiness that most people aim for. From Alfred Jarry, with his absinthe drinking, to the Marquis de Sade, from whom the name "sadism" derives, the surrealist notion of a canon was based on a group of destructive individuals whose idea of revolt specifically excluded the domain of domesticity.

When we think of the surrealists and their most famous practitioners, it is almost always a radical sense of impiety that is brought forth. This seems linked to a generalized absence of care in the home. The list of abandoned children who later became surrealists, or those with cold and rejecting mothers or problems with both parents, would essentially make up the entire list. Corso's case is not an exception; it is the rule. Richard Brautigan was abandoned by his mother in a Montana hotel in his very early youth; Charles Willeford was abandoned very early and later hit the road at age fourteen. Leonora Carrington hated her wealthy British parents with a sarcasm that bordered on rage. Salvador Dali spit on his mother and was disinherited by his father; Philippe Soupault's father died when the future surrealist was seven, and his mother was apparently too busy with her social life after this to be of much comfort. André Breton's mother slapped him senseless at regular intervals during his upbringing. Mark Polizzotti writes in his biography of André Breton:

> Breton's aversion to children, and to families in general, was as long-standing as it was violent. Georges Hugnet remembered him yelling several years earlier at a young mother whose stroller had accidentally brushed his leg: "Just because you've shit out a kid doesn't mean you have to rub everyone else's nose in it!" And during a "discussion on sexuality" at around the same time, Breton had declared that he would refuse ever to see a child born to him, adding, "The sad joke that began with my birth must end with my death." (429)

Polizzotti is quick to add that Breton's heart changed when his own little girl was born, but even this "seems to have had little impact on his public stance regarding the family" (429).

Suicide was a common fixation among the members of the surrealist group. Their great cultural heroes included Charles Baudelaire, Arthur Rimbaud, le Comte de Lautréamont, and the Marquis de Sade, all of whom, it can be said as well, sprang from troubled families and none of whom ever created any emotionally stable family units of their own.

If the nuclear family, the site of the only unconditional love that most people ever get, was considered a hell, or even a toilet, what, then, did the surrealists value in art? What was this rather large and extremely talented group of men and women aiming for? While the vast majority of people take comfort in their families and in conventional religion, surrealists seem to turn these institutions upside down and inside out in order to create fleeting moments of beauty that have a large share of imagination in them, a large share of a different order of reality altogether. Forced to think about the role of humankind in the universe due to their discomfort within their own families, surrealists are free to reimagine society from the ground up and to rethink the place of beauty and poetry in the creation of a better world.

In reflecting on Corso and his relationship to surrealism, I often think of surrealist precursor Alfred Jarry, whose incredible poverty combined with intellectual brilliance made him rise briefly to the top of the Parisian art world before he sank out of sight from an absinthe addiction and perpetual overwork, leaving a strange aesthetic legacy that was highly appreciated by the surrealists. "It is conventional to call 'monster' any blending of dissonant elements. . . . I call 'monster' every original, inexhaustible beauty" (Alfred Jarry cited in Shattuck 239–40).

Like Jarry, Corso was obsessed with the Passion of Christ and with trying to understand its aesthetic power. Also like Jarry, Corso wished to subvert the piety of the Passion and to turn it into something paradoxical, ambiguous, rather than something that would simply comfort humankind. What is the Passion in a surrealist's eyes but a monstrous look at how God's children killed his only son?

Ecce Homo
Inside the wounded hands and feet
the fragments of earlier wounds (almost healed)
like black almonds crusted
are answer enough
the nails went thru the man to God.

The crown of thorns (a superb idea!)
and the sidewound (an atrocity!)
only penetrate the man.

I have seen many paintings of this;
the same inflictions
subject of proof; *ecce signum*
the same sad face;
I have forgotten them all.
O Theodoricus, youth, vagueness, my fault; yet yours!
What grief! this
impossible to forget.

(*G* 28)

The images of the Crucifixion that have been painted for millennia would seem to bank on the amount of sensuous pain that they offer. "What grief!" Corso writes; "this / impossible to forget." The crown of thorns, the side wound, and the wounds in the hands indicate intensity of sensation as the aesthetic of evaluation in this picture and in others in the surrealist tradition. In other words, compassion is set aside and intensity instead takes its place. Nevertheless, in Corso's brief poem, there is genuine pain, and there is also a capitalization of "God," which one would not find in a poem by Benjamin Péret, a violent atheist, or indeed in the works of Breton himself.

Corso had five children and loved them, although his marriages didn't remain intact. His affection for the children is made clear in some of his shorter lyrics.

> **For Lisa, 2**
> I saw an angel today
> without wings
> with human smile
> and nothing to say
>
> *(HA* 54)

In general, the surrealists turn the normal realm of positive feelings inside out and instead value only intensity, disregarding the positive or negative aspect of that value. The Marquis de Sade was valued precisely because of his voluptuous intensity, and no regard was given as to the ethics of the Sadean worldview. How is this possible?

What the surrealists seem to object to is the absence of feeling in their respective families. Whereas the average citizen grows up in a loving home, surrealists seem to have despaired of the prevailing conditions in their childhood. Absence, loss, overwork, and the other conditions common under Western capitalism create a longing for love, beauty, and poetry. This is most keenly felt by those whose families were most cold or whose cultures were most unpitying. It should be of some alarm that surrealism is becoming a major aesthetic attitude, a major source of comfort to an alienated youth to whom the Marquis de Sade is about as scary as an episode of *Batman*. Surrealism is a reaction against the values of cold, rigid material progress and an insistence on strange beauty in the present tense. However, because the attitudes of many surrealists have been warped by their upbringing, the vision of warmth that they seek to project is itself often warped. The psychiatrist Charles Rycroft comments:

> This capacity of the mind to endow all its perceptions with additional symbolic meanings can be exemplified by our responses to scenery and architecture. It is, for instance, what makes us feel that bleak landscapes are unfriendly and unwelcoming, but that lush valleys are not, that mountains, cliffs and large buildings, particularly if they lack windows, are austere and forbidding, and that houses with bay windows and wings coming out to meet one are inviting. It seems that we react to things—scenery and buildings—as though they were people who might embrace, ignore or cold-shoulder us. (165)

However, if a writer has twisted perceptions and comes to identify himself with outcasts, as Corso does with warthogs, then the usual affections might be reversed and create a rich, private language that needs to be pondered before it can be understood. Where an average citizen might value a golden retriever, a surrealist poet might value a warthog; where an average citizen might link beauty to a birthday, a surrealist poet might link beauty to being chased down the street by killer parents. In these cases, how do we value a surrealist poet's world when it is at variance with our own?

In his most important book from his later period, *La Monnaie Vivante,* the extreme surrealist Pierre Klossowski goes off the gold standard, away from external standards of value measurement, in order to speculate that the origin of all value is in "voluptuous sensation." Does this mean that all morality goes out the window in terms of evaluation? If only raw sensation is counted, then it would seem that morality no longer has any place. However, as it turns out, voluptuous sensation is utterly dependent on morality. For without morality, there would be no shock, no sense of shame, which gives rise to the most important voluptuous sensations. Feelings are dependent on morality. The shock of immorality produces exquisite feelings, which Klossowski says are better than money in a bank. While most see Jesus within the framework of compassion, that he gave his life in order to save humanity, a surrealist may see only the monstrousness of the act from an aesthetic viewpoint, and even see it backward, as if the monstrousness of the act was linked to its aesthetics. What is more immoral than to nail Jesus Christ, the Son of God, to a cross? It is this image that founds Western civilization in Klossowski's view, providing a gold standard of absolute surrealist value, it being the most horrible image imaginable and thus paradoxically found at the center of every Christian church. This image brings out the other side of Christ, Christ as Dionysus, which Nietzsche did so much to foster and which was picked up by Nietzschean postmodernism. Nietzsche is often interpreted as anti-religious, but as Nietzsche scholar Julian Young remarks, he had also seen "Lutheranism . . . as a rebirth of the Dionysian" (cited in Young 49).

From this viewpoint, we can ask which is more powerful, Corso's poem about Theodoricus's depiction of the Crucifixion, or the original painting? Following the surrealist viewpoint, we can ask which is more powerful, the painting by Theodoricus, or the original, in which Christ is actually on the cross? Is the Passion of Christ, as seen on a postcard, truly the Passion? Is a painting closer to the truth of the Passion than a postcard of a painting of the Passion? If Christ were posed like an androgynous pinup on the cross with miniskirt and naked breasts, his eyes crisscrossed Ben Turpin–style (silent film comedian who specialized in crossing his eyes), would it be preferable to the original? The image of the Passion drives us to ask such nonsensical questions, because it is itself nonsense when compassion is left out of the picture, especially as it is seen in the eyes of convulsive surrealism from Salvador Dali to Gregory Corso. How could God, the most powerful being in the universe, the Alpha and Omega, in which all things reside, permit himself to be martyred by Roman soldiers using ordinary wood and nails? The image has to be understood through the heart, but to those whose hearts are closed, the image can be understood only intellectually. The early Christian theologian Tertullian, a favorite of Klossowski because of his strange theology, "speaking of the absolutely absurd supposition that God was a man and suffered martyrdom, said: 'I believe it because it is absurd'" (Saw 35).

In order to discuss the criterion of voluptuous emotion, which seems to go against sense, against the rational, and specify how a "libidinal economy" differs from classical political economy (based on the distinction between use-value and exchange-value), and to speak in particular about how Klossowski's libidinal economy differs from his close friend and associate Georges Bataille's notion of unproductive expenditure, it will be necessary to draw in Marxist notions of what happens when the economy becomes libidinal and feeling becomes economic in order to reveal the distinction between surrealist and Marxist thought and in order to show how each can be applied to axiological theories of literature and why the surrealist position is clearly the more interesting from an aesthetic vantage point. Whereas Marxist thought attempts to formulate objective theories of value, the surrealist mode favors a theory of value based on voluptuous emotion.

Pierre Klossowski, a member of the College of Sociology, was closely associated with Georges Bataille, Roger Caillois, and Maurice Blanchot. The College of Sociology was a surrealist splinter group; many of its members had started off in surrealism but found it didn't go far enough for their tastes. They maintained a parallel but intense relationship with André Breton and were perhaps even more surrealist than the surrealists themselves. Klossowski's essay *La Monnaie Vivante* takes off from an incidental remark by Raymond Aron, that "l'érotisme— échappant à l'urgence des besoins vitaux—n'a pas été thématisé par la théorie économique" [eroticism, escaping the urgency of vital needs, has not been thematized by economic theory] (cited in Monnoyer 241). Klossowski's proposition highlights many of the problems in economic and literary theory and the theory of libidinal circulation as proposed by Jean-François Lyotard, among others, to replace Marx's objective theory of circulation and is thus a perfect site from which to create a foundation for a postmodern theory of artistic value.

Marx writes, "A commodity is, in the first place, an object outside us, a thing that by its very properties satisfies human wants of some sort or another" (*Capital* 35). Is a poem a pragmatic commodity in this sense? If the object is exterior and the wants are by definition interior, then the satisfaction of these wants comes about as a relation between interior and exterior. To take a concrete example, a McDonald's burger, as it makes the transition from exterior realm of Golden Arches foyer to interior realm of stomach, satisfies partially in that it is cheap. For less than a dollar, one pays for the value of the labor that has entered into the equation of the McDonald's burger, from farmer's cow munching grass to slaughterhouse to U.S.D.A.-inspected meat factory to proletarian slinging round meat unit between buns. But can we think of the McDonald's burger as a reasonable means of universal exchange? Marx praises the beauty of metals as means of exchange: they are extremely durable and uniform. Moreover, precisely because they have limited use in and of themselves, they can serve as a purely symbolic value:

> If, for instance, one evaluates all commodities in terms of oxen, hides, corn, etc., one has in fact to measure them in ideal average oxen, average hides, etc., since there are qualitative differences between one ox and another, one lot of corn and another, one hide and another. Gold and silver, on the other hand, as simple substances are always uniform and consequently equal quantities of them have equal values. (*Contribution* 153)

The nature of a hamburger is that it does not keep. Whereas a nickel can circulate for twenty years without remarkable depreciation, a hamburger after twenty years would hardly be in the same state. Thus, one principle of Klossowski's *Monnaie Vivante* is seemingly weak. Unlike coinage, art fluctuates in value according to the amount of shame and resistance felt by the viewer. In the Theodoricus painting, Corso congratulates the painter on "[t]he crown of thorns (a superb idea!) / and the sidewound (an atrocity!)." This praise has to be seen within the realm of humiliation and atrocity—the intensity of these wounds shames the viewer into a heightened appreciation of the paradoxical suffering of the Son of God, which is so close to the suffering of Dionysus.

Klossowski claims that the body is the equivalent of wealth and is wealth itself. The final source of value in Klossowski is voluptuousness. Whereas Marx puts labor value beneath everything else, Klossowski outbids Marx by implying that all of that labor value goes merely to purchase sensation. According to Klossowski, our emotions are interpersonal. Our emotions depend on the distinct emotions of the other. There is the problem here of intersubjectivity. Money does not look us back in the face. It is a standard measure agreed upon between two consumers.

Marx's problems were how to feed and clothe people. Although we have not entirely achieved even that, a surrealist economist jumps ahead to solve the tricky problem of how to thematize the vagaries of sensation while the literary theorist must attempt to theorize the vagaries of value of the written page, perhaps the most ephemeral and subjective of all economies. Klossowski, in theorizing the two together, shows us an entirely new paradigm: one in which intensity of emotion is the criteria by which art can be judged. The greater the emotion, the greater the art. How do we quantify an emotion? Is it possible that every reader will value the same page of literature in exactly the same way?

At each new level of axiological examination, the problems multiply interestingly. To return to the experience of the McDonald's burger: I sat down with one of my more carnivorous friends in the spacious McDonald's parlor, and as I ordered a salad, she stacked bacon burgers on her tray. I immediately indulged in the ritual embarrassment technique practiced by vegetarians toward carnivores (I gave up meat many years ago, picking up on Corso's anxiety about it), which changed her experience from one of the kind of delirium that can accumulate around a single name (Big Mac) to one of meaning inscribed within an exterior system of ethics and laws. Her taste, however, didn't vanish entirely, nor was the phantasm or originary and incommunicable pleasure gone and only the ethical meaning of her tasteless act of consumption left on her tongue, but rather, my teasing augmented my pleasure as it lessened hers, making her more and more aware of the flavor of the flesh she was eating and making her want to throw it up. One might almost say that my pleasure was heightened by her discomfort as she felt my shock and horror as a moral shock that ruined her appetite, which nevertheless improved mine. Others are necessary to participate in acts of Sadean voluptuous sensation, but this has to be seen as a relation without compassion, without any real emotional empathy.

In other words, another who resists simply adds to the sensation. To have this sensation, however, we must agree on a meaning for the act of consumption. We must have to some extent the idea that eating another being is harmful. Therefore, the perpetration of a Sadean act must not be crazy but rather be a borderline case, in which morality is understood, but only as a rule of law, not as some deep inner emotional logic. Corso's writings depend on this to a large degree, from the beginning to the last, as the reader shares the narrator's joy. Shame is communicated. Without that shame of eating and killing, there would be no psychic intensity.

The serial killer, such as Ted Bundy, takes great delight in the narration of his acts in newspapers and television. He enjoys the shock and thrill of a community of disgusted and concerned citizens. Without that shock and disgust, his pleasure would not be there. However, Bundy's act is not aesthetic, as it is not shared by a willing audience eager to participate in an art event. When Corso narrates the killing of beauty in "Don't Shoot the Warthog," a similar baiting of the audience occurs as the poet plays with cultural tensions surrounding sacrilege, especially concerning young children, and manages to make us briefly glimpse the warthog as sacred, which is both laughable and morally mind-numbing as it opens the heart to the endless suffering of the world. If Corso's act differs from Bundy's, it is in that it invites an audience to judge it and by doing so to judge themselves, whereas Bundy's act is forced upon the audience.

To destroy another human being, as one destroys a cow, is a capital offense. To make the ontological equation between human beings and animals is disallowed in almost every society. It is one of the major taboos of Western society. Therefore, to break such a taboo creates a major sensation, not only for the taboo breaker but also for the entire community. Serial killers break this taboo in order to feel the thrill. But the thrill is connected, definitively, to the morality of the matter. Without morality, there would be no resistance, and without resistance, there would be no narration, and without narration, there would be no pleasure. Ted Bundy deliberately moved to Florida, the state that was the most stringent in its application of the death penalty. Bundy wanted the final drama and the torrent of confessions, because without this, he would not have gotten any pleasure. Pleasure is shared by a community or else it is no pleasure at all, and Sadean pleasure is always had at the expense of a reluctant community.

Meaning is closely linked to value and regulated by "community standards." The abuse of bodies, whether through the eating of cow parts or the fetishistic murder of victims, intensifies meaning and produces a volcano of blasphemy, an epical sensation, a delirium, just as the Passion is meant to do. As Lyotard writes, "Le phantasm Klossowskien veut, quelque part, au moins un corps à transgresser: car il consiste précisément en un usage parcellaire du corps de la victime" [The Klossowskien phantasm wants, somewhere, at the least a body to transgress: because it consists precisely in a portioned-out use of the victim's body] (*Economie Libidinale* 94). Laws, of course, protect us to a certain extent from these phantasmic seekers of experience. But just as certainly, they also provoke and inspire them. The question remains whether we can incorporate libidinal experience within a general political economy, especially when it is the transgression of the political and legal that creates the value for early Klossowski and his greatest precursor, Sade, as well as for serial killers like Ted Bundy. The Crucifixion, from within the surrealist viewpoint, is simultaneously an outrage and a cry for mercy, as are the shocking transgressions of the serial killer.

Bundy operated in the shadow world of political meaning, in a libidinal economy of nameless and meaningless intensity, but he ultimately sought to recuperate this intensity into a coherent narrative that he could share with other members of the community. Through recounting his story, which he was forced to do, he had the double thrill of being both victimizer and victim. Intensity itself became the only differential, as it is for Klossowski's Nietzsche in *Nietzsche et le Cercle Vicieux:* "Nietzsche, dans son phantasm, voit flamber les merveilles du Louvre. Ce ne sont pas les merveilles qui importent, mais les émotions à l'origine de celles-ci. Or ces emotions font régner l'inégalité" [Nietzsche, in his phantasm, sees the marvels of the Louvre ablaze. It is not the marvels which count, but the emotions at their origins. But these emotions begin the reign of inequality] (*Nietzsche* 33). The reason that art was outlawed in the first commandment is that it brings forth a monstrous logic in which, even in those images allowed in the church, it is always the most powerful sensations that the artists are provoked to create. Nightly, our television screens explode in visual mayhem.

Murder is the backbone of the fiction industry. It is the highest emotional experience, according to Aristotelian notions of catharsis. Aristotle's notion of catharsis is advanced in his *Poetics,* which is most certainly about narrative. We can only understand or appreciate murder as it is represented in a meaningful story. Outside of a communicable story, murder means nothing; even the word "murder" cannot be attributed to a community that does not recognize murder as an officially banned act. This is where surrealist aesthetics differ from classical aesthetics. While Aristotle's *Poetics* is meaningful within a community and is meant to expurgate negative emotions so that the community can live together more peacefully, surrealist aesthetics create powerful emotions that a solitary individual can relish, especially at the expense of another, in order precisely to deny that there is any community at all, and yet this very act paradoxically proves the sense of community.

If eating the dead body of a cow is wrong, it is wrong because it doesn't fit into a narrative that we tell about ourselves and the cow. If even a stupid cow has a soul and is thus continuous with ourselves, we cannot eat it, because it has rights. If other human beings have the same kind of soul that we do, it is necessary to turn them into another species in order to justify their killing. If Bundy is a killer, then his soul doesn't count, and thus we kill him. This gives the entire population a huge moral thrill, which some think of as immoral. We increasingly feel that a transgression upon the bodily space of another being is inconsiderate, to say the very least. However, it is this transgression upon the body parts of another that is at the basis of the value of Corso's (and most surrealist) writings. Throughout his writings, from the earliest to the last, we are continually reminded of the cannibalistic nature of the food chain, its predatory aspects, and to some extent this constitutes its beauty, its voluptuousness. We live in a world that is a perpetual motion machine of eating. The taste of the food chain is our most constant source of voluptuous pleasures: we spend our days planning lunch and dinner made up of other creatures whose carnal delights are heavily advertised. Klossowski's voluptuous capitalism turns Marx's ascetic denial of the beauty of exploitation on its head.

While Marx says that all inequitable exchange is a form of prostitution, in that unlike things (labor and money, for example) are unfairly exchanged at arbitrary levels of value, Klossowski playfully but literally attempts to put what is bodily and fetishistic back in as the only value. Klossowski's is a radical positioning of the scale of values, a Sadean attempt to go beyond material things and back to what really matters. Only that which cannot be exchanged has any worth. The body cannot be exchanged. Although Klossowski's system does not register on any common ethical scale, it does make sense, and it does portray a deep insight into surrealist aesthetics.

Marx's willingness to strip away the personality, or what Marx called the fetish quality, of products in order to affix a standardized and general meaning on a product, a meaning determined once and for all by the State, is exactly what Klossowski fought against. The correspondence between use-value and exchange-value can only be achieved where what is made and its meaning is strictly controlled by the State. Where meanings can be twisted, a new sense of values is free to arise with the introduction of imagination. Individual imagination is exactly what Marx sought to eliminate from his system, whereas the surrealists saw it as the primary aspect of their own.

In the very first portion of *Capital*, Marx sought to destroy fetishization. This monopoly on meaning is given such a major role that it deserves to be cited at some length:

There is a physical relation between physical things. But it is different with commodities. There, the existence of the things qua commodities, and the value-relation between the products of labor which stamps them as commodities, have absolutely no connexion with their physical properties and with the material relations arising therefrom. There it is a definite social relation between men, that assumes, in their eyes, the fantastic form of a relation between things. In order, therefore, to find an analogy, we must have recourse to the mist-enveloped regions of the religious world. In that world the productions of the human brain appear as independent beings endowed with life, and entering into relationship with one another and the human race. So it is in the world of commodities with the products of men's hands. This I call the Fetishism which attaches itself to the products of labor, so soon as they are produced as commodities, and which is therefore inseparable from the production of commodities. (*Capital* 72)

In this passage, Marx seems to indicate that this fetishization cannot be stopped, and yet at the same time there is a heavy sarcastic inference that it should be, both from the use of the (for Marx) pejorative term "fetishization" and the sarcasm inherent in Marx's reference to the "mist-enveloped regions of the religious world." The term "fetish" was originally applied to West African idols and religious artifacts, or those objects endowed with supernatural and otherworldly powers and is used here to ridicule the unscientific thinking of consumers who are too easily fooled by this mystification. In Marxist societies, things are to be valued for their use-value alone and to be stripped of any fanciful exchange value added by imaginative marketing gimmicks.

Against this rather intolerably sane appraisal of commodities, most cultures do fetishize, exploiting the human capacity for imagination and often turning the most volatile criminality into the highest aesthetic good. In his polemic against the Gnostic heresiarch Carpocrates, the Bishop Irenaeus mentions that the cult had, amongst their relics, paintings done by Pontius Pilate of the earthly life of Christ (116). They worshiped these paintings and considered them to be the equal of the works of Pythagorus, Plato, and Aristotle. "Ils rendent à ces images tous les autres honneurs en usage chez les païens" [They rendered unto these images all the honors customary among the pagans] (Irenaeus 116).

Although Klossowski does not mention Pilate's paintings, perhaps it is through them that we can best understand the Klossowskien usage of the word "render," meaning not only to fork over, or to pay tribute, but also to depict:

Pour eux [the Carpocratians], l'Evangile enseigne aux hommes comment il faut rendre à la lumière ce qui est à la lumière en restituant aux ténébres ce qui est aux ténébres. [For them, the Gospel teaches men how it is necessary to render to the light that which belongs to the light and returning to the shadows that which belongs to the shadows.] (*Sade Mon Prochain* 188)

Pierre Klossowski, like Gregory Corso, was born a Catholic and thus was under the general Christian ordinance not to render graven images. Klossowski found support, however, for the rendering of graven images not only in the Gnostic heresiarchs and Sade but also in Freud's postulate of an originary violence that finds its release in therapeutic catharsis, which Klossowski compares to medieval exorcism (*Ressemblance* 105–9; Monnoyer 32–36). Corso's writing, I believe, follows a similar "logic," which will have to be discussed in some detail.

Klossowskien irony inverts not only Plato's hierarchical schema of tragedy and comedy but also their analogues: model and copy. According to Plato, the original forms are the only reality, and the further we get from these models, the more debased and less real the copy. However, if we see the simulacrum as a new model, completely distinct from what came before, then we should see a bad copy, a deliberate counterfeit, as a new original, because, since it does not pretend to be the original but even brags about its own status as simulacrum, it perversely founds its own originality while calling into question the originality of the original. The radical subversion of patriarchy (retained by critic Harold Bloom in his notion of the Oedipal jealousy of poets) instituted by the parodic simulacrum begins when the statue sticks his or her tongue out at the sculptor behind the sculptor's back; the Gnostic libertine ethos, similarly, is about the creation of a Frankensteinian monster whose rebellion is total insouciance against the reverence toward the father (the model, or the ideal form) privileged by Plato, but obsession with him nevertheless. We have seen this Gnostic insolence toward the divine Father in Sade, and now we will look at it in more detail in Corso's oeuvre.

Corso's poetry possesses a twisted moral vision, a moral vision from the street, which has only the most tangential connection to the moral vision of most of contemporary America. While most Americans accept the idea of God without great trouble, and perhaps pray once in a while when they need a new refrigerator, or even think of God as a trusted friend, Corso, on the other hand, is obsessed with his lack of trust in a God that he can nevertheless not leave, which symbolizes perhaps a larger distrust of every value. Corso writes a poem to the medieval French poet François Villon, who had been hanged for being a thief. Corso had been imprisoned in his teens for stealing a coat.

> **Dear Villon**
> Villon, how brotherly our similarities . . .
> Orphans, altar boys attending the priest's skirt;
> > purpling the coffins
>
> Thieves: you having stolen the Devil's Fart
> And I stealing what was mine
> . . . .
> . . . Nothing is mine, a Prince of Poetry
> made to roam the outskirts of society

> taking, if I needed a coat, what was taken
> from the lamb
>
> (*HA* 24)

Corso's poetry marks a reversal of contemporary values. He denies the original ownership of a coat, claiming that since it had once been stolen, it was his right to steal it a second time. Obviously, the law did not recognize Corso's right as a teenager, and he spent a few years in prison for it, but this did not change Corso's opinion of anything except the law. Corso's marginal sensibility does not allow him to be understood within the moral framework of American life, or within the moral framework of any life. He is a surrealist poet, not a preacher; his art is to deterritorialize any boundaries of sense and to give a new freshness to mental experience, but to do this, Corso has to deny truth and argue instead that the creative power of the imagination has a legitimacy equal to the certifiably and objectively real, making that which is invented the equivalent of that which had priority, or that which was given by God. Since for Corso there was no trustworthy parental figure, there are no principles at all. This puts him into the categories of a permanent doubter, a sophist, and iconoclast, and yet his argument over stealing does make sense in that it is indeed true that the coat was stolen from the lamb, and Corso, being a lamb of God, therefore has a right to it. His logic is arguably Christian and yet against American laws regarding property. How do we evaluate such an individual? Corso's work itself cannot seem to make up its mind whether this world has any value or not, although he often veers toward optimism. This optimism, however, is always offset with a question: Is the food chain based on bad taste, or good taste?

Is it some riotous combination of the two, in which darkness and light commingle in some paradoxical way that has never been quite fully articulated by any philosopher? Are morality and aesthetics possible in our particular food chain? These questions are reopened in every one of Corso's poems and are never settled. Without God, the question of a foundation is negated, and only laughter, doubt, and iconoclasm are left as implicit sources of value. These values, in turn, are the classic values of the major surrealists with passion perhaps as the only standard. Mark Polizzotti writes that André Breton, "the man who had unmasked a Rimbaud forgery through its lack of internal passion[,] never ceased judging works and individuals by the emotional 'shivers' they could generate" (599). Corso's difference with the surrealists is that while they let the shivers have the last word, Corso always returned to talking about God.

7

Corso's Inquisition of Christian Metaphysics

The aesthetic philosophers of the Middle Ages, stemming from St. Thomas, would find it difficult to see the greatness of Corso. According to Hugh Honor and John Fleming in *A World History of Art,* "St. Thomas Aquinas or a close follower, defined beauty as 'a certain consonance of diverging elements'" (362). The idea of unity is rarely one of Corso's driving motivations. And instead of the humility of a medieval monk before God, Corso saw himself as divine and thus felt that what he wrote was divine.

Corso's poetry has offered a difficult and ambivalent access to the eternal spirit of the Dionysian trickster, which, he wrote, "comes, I tell you, immense with gasolined rags and bits of wire and old bent nails, a dark arriviste, from a dark river within, *How Poetry Comes to Me,* page 1369" (*G* frontispiece). Even when Corso discusses his own poetry, he uses the term "arriviste," implying in advance that he is a pretender, and yet he comes from a "dark river within," implying that he is the real thing. Corso destabilizes the regime of reason and offers instead limited but precious access to other aspects of the mind that are terrifying, beautiful, humorous, and best appreciated in the intense ambivalence of his search for authenticity, which is simultaneously a fraudulent performance based on an unreliable sense of self.

Corso's dated language, his perpetual resort to "thee" and "thou" that he mixes with street language, heightens this sense that he is a street hustler, or one of these new age gurus who "channel" voices from the great beyond in Scotch brogue mixed with Low German. Corso, an autodidact, must have found biblical language thrilling to come across when he was in prison as a youth, as he often mixes this with Shelleyan "ayes" and other pompous language, but somehow one has the sense that there is something genuine here just the same and that the very fraudulence of the whole performance is a testimony to its authenticity; the effect of his hesitations is sometimes deeply moving. In the poem "Writ on the

Steps of Puerto Rican Harlem," Corso writes of the various oppositions within himself: "I'd an innocence I'd a seriousness / I'd a humor save me from amateur philosophy / I am able to contradict my beliefs" (*LL* 77).

It is Corso's humor that provides a locus for his contradictory character, but I want to stipulate that Corso's humor is not wit or something polite. It recalls Jarry's "monstrous and inexhaustible beauty." His humor roars with agonized humanity and is thus emotionally rich rather than merely intellectual, but it lacks the sense of "a certain consonance" that has been an important criteria of art critics since the medieval era. Humor is itself often built on contradictions, and Corso's strength is to build his poems at the intersections of worlds that do not intersect: morality and the food chain, humanity and animality, pain and beauty. In Corso's poem "Writ in Horace Greeley Square," he discusses his own capacity to live with contradictions.

> I know I'm one who
>   even if he does see the light
> still won't be completely all right
>   and good for that
>
> Yesterday I believed in man today I don't
>   and tomorrow
>   tomorrow's a toss-up

(LL 84)

The *Oxford English Dictionary* discusses the term "contradictory" as

(i) disagreement in character or qualities; want of accordance or harmony; discrepancy; inconsistency. (ii) Want of accordance with what is reasonable or fitting; unsuitableness, inappropriateness, absurdity. (iii) Want of harmony of parts or elements; want of self-consistency; incoherence. (cited in Martin 175)

Corso's contradictions range from the tragic to the humorous to the poignant to the irrelevant. Corso's art doesn't make one laugh out loud—the about-faces that he performs between cheerfulness and despair come so suddenly that one doesn't guffaw, exactly. A short and rather typical poem for Corso is "A Guide for My Infant Son":

> Simple perfection
> Perfect simplicity
> It's easy
> like painting a flower
> or
> snapping it dead

(HA 56)

The sudden turning from the perfection of the flower to a nasty "snapping it dead" illustrates the hair-trigger mentality of Corso, who is either enormously pleased or filled with despair, or often both, at the slightest incidents. He is an unpredictable, unstable character, which is why he is best observed at a distance, or between the covers of a book. Most of Corso's poems lie on the border between the monstrous and the amusing, as if the humor is used to keep terror at bay and the terror is used to keep humor from forgetting about reality. Corso mixes aesthetic appreciation (painting a flower) with the jolt of viciousness (snapping the flower dead) and puts this under the title of a "Guide" for his infant son. What kind of a guide is this? Is it a trustworthy guide? Characteristically, the poem brings up morality, but inconclusively. We are tempted to intervene and say to the child, "This is no guide!" On the other hand, there is nothing really very wrong with "snapping it dead," as long as it is only a flower and not a person. But as usual, Corso is also bringing up the ontological distinction between flower and person and asking why we snap one and not another. This is not so much a guide as a kind of Zen koan, which forces the child (and the reader) to sort out things that can't be sorted, asking us to run through all the possibilities that would set this poem right, but the poem, characteristically, resists any kind of reterritorialization by reason or morality. This pile of contradictions gives us pleasure, but why? Perhaps it goes back to the surrealist distrust of the faculty of reason, a distrust that Corso shares. Arthur Schopenhauer writes that we like humor because it is "delightful for us to see this strict, untiring, and most troublesome governess, our faculty of reason, for once convicted of inadequacy" (cited in Martin 185).

Corso, like the surrealists, wanted to attack the real and usher in a regime of humor and the marvelous. The question of which is the real and which is the copy, which is the true philosopher and which is the philosopher villain, has been around at least since Plato. Who is a real poet and who is a hustler? What makes Gary Snyder a real poet, doing the "Real Work," as he puts it in the title of one of his books, and Corso a fraudulent huckster, a pseudo-shaman? Is it merely class origin, connections, and cultural prestige? Diogenes the Cynic made no distinction between the true and the false. When accosted with the comment, "You don't know anything, although you are a philosopher," he replied, "Even if I am but a pretender to wisdom, that in itself is philosophy" (Laertius 65–67).

After all the charlatanry, crazy humor, and what Derek Parker has called "ill-digested" influences in Corso's poetry, there is finally something that is as close to divine as a simulacrum can be in Corso's poetry:

Inter & Outer Rhyme
Last night was the nightest
The moon full-mooned a starless space
Sure as snow beneath snow is whitest
Shall the god surface the human face

(*HA* 21)

What god is it that surfaces here in this late poem? Whatever it is, it is not warm but rather like "snow." There are divine references throughout Corso's poetry to Hermes, the trickster god, but they also point to Hermes Trismegistus, who, as Barnstone explains, was the foundation for the myth of Faustus (606). Hermes, a Hellenistic pagan god, is linked to Hermes Trismegistus. Barnstone writes, "Hermes is the common translation of the Egyptian god Thoth and is identified with his attributes" (567). Could it be as well that Shelley's "Intellectual Beauty" is also a variant of this speedy messenger of the gods? According to Ernest Lee Tuveson's *Avatars of Thrice Great Hermes*, the continuity of this overreaching figure, from Simon Magus to Faust, extends from Shelley's "Intellectual Beauty" and beyond to Walt Whitman. Corso's Hermes is also Hermes Trismegistus, also Faustus, but lit with the bizarre sense of humor of the very first Hermes, who stole Apollo's cattle on his first day of life and then later presented Apollo with the first lyre as a makeup gift. Corso combines this sense of humor with the speculative nature of the early Greeks. Corso found himself incarnated as a poor orphan of the city streets in Little Italy and apparently thought this to be too limited a circumstance; he wanted to enlarge his persona until he became something great. Toward the latter part of his poetry, he reinvests nature with spirit, with an ontology of its own, mysterious and yet briefly beautiful, a brief culmination of the entire wisdom tradition beginning with Hermes Trismegistus and ending with himself as magician and alchemist, capable of transforming nature into spirit.

Corso's poetry has often been seen for its hesitating, truncated quality, a quality the surrealists prized. When he hits a harmonious note, as he does now and then, he touches it so ever so briefly because it is seemingly all that he can sustain. His most frequent note is humor. According to the Thomist tradition, and the tradition of the classical canon itself perhaps, "[L]aughter [is okay] if it is sincere and tinged with gravity," as St. Bernard de Clairvaux wrote (cited in Eco, *Aesthetics* 11). Corso's laughter, however, is almost never grave and is too often filled with doubt to register within this classical criteria. Like the comedians among the monks in Eco's *Name of the Rose,* who were being offed by a graver Borgesian older monk for blasphemy, Corso is busy scribbling a monstrous hilarity in the margins of poetry and would thus be likely to continue to be marginalized except that his aesthetic is now beginning to match the worldview of a growing number of people who no longer believe in a Catholic God or any God whatsoever. And yet, even here, in Corso's atheism, is a paradox. As he puts it in the last lines in his *Mindfield:* "like Holderlin sayeth I am closer to god / away from Him . . ." (268).

Which God is it that Corso refers to here? The God of the Thomists, or the God of the Protestant romantics? Is it a static and hierarchical God, or a progressive God, or some slippery combination? In this instance, it would seem to be a Protestant God, one who reverses the Thomist notion of the hierarchy. As Edward P. Mahoney writes about Thomism, "The notion that God is the basic measure and that things take their places in the hierarchy of being as they 'approach' toward him or 'recede' away from him is of major significance" (223). And yet, summarizing some of the Italian Renaissance debate on this topic, Mahoney writes:

> George of Trebizond denies that one creature could be any closer to God than another, since all of them are instantly distant from him. Bessarion, his distinguished adversary, replies by suggesting that God can be considered not only as infinite but also as that being which is more perfect than all other beings and the highest being, though not infinite. God as creator must be taken in the latter sense and is therefore not infinitely distant from creatures. (224)

Corso's poetry, rather than closing ontological questions, raises them and in the process evokes, in a vivid and puzzling manner, ancient arguments that have yet to be resolved. Corso's poetry often invokes Hermes, as a humorous contrast to his early Catholicism, but there is a darker god, a more disruptive force, who surfaces in his most outlandish creations, such as "Don't Shoot the Warthog." This god is Dionysus, who seemingly enters Corso's poetry as a "dark arriviste," one of the last of the gods to enter the pantheon, the god of tragedy, as Nietzsche pointed out, bringing "the spark of life from the marvelous" (Otto 27). With this spirit comes not a sense of harmony and concatenation as in the Thomist tradition but another order altogether. As Robert B. Palmer writes in his introduction to Walter F. Otto's book *Dionysus: Myth and Cult,* this god is a stranger who appears from nowhere, "a God of paradox who cannot be understood outside the language of poetry" (ix–xx). This god, in turn, is linked to Christ in Gilles Deleuze's book on Nietzsche: the force of the marvelous with at least two faces. Whatever this god is, it isn't the god of the suburbs.

8

Would You Rent Corso an Apartment?

G. K. Chesterton wrote:

[T]here are some people, nevertheless—and I am one of them—who think that the most important thing about a man is still his view of the universe. We think that for a lady considering a lodger, it is important to know his income, but still more important to know his philosophy. (*Heretics* 15)

Corso's view of the universe is mercurial. In one poem he believes that he stands alone before the universe with the ring of poetry on his finger; in another, that gods exist (pantheism); in still another, that Jesus Christ was a spiritual reality; in another, that he is himself a Greek god. What should Chesterton's landlady have thought of the following poem?

> **Spirit**
> Spirit
> is Life
> It flows thru
> the death of me
> endlessly
> like a river
> unafraid
> of becoming
> the sea

(*HA* 41)

Corso is split between two paradigms. One paradigm is the ancient Christian tradition in which spirit is trapped in matter and must find a way to return to its heavenly source. The other is the post-Darwinian paradigm in which humanity lives on an immanent plane with other animal life in a world without the possibility of transcendence. In the poem just cited, the spirit flows through the "death" of the narrator, unafraid of becoming the sea. The sea is the sea of spirit—or is it the actual ocean? Is his body dead matter, and only the spirit alive? Corso's ambiguity on this point is an ambiguity that cuts across all of his poetry. Through these two systems runs magical thinking, an Orphic thinking that can be expressed only in poetry.

Should a landlady rent him a flat? Corso was by turns a pagan, a pantheist, a Christian, an alchemist, a free-thinker, an agnostic, a believer, a Gnostic, an aesthete, a trickster, a romantic, a rationalist Darwinian, a heretic, a surrealist, a classicist, a postmodern, and influenced by Zen Buddhism. He changed beliefs like Mrs. Marcos changed shoes.

Corso's motivation in regard to metaphysics is to find some way to guarantee continuity through God, who is coextensive with all of space and time, while also granting himself the total freedom that the Darwinian paradigm permits. The psychoanalyst Charles Rycroft comments:

> Those who adhere to the scientific stance can find no place in their philosophy for art or intuition; those who adopt [T. S.] Eliot's own solution can make nothing of technology; while those who adopt the psychotic solution of jumbling the two together become confused, bewildered and incomprehensible to their fellow men. The God that is really wanted, as opposed to the God that I personally want, is one Who would annul this "dissociation of sensibility" by an act of synthesis. I doubt, however, whether any self-conscious attempt to synthesize such a deity would be any more successful than those of the God-creating schizophrenics, who usually . . . end by asserting that they themselves are God. (285)

Corso's mental health was certainly undermined as he tried to make a bridge between classical religious thought and post-Darwinian thought. The problem is one of ontology: are we human, animal, or divine? If the central concern of many American liberals as this century begins is to question the ontology of who can speak, and who thus has rights, from the perspective of race, gender, and class, then Corso could be seen to be a participant in this revolutionary attack on Aristotelean ontology, which offered full being only to white men with property.

With Christ, the assault was launched on this ontological system. If a common itinerant preacher could in fact be the Son of God, then any individual—even a prostitute, even an orphan—could be seen as part of God. This was the appeal of Christianity, as it toppled values. Christ fractured the identity of the community and began a reversal of values that continues to this day and that, having started, will never cease, causing us anxiety and questions about who and what we are—the children of an absent God, or the result of evolution, or both? If mental health is defined as mental unity, as possession of a singular identity or a single paradigm, then possession by multiple identities or multiple paradigms is an active evil, a sign of mental imbalance.

Can we continue to base our perceptions on the Bible, even though much of that worldview has been disproved by science, or can we live in a world with no value except survival of the fittest? Is there any mercy within nature? Not all animals seek to devour one another in the same way the tiger seeks to kill the gazelle or the wolf the lamb. Between themselves, wolves are cooperative, as are many of the larger apes and as are certainly most humans. Even animals recognize certain taboos, as do dogs who playfully bite but seemingly get angry if one dog doesn't get it and bites too deeply. A state of permanent warfare (Darwin) or welfare (Christ) within our species would quickly lead to self-extermination. If men really sought to prey on women in the manner described by Sade, there would soon be no women remaining. In Sadean ecology, balance is gone: it is a nightmarish world of the appetite of man for female flesh. The system is unbalanced, untenable, haywire.

Since the eighteenth century, various philosophers of nature have added subtlety to the picture. New Darwinian thinkers posit survival as a matter of teamwork. Matt Ridley writes:

> The first life on earth was atomistic and individual. Increasingly, since then, it has coagulated. It has become a team game, not a contest of loners. By 3.5 billion years ago there were bacteria five-millionths of a meter long and run by a thousand genes. . . . By 1.6 billion years ago there were complex cells a million times heavier than bacteria and run by teams of 10,000 genes or more: the protozoa. . . . The blue whale has 100,000 trillion cells in its body. But already a new form of coagulation is occurring: social coagulation. By 100 million years ago there were complex colonies of ants run by teams of a million bodies or more and now they are among the most successful designs on the planet. (*The Origins of Virtue* 14)

Against Ridley and the new optimists of ecology there remains the fact that when we eat, we must violently dissolve another corporation, doing violence to it, or else we ourselves perish.

We are between philosophical systems, in an ontological uproar. Many of the renegade surrealists saw this and reflected this in their art, much as Corso does. Kenneth Burke describes a surrealist painting in which the right attitude toward our cosmos is difficult to ascertain.

> Thus a surrealist might feel pity for a steak, yet eat it nevertheless. This he would do by eating the steak, not as a meat-eater, but as a vegetarian corrupted. And he might symbolize all this by doing a quite personal portrait of the steak he was about to eat (the "alienation" here taking the form of *less* alienation in a situation which would normally show much *greater* alienation)—and he might "solve" the problem by placing, right in the center of the steak, an accusing eye. (*Surrealism* 65)

For many, it is only with humor that we can begin to accept the contradictions. When we move from a vertical transcendent economy to natural systems theory, therefore, it is important to look beyond Sade and his contemporary inheritors such as Sigmund Freud and Georges Bataille, who in their fury against Christian hypocrisy still seek to replace Christian compassion with its opposite. With many of Christianity's basic tenets (the age of the earth, the creation of women, the creation of animals) undermined by science, as we move into a new millennium, it is possible at last to think of humanity's immanence within nature and to refigure a philosophy that is adequate to our place within that nature, not one that was innocent or suspicious of nature, as was much of early Christianity, or its most destructive variant, Gnostic libertinism; rather, the synthesis will have to be partially managed through humor, which is the reconciliation of opposites, or the bringing together of two things into a new machinic counterpart. At the same time, the better aspects of Christianity, such as compassion for the poor and the orphaned, ought to be worked into the paradigm, but on what basis? The philosophical tools for such a paradigm shift have only partially been forged.

Distracting our vision from biological life toward a world of ideal forms, Augustinian Christianity took over from Plato in moving us toward closed systems, which remain static and eternal. The Gnostic libertines sought to create a partial antidote, but in doing so they destroyed the value of this world. If we are to recover from Platonic philosophy, we must look into the non-Platonic pharmacy cabinet.

Corso's conception of the universe, while mercurial, is at least large enough to be worthy of consideration. He questions the meaning of the universe and his own role in it, which is why he has to try out so many different roles. His argument is with the Catholic God, but he interrogates his early worldview from within many alternate metaphysical systems.

One of his favorite guises, it seems, is a role as magician, as poet, as great spirit, but this is undercut with humor. In a former society, he might have been considered a shaman, a role seemingly reserved for what at a later time would be the surrealists. Anatole Lewitzky discussed the role of the shaman in a special session of the College of Sociology before Georges Bataille, Roger Caillois, and other members of an intellectual elite in the late 1930s. Among other things, he discussed the "frankly pathological personality of the shaman, the idea that he was profoundly intimate with the representatives of the spirit world and the notion of levitation and, in a more general manner, with penetration into other worlds" (584). Furthermore,

> [w]e only become a shaman if we have a nervous system predispositioned so as to be interpreted as to be in direct contact with the spirits. . . . In order to become a shaman, one must have a strong soul. To be noticed by the spirits is a proof of exceptional power. . . . The shaman in mythology is more than an intermediary between men and spirits, he is himself a spirit—he has his own independence and his own power. Far from being

the servant, he himself has numerous secondary spirits which serve him, that he takes under his own authority. (585–86)

This figure, the shaman, presupposes a spirit world above and beyond the simpler animal world that we inhabit. It is a world that science, with its logic, with its need for proof, has never condoned, as it has yet to be proven. This is a world not of realism but of symbolism. Corso himself is a figure at the crossroads of these two worldviews, between realism and symbolism, between science and mythology, between the figure of the reporter and the figure of the shaman. Corso's worldview is one that is ours in many ways. He does not want to abandon hope and give in to the nihilism of the scientific viewpoint. He can't, however, bring himself to collapse into a new age viewpoint or mindlessly follow a religion led by a guru. These are hard times for poets and shamans, who have lost their function without a transcendent realm. The role of the poet is an irrational one, bringing the paradoxical logic of the emotions into a world that seems to think it no longer has need of the passions, that it can live on reason. But, as Walter Otto writes, "[P]aradox belongs to the nature of everything that is creative" (31). At the root of our being, at the root of our life in this world, is this sense of paradox and irrationalism that the poet alone can fully articulate.

Corso isn't able to be reverent—or completely irreverent. He moves between paradigms, interrogating, yet never settling in, never resting upon his laurels. His poetry offers no secure wisdom and jumps between the shaman and the trickster, between the genuine poet and the con man, between the optimism of Christ and the staggering pessimism of Dionysus. Corso is a double figure, moving back and forth between different worlds, leaving logic behind in order to create a world of enormous fun to patch over doubt and emptiness and despair. Corso questions every narrative, interrupting them, splicing them together, and playing with them, the way Hermes himself played with what came before him. There is no finality in this story; it is a relay. Unlike Zeus, Hermes plays tricks and is mischievous. Unlike Plato, Diogenes plays tricks and tells jokes.

Separating modernism and postmodernism, Lyotard writes, "Modern consciousness, in full confidence, places its fate in the hands of a single just and good father" (*Postmodern Fables* 97). Lyotard argues that modern consciousness goes back at least to Plato. Such a consciousness, as in its contemporary epigones within Marxism or other religious systems, asks only to be believed. Corso isn't a follower, in the sense that he has no leader or Messiah, and he identifies himself with a baby god, Hermes, when he argues with Catholicism. His is not a new system of belief or a system of elegant proofs but a system of anguished and tortuous knotted paradoxes that ask us to struggle with them, to reflect on them, as Corso struggled with all the systems of the church fathers in order to help usher in a new kind of contingent, irreverent thinking. I would argue that this new kind of thinking feels postmodern rather than modern, but it may in fact be postpostmodern in that Corso returns to modernism but only by exhausting postmodernism even while it was being invented. Lyotard writes:

When the head of Louis XVI was cut off in January 1793 in the Place de la Révolution, God was the one whose head was cut off. The republic, and hence interlocution, can only be founded upon a deicide; it begins with the nihilist assertion that there is no Other. Are these the beginnings of an orphaned humanity? (*Postmodern Fables* 211)

Corso, an orphan, begins with this terrifying situation and describes what it is like to have no father, no God, no sense of a moral guide. There is no moral guide any longer, and everything is up for reinterpretation. The result is terror. Everyone contests everyone else and refuses consensus. Consensus would mark the return of God. Corso contests this return. While the other Beats were coming to a new conclusion, one based on Buddhism and ecology, Corso kept the door open to a different kind of faith based ultimately on ambiguity and paradox and agonistic wrestling against every totalizing system, and yet, as he put it, the further he went from God, the closer he remained. His work doesn't offer logic or understanding. Corso offers feeling, a depth of voluptuous emotion, a physical answer, an event that sets in motion a temporary soul, a split in consciousness effected through paradoxes and humor, which returns us momentarily to our senses and to a fleeting feeling of health and occasionally a glimpse of heaven. Shaman, poet, and questioner, Corso collapses the rational mind by invoking all the theories of science, then leading them into dark places of paradox. From there, he leads nonsense back into the heart of the mind and lets it reign supreme for a moment. This is Corso's version of shamanic alchemy with which he tries to subvert death, which for him is primarily a temporary death of the soul, a dead feeling.

Lewitzky, discussing the shaman's familiar, says that one bird in particular is often associated with this profession. "There is, finally, one bird whose importance in the whole area of Asia and into China is not well enough known, it's the owl, or the grand-duc. It is the bird of the metal-worker, and also of the shaman. It symbolizes underground fire" (605). Corso's poetry often spins changes on this strange bird. In the poem "Death," Corso uses the symbol frequently:

> Before I was born
> Before I was heredity
> Before I was life
> Before I was—owls appeared and trains departed
> . . . .
> Owls hoot and the train's toot deflate
> I beg for the breath that keeps me alive
> . . . .
> And the owl sobs
> The vizer Croat
>   is scratched a tally
> Hear the owl rally
>
> (*HB* 38–42)

In this poem, Corso's narrator is a medieval alchemist who learns the secret of life and brags of it. His familiar is the owl, who rallies at the end of the poem, because death, figured as a "vizer Croat," is scratched a bit. Corso's recipe seems to be humor mixed with melancholy, paradoxes, and a strange language to give the soul a sense of being alive, a sense of freshness. It is this soul-making through feeling, through aesthetics, that is the proper end of his art. Those poets who have forgotten this in their rush toward new religions, philosophies, and systems have abandoned aesthetics. Alone among the major figures of the Beat generation, Corso remembered that his shamanic act was to bring the soul back to life. The extremely obscure poem "Heave the Hive with New Bees," published in *The Happy Birthday of Death,* appears to be a shamanic incantation, or recipe, for bringing the body back to life:

> The dead a wildcold body must bear
> Follow through with fineries
> —an exact mandate
> Sick and violent the senses
> regain the catch old feelings difficult to rejoy
>
> (*HB* 71)

In this first stanza, the dead body finds it difficult to "rejoy" the old feelings. That is the only easy line. The opening line seems to be a flat statement, which is that, to paraphrase, "a wildcold body must put up with the dead," then follow through with certain mumbo jumbo so that the incantation is beginning, and then you have an exact mandate. The senses will then become sick and violent, and there will follow through the old feelings.

> Sursum corda O dead! With a bragged requiescat
> spray blood Deathdrench the dash of life
>
> The dead are born in Cheeryland
> Their buttocks neigh
>
> (*HB* 71)

The exceptional weirdness of these last two stanzas can be understood when we remember that "Sursum corda" means "Lift up your hearts" and are the first words of the Catholic Preface of the Mass, while a "requiescat" is, on the contrary, a wish or prayer for the repose of the dead. Which does Corso want, to raise the dead or for them to sleep in peace? Seemingly, he wants both: first, to lift up your hearts, and then, while asking for the repose of the dead, to "spray blood Deathdrench the dash of life." He wants, through a violent clash of opposites, to create life anew in order to "Heave the Hive with New Bees." Through his magic technique, "The dead are born in Cheeryland / Their buttocks neigh." The music of animal life is born from the collision of spiritual opposition. This strange act of calling up the dead can be seen either as blasphemy against the

Catholic Church or else as a personal resurrection in which poetry resuscitates spirit. Blasphemy, also, may be what in fact resuscitates spirit.

Aquinas, in the *Summa Theologica,* spends about fifty pages describing the resurrection and the exact qualities of those who will arise. Only the good will rise up, and they will be as they were at the peak of their lives, without mutilation, and their fingernails will grow, and they will have sexual organs (which do not function in an "animal" manner) ("Treatise on the Resurrection," 885–996). Nowhere does Aquinas mention that "buttocks will neigh." Therefore, this magical incantation can be seen as non-Christian at the very least. Why will the buttocks "neigh"? Horses often have a sexual connotation for Corso, as they do in the poem by that name in *Long Live Man,* which goes:

> Joy to horses!
> Horses by the sea are listening to me;
> do you suppose they are listening to me,
> breathing and heaving and neighing to me?
> Horses of night are there;
> Horses of light and delight and nightmare,
> they are there,
> completely satisfied with the sea,
> completely satisfied with me.
>
> (*LL* 29)

Corso's poem that brings in neighing buttocks can be seen from intertextual comparisons to be about raising the animal aspects of humankind, which Aquinas specifically says in the *Summa Theologica* will not be needed after the resurrection:

> Consequently those natural operations which are directed to preserve the primary perfection of human nature will not be in the resurrection; such are the actions of the animal life in man, the action of the elements on one another, and the movements of the heavens; therefore all these will cease at the resurrection. And since to eat, drink, sleep, beget, pertain to the animal life, being directed to the primary perfection of nature, it follows that they will not be in the resurrection. (967)

Corso's alchemical act is specifically linked, therefore, to the needs of the Dionysian artist and not to the Christian afterlife as such, although he blasphemously utilizes Christian liturgy in performing his incantation. This kind of Dionysian shamanism is increasingly forgotten, or not understood, as academics have turned toward a rationalistic behaviorism in terms of artistic function in which the goal of art is to engineer a broader consciousness concerning maligned classes. Instead of aesthetics, most of the humanities at this point are concerned with politics. Corso's use of shamanism works on a different scale of values. Lyotard writes:

> A poem retains the unspoken within its words. "To speak without having nothing to say," writes Paul Eluard in *Capitale de la Douleur [The Capital*

of Grief]. The god of the invisible, says Sam Francis, a blind god, awaits the company of painters to make visible to us what he "sees." The music of John Cage is an homage paid to silence. Art is the vow the soul makes for escaping the death promised to it by the sensible, but in celebrating in this same sensible what drags the soul out of nonexistence. Burke describes exactly this *double bind.* The *anima* is threatened with privation: speech, light, sound, life would be absolutely lacking. That's *terror.* Suddenly, the threat is lifted, the terror suspended, it's *delight.* Art, writing give grace to the soul condemned to the penalty of death, but in such a way as not to forget it. (*Postmodern Fables* 244–45)

Corso's poetry doesn't want us to forget death, or to conquer it, but to have the sudden pleasure of confronting it successfully for a moment, to have a moment of pleasure in spite of it, which gives the soul temporary courage to blossom. From Corso's earliest poems, such as "Greenwich Village Suicide" and "Amnesia in Memphis," through the middle poems, such as "Uccello," up to his latest poems, such as "Field Report," death lurks in the foreground. Lewitzky writes:

A shaman seems thus to be especially a kind of magician, but a magician fulfilling a function consecrated by society, that is to say a kind of priest. When he combats divinities, he does so in order to defend humans. He is not however the only one to have this attitude towards divinities. The collectivity itself, in the case of need, confronts invisible powers, and opposes itself to their intervention. There is in sum between the attitude of a shaman and that of a secular man only a difference in degree and not of nature. (605)

Corso works against the general deadening of the soul created by an undue emphasis on external acquisition in capitalist culture. Corso's poetry is meant to create an inner richness that will allow us to feel as deeply as we think. Without feeling, life is not worth living. As Corso writes in his poem "Ancestry," "I would jot down for all blessed things / the equal balance of heart and feather / on the scale of life" (*HA* 20).

Equal to the feather, which symbolizes flight, a constant feeling in Corso's poetry, is the feeling of the heart, the voluptuous emotions that make us aware of being alive. Philosophy doesn't offer this, nor does economics, nor does owning a big house. It is an inner richness, which is the domain of the poet to offer. Hermes is a totemic figure, a force that Corso uses to help him bring his poetry to life. The owl is the same. Surrounded by these figures, Corso, between worlds, between paradigms, brings the soul to life without advancing any politics or any philosophy. His is not a program but an aesthetic act meant to create a flood of feeling, a rich dark river of emotion, mixed with humor and irreverence, where the rational mind is temporarily eclipsed in favor of imagination, compassion, and physical feelings. In his poetry, it is not reason that triumphs or has its day but mystery, beauty, feeling, and the irrational marvel of humor. Corso uses his body like the ancient alchemists used a dull metal, experimenting and trying to turn his experiences to gold. Often, he succeeds.

Corso's mercurialness and need for risks would make him a poor prospect as a tenant, but he is a great poet in that he often triumphs in creating this explosive change of one thing into another, translating his experience into golden words. We are animals, and we are also human, but most importantly for Corso's shamanistic investigation, we are divine as well. If we go that far, we can go one step farther and say that our invention of infernal horrors in hell is also human. Marilyn Schwartz, in her perceptive study of Corso's work, writes that for Corso, "any fear to gaze straight into hell for a vision of its opposite resembles the superstition of primitive man in inventing gods and attributing to them his own power" (135). God, Schwartz argues, represented a limit to Corso, which kept primitive people from recognizing their own power and gave a limited meaning to the universe. Without this limit imposed by priests, humanity is now free to see themselves as divine and their powers as limitless in terms of either hellish or heavenly creations. When something is evil, we can look into it for its opposite. "By affirming the unity of human and divine, Corso discerns the poetic reality of the uncreated heaven which pervades the hell of this world" (Schwartz 134).

Between heaven and hell, there is the poet, mixing the two together and becoming more human in the process. In the vision of hell is Corso's glimpse of a celestial city, using his imagination to extract poetic gold with his characteristic alchemy, in order to create a new world. What I would argue, however, in contrast to Schwartz, is that this world is not an outer world but an inner one. Corso is a shamanic alchemist as opposed to a city planner.

Corso is an experimenter, and as such, not all of his poems are successes. Some of them are duds, but never count a Corso poem out. Some of his poems have lain dormant on the page for decades when suddenly one can get a handle on them, and they explode. The key is always to think about Thomism, Darwinism, and magic. With that sequence as key, almost any Corso poem can be opened. With these elements, quite frequently he manages to create a blinding flash. The poet Kenneth Rexroth described Corso as a "real wildman" and that "at his best, his poems are . . . poetic cannon crackers" (194). It is for this reason that I would rather rent an apartment to an orthodox Thomist, because a stable worldview would probably create a more stable tenant. Corso would have been last on most lists of prospective tenants but first in many lists of American poets. Due to his interest in creating a celestial city in the heart, he was willing to create a smoking hell in the apartment. Drug fiend, chain smoker, all-night conversationalist, violent drunk, Corso used his body, his writing utensils, and the bodies of others the way the alchemists used common metals—in order to transmutate them into lyric intensity.

9

Conclusion

Corso wandered a long way from his Thomist beginnings, thought intensely about Darwinism, and went toward a violently Dionysian viewpoint on art, yet he retained his interest in his religious origins. From the Middle Ages, with its static conception of a chain of being, to our own confusing time, in which an artist is more like a shaman than a tranquil priest, there has been a rapid decline in rationality and a consequent upsurge of the irrational, all of which, ironically, has been set off by the rationalist undermining of faith. This has split our minds into a rationalist and a believing sect, the two of which are at odds. The nature of the great chain of being has been altered, and Corso's poetry reflects those momentous changes.

> Francis Baumer, in *Religion and the Rise of Scepticism* writes, "It is a fascinating thing to watch this *reductio* [whereby divine activity in nature was significantly reduced if not eliminated] proceed, almost ineluctably it would seem, from Galileo to Newton and Leibniz." (cited in Oakley 239)

Although we can't go back to the Middle Ages, we can mark in Corso's work and life how much has been lost and look back with nostalgia toward the Paris of St. Thomas, as Corso did at the beginning of his career.

What did Thomist aesthetics offer that has now been lost? Umberto Eco writes in *Art and Beauty in the Middle Ages,*

> It [medieval aesthetics] can foster a conception of art as something constructive and technical, thus serving as an antidote to an Orphic one, typical of post-Romantic aesthetics. It can inspire critical methods committed to rigour and rationality. (119)

Thus, the idea of beauty and rationalist inquiry were still seen as part of one coherent investigation into God's world. While beauty and goodness were often unproblematically linked in Aquinas, Eco writes in *The Aesthetics of Thomas Aquinas* that

> [w]e shall see, in connection with the neo-Platonic elements in Aquinas, that for the medievals the aesthetic moment was characteristically theophanic. They had a sense of universal harmony, in which all beings sing of the presence within them of an emanating Principle in whose power they share; this is the significance of St. Francis' *Cantico delle creature.* (14)

This worldview has been slowly turned upside down and inside out by a millennium of free thought, which has recently turned into a frenzy of sarcasm and rage. The twentieth century was marked by two cataclysmic wars, mass genocides, the introduction of the atomic bomb, the idea of the unconscious as being at least as important as rationality, and the idea that people are nothing more than animals. When we compare the rationalist ideals of St. Thomas, we can get a glimpse of how far we have fallen. According to Eco, "Aquinas says that intemperate behavior is ugly, because it does not possess the light of reason which would make it beautiful" (*Aesthetics* 116). We no longer have any firm standard by which to critique intemperate behavior, and it is in fact temperance that is often treated by psychiatrists as repression.

The very fact that poetry still continues to exist, however, and is still taught in universities is one positive sign that we haven't given everything over to rapacious productivity or explosive nihilism. Poetry is the attempt to link rationalist inquiry and interest in form with theophanic inspiration. That there is still an audience for this kind of inquiry indicates the importance of somehow linking these two areas to create the conditions for which a great number still yearn and for which probably everyone except the most hardened scientist feels some nostalgia. Being moved by a sunset or a poem or a beautiful mathematical problem points out to us how deeply we feel the need for a spiritual life that goes beyond mere survival, which is what the Darwinians tell us life is all about. Increasingly, rationalism has sought to explain everything and has been successful in turning the marvels of the Middle Ages into dreary if predictable scientific laws. The Ascension of Christ is contradicted by the laws of gravity, and anyway, where was Jesus to ascend toward? After Copernicus, there was no up. If that's all there is, what about poetry? Does it fit the Darwinian vision? It certainly did fit into the Thomist vision.

Summarizing Aquinas, Eco writes:

> Pure disinterested contemplation is similar to play, because it is an end in itself. It also resembles play in that it is not a response to some compulsion rooted in the exigencies of life, but it is rather a higher activity appropriate to a spiritual creature. (*Aesthetics* 17)

Poetry is labor-intensive but doesn't produce anything and is not rooted in the "exigencies" of life. Focusing on an aspect of the Thomist aesthetic, Eco notes:

[I]n humans alone there exists the possibility of a pleasure quite extrane-
ous to tactile pleasure. And this is aesthetic pleasure. A lion experiences
pleasure when he sees a stag, but it is not a pleasure in its shape nor in the
sounds it makes. . . . Man, however, enjoys these sensations not just be-
cause they promise a prey, but also because they are pleasing to sense. (*Aes-
thetics* 17)

Corso's work is founded in St. Thomas Aquinas. Without this initial onto-
logical system, there would have been no Corso oeuvre. As he moved away from
his early Catholicism and God, he also moved away from poetry toward gam-
bling, drug use, and cynicism but also toward a less abundant Orphic poetry that
would occasionally reassert itself with magical force in a tradition of liberation
markedly different from Aquinas and the legacy of the Catholic Church. To re-
constitute Aquinas's aesthetics today would for many necessitate undoing a mil-
lennium of ethical wrongdoing on the part of the church: systematic oppression
of women, non-Catholic peoples, and those who tried to think freely within the
church, such as Galileo and all those who died in the Inquisition. All of this vio-
lence was predicated in Aquinas's own words.

The punishments of the present life are medicinal, and therefore when one
punishment does not suffice to compel a man, another is added, just as
physicians employ several bodily medicines when one has no effect. In like
manner the Church, when excommunication does not sufficiently restrain
certain men, employs the compulsion of the secular arm. (2:577)

God was used not only to guarantee beauty but also to justify terror in Aquinas's
vision. In our new democratic societies, we have exchanged the Almighty for the
chance to think for ourselves. What has happened to poetry in the process? Corso
went from a reasoned, orderly beauty in his early poetry to "convulsive beauty"
in the later and finally almost dropped poetry altogether. It seems that more than
this "convulsive beauty" is required for earthly happiness, and yet this Orphic
beauty is also in a lineage of beauty and freedom, from the days of the ancient
Greeks up to our own time, providing humanity with some of its most stirring
evocations of what is in store.

Against the rational appeal of Thomism, the Protestant Reformation ushered
in a thunderous cry. Nietzsche writes:

Luther's chorales, so inward, courageous, spiritual, and tender, are like the
first Dionysiac cry from the thicket at the approach of spring. They are
answered antiphonally by the sacred and exuberant procession of Dionys-
iac enthusiasts to whom we are indebted for German music. (*Birth of
Tragedy* 138)

The torrential outpouring of instinct over reason, as implied in this passage,
marked the rebirth of the overpowering aesthetics of Dionysus as opposed to the

good form of Catholicism. The *Sturm und Drang* of German romanticism resulted from Luther's change in musical styles. The dried-up ritual of the Catholic Church was changed for the direct and powerful emotional upsurge in each individual, the force of emotion like the thunder of Luther's speeches. In this sense, Luther was bringing back another side of Christ's message, the thunderclap of righteous delirium that made the Son of God overturn the tables of the money changers. Corso found this inspiration quite late, as he appears to have discovered a sense of tradition in the German romantics (especially Hölderlin), a tradition that was in turn held sacred by the surrealists.

We seem to require what Charles Rycroft calls "a sense of continuity" (293). This sense comes to most from family tradition, national tradition, or religious tradition. Without a religious tradition, family and nation are undermined. Without a sense that God has been at the beginning and will be there at the end, without the sense that God stretches from one corner of the universe to the other, we are left with a sense of being lonely particles in a war of all against all. Corso was given a sense of God in his upbringing, but his upbringing also challenged this tradition. What he found was a sense of community through surrealist art. For humanity requires not only a past but also a sense of a golden future, a dazzling world where the noblest dreams of the poets can be realized. I have intended in this book to show how Corso belongs within the literary romantic and surrealist tradition, how he questioned the Thomist tradition, and how he saw himself as a messenger in a vast system of Hermean relay. André Breton wrote:

> Un jour viendra où il ne pourra cependent plus s'en remettre, pour juger de sa propre déterminabilité, au bon plaisir de l'organisme social qui assure aujourd'hui, par le malheur de presque tous, la jouissance de quelques-uns. Je pense qu'il n'est pas trop déraissonable de lui prédire pour un jour prochain le gain de cette plus grande liberté. [A day will come where he will no longer be able to set his dreams aside, and each will be able to see for himself that the social organism today assures the unhappiness of almost all in order to guarantee the pleasure of a few. I think it is not too unreasonable to predict that in a future day each will enjoy this great liberty.] (*Vases* 168)

Art, however, especially surrealist art, implies continuity and seeks the marvelous and thrilling—even if monstrous—incidents, as Corso does in his poem "Happening on a German Train." He writes that "on my way to King Ludwig's castle" he sees "a white American jet fighter plane / CRASHBOOM and billows of orange" (*LL* 33). What continuity does the poem offer? It offers the pleasure of mysterious communication put forward, interestingly, while Corso is on his way to a surrealist mecca—that of mad King Ludwig's castle in which, in the romantic utopian future, every single individual could choose to live.

Rycroft writes:

But Continuity is not only past-seeking, and it should not be confused with either nostalgia or traditionalism. Continuity implies growth and change and, if deified, it would be two-faced, looking forwards as well as backwards. . . . Towards the future he will have to have faith that something will continue for ever to be as it was in the beginning. (294)

Throughout Corso's poetry, he has managed to have glimpses of this sense of continuity and to affirm it in himself. It is for this reason that his poetry will continue to be so valuable. He takes up the exploded tradition of St. Thomas and questions it within the surrealist and alchemical traditions, providing a sense of interrogation of our collapsed value systems, which provides a unique vantage point to create a larger conversation about the future of poetry and community. Richard Gray, British critic of contemporary poetry, summarizes Alexis de Tocqueville on literature in democracies:

"[A]ristocracy brings everyone together, linking peasant to King in one long chain," one thoroughly articulated, hierarchical framework; "democracy breaks the chain and separates each link." As a result, people "become accustomed to thinking of themselves in isolation, and imagine that their entire fate is in their own hands." "Each citizen in a democracy," he insists at one point, "usually spends his time considering the interests of a very insignificant person, namely, himself." (Gray 5)

Gray writes that this tendency to be locked into the "separate self" is something that can be seen throughout American poetry. And yet, what Gray overlooks in this atomization is that the future will belong not only to those at the top of the hierarchy but to all in a democratic society, and that everyone, from the lowliest member on up, should have a right to sing the song of his or her existence. Isolated in the manner of Dionysus, the stranger god, the American poet is skeptical of ritual and tradition but trusts in the emotional power of the lyric. No longer linked by the hierarchical system that holds a society together by formality or intellectual decree, American society is held together by emotion. Intensity of football games and other sports, intensity of argument, intensity of soap operas, the god of American life is an homage paid to the instincts and is Dionysian rather than Apollonian. In a violent, stormy country, stern and harsh, America's crazed Puritan preachers and believers whip up powerful feelings to the neglect of minor points of theoretical nicety.

Corso offers a fragmented echo of humanism and hope to future generations but also shows the difficulty of putting together a closely knit community without God. Corso's vantage point of Thomism within a democratic framework inspires us to see him as a singular singer, alternately bemoaning and laughing over the lapse of a great world tradition and the death of God. As counterbalance to this negation of a tradition that supported hierarchy and was held together by the aristocratic philosophy of the great chain of being, Corso picks up the surrealist notion that the power of God is a power that each one of us had all along in our unconscious, a power we only need to open in order to continue our evolution toward a utopian society. This legacy stems directly from the Protestant tradition and the Dionysian upsurge that Nietzsche traces to Luther.

Gregory Corso's writing is a mental map of our own day, a day heaped with confusion and strained attempts at recovery of some logic that would allow the divine to shine once again on the faces of what Lyotard has called "an orphaned humanity." And yet, in the face of nihilism, Corso posits beauty and the power of feeling, and surely this beauty can have come only from his religious origins, as a light from a sun reflected through many mirrors. Surely beauty must matter to us as a species, as a response to the strange universe we've inherited. But there are many kinds of beauty. The two most potent kinds of beauty in the Western tradition are the Thomist beauty of Apollonian intellectual clarity and the roar of Dionysian tenderness, drunk with feeling, in the Protestant tradition. In a thousand years, someone who comes across the poetry of Gregory Corso may see his poetic marvels as one link in a long chain of surrealist relay, but it is important not to occlude his faith. As Michael Skau notes, "Despite his renunciation of religion, Corso seems to retain a Christian perspective" (141). He has surrendered neither the beauty of the Catholic chain of being nor the rightness of democracy. Faced with two equally valid choices, he has "chosen both."

Corso was chosen by the muses and favored by God. Unusual among American poets, he writes of his close association with these figures throughout his poetry, which for most of us are matters of myth or to be attended to only at Sunday service. Corso manages to bring together the formal qualities of Catholic ritual and the intoxicating passion of the romantic Protestant tradition, thus creating a powerful synthesis of Apollonian and Dionysian. Walter Otto writes of such a combination in the festivals of the Greeks:

> In this union the Dionysiac earthly duality would be elevated into a new and higher duality, the eternal contrast between a restless, whirling life and a still, far-seeing spirit. . . . [W]ith this marriage, Greek religion, as the sanctification of objective being, would have reached its noblest heights. (208)

Nietzsche, likewise, in the close of *The Birth of Tragedy,* celebrates the brotherhood of these two divinities, forces from beyond this world, which transcend our condition and inspire aesthetic delight. Trapped in a food chain in which death is a certainty, the gods of the Western tradition have opened a view of beauty that makes terror palatable. "Confident of their supreme powers," Nietzsche writes, "they both toy with the sting of displeasure, and by their toying they both justify the existence of even the 'worst possible world'" (145).

History and philosophy, after postmodernism, are increasingly seen, once again, as inferior to poetry. Ludwig Wittgenstein, among many other contemporary philosophers, has said that he sees the future of philosophy as a kind of poetry; as for historians, the idea of an objective telling of a series of events is now seen as out of the question. The Platonic tradition of philosophy that has eclipsed poetry for so long is in the process of being dismantled, leaving poetry as once more the most important of the humanities. As the German romantic poet Friedrich Hölderlin wrote in his *Remarques sur Oedipe, Remarques sur Antigone,*

> La poésie reçoit ainsi une plus haute dignité, elle redevient à la fin ce qu'elle était au commencement—l'institutrice de l'humanité; l'art de la poésie survivre à toutes les autres sciences et à tous les arts. [Poetry receives thus the highest dignity, it becomes at the end what it was at the beginning, the tutor of humanity; the art of poetry survives all the other sciences and arts.] (165)

Philosophy, with its basis in reason, cannot sing of beauty or emotion; only poetry can do this. Traditional philosophy, stemming from Plato, with its emphasis on the rational, can thus be seen as a forerunner of science, which cannot tell us what the value of life is or how it matters. Only those arts steeped in the tender madness of the lyrical can achieve this.

Acts of tragedy create moving events, which set in response emotional and ethical reactions among the population at large. Jean-Jacques Lecercle writes of the philosopher Alain Badiou's philosophy.

> His concept of the event involves a given situation—the *status quo* that imposes itself on us, shattered by the emergence of the radically new, the event, which revolutionises it; such events may occur in the four fields of politics (a political revolution), science (the emergence of a new paradigm), art (an aesthetic sea-change), and interpersonal relationships (a *coup de foudre,* love at first sight). For the subject who is embarked on this emergence, the event is a shattering experience which changes her life completely, turns her into a militant engaged in a process of fidelity to the event. ("Alice and the Sphinx" 25)

The greatest such momentous occurrence in the West, an event that has affected the lives of many hundreds of millions over two millennia, was the life of Christ. The most tragic and powerful part of his life, given description in Corso's brief poem "Ecce Homo," remains the Crucifixion. Lecercle doesn't mention religion as one of the great events that can stir a soul to militant fidelity, because the philosopher he's discussing, Alain Badiou, is Marxist. However, the event and advent of Christianity is often overlooked and derided in our postmodern era as antiquated and insufficiently logical. At a post-positivist period in our philosophical history, when it is generally agreed upon among the academic elite that almost nothing is certifiably true, it is somewhat strange that positivism remains the first line of defense for those very post-positivists who wish to wave away religion. Nevertheless, religion remains at the very center of the majority of ordinary people's lives throughout the world, and an estimated 85 percent of Americans. The acts of Jesus framed a set of important values that have set a high-water mark in Western history. Jesus could be seen as the initial surrealist who overturned the tables of logic and good sense and ushered in a regime of the marvelous.

America's greatest poet, Gregory Corso, spent his life alternately doubting and responding fervently to that life and to the faith Christ created. Corso's ambivalence in life was no doubt caused by his abandonment as a child, but his subsequent strict Catholic upbringing gave him a strong sense of belonging. His poetry records his doubt but also, and most importantly, the power of his belief. Corso saw Jesus as his model in his autobiographical poem "Fire Report—No Alarm," where he says that he aided the poor, old, and young throughout his life, "like an act of Jesus" (*M* 235). Corso retains a strong sense of the afterlife in his later poetry, as in "When We All" (*M* 201) and "Feelings on Getting Older" (*M* 203–5), and in "For John Lennon," he makes his belief clear in the aftermath of the singer's assassination:

> Yea we'll walk the vast savannahs
>   alongside your resurrection
>   and with legs of spiritus
>   we'll wade in the hosannahs
>   of new water
>
>   (*HA* 28)

Corso often allied himself with Christ, and yet he never denounced laughter, which seems again to contradict the Christian sensibility. Karl-Josef Kuschel writes that laughter is Christian in that

Christians who laugh are insisting that the stories of the world's sufferings do not have the last word, and are also offering sufficient opportunity to penetrate an attitude of "postmodern optionalism" and an aesthetics of irony and enunciation and to show solidarity with those who have nothing to laugh about in this world. (133)

Gregory Corso died on January 17, 2001, at the age of seventy in the city of Minneapolis. A newspaper obituary in the *Minneapolis Star-Tribune* on January 19 written by Kristin Tillotson said that he recorded a CD with singer Marianne Faithful a week before his death, he continued to play card games with his friends, and he had recently won $1,200 in a gambling casino playing blackjack in spite of suffering from prostate cancer. In the last eight months of his life, he was tended to by his daughter Sheri Langerman, a professional nurse. Since his death, there has been an outpouring of public support and a wide variety of testimonials in journals such as Edward Sanders's *Woodstock Journal* (Autumn 2000 and Spring 2001) and *Long Shot* (vol. 24, Summer 2001) as well as conversations about his importance in myriad web-zines and chat lines. His prose, letters, and often charming drawings have yet to be collected; poems he wrote in his final year are scheduled to be published in 2002. Although all the work is not in, a kind of consensus is forming. Corso's paradoxical poetry helped to lift himself and his generation out of cynicism and despair and toward a poetic engagement with the realms of uplifting humor and religious faith. Corso gave his generation a sense of continuity with the past and a hope in the future.

Hundreds of people helped to pay for his burial, contributing as little as five dollars and as much as several thousand. In the summer of 2001, Corso was laid to rest near the atheistic poet Shelley in Rome's non-Catholic cemetery—Rome, the heart of the Catholic Church. The place of burial is a perfect symbol of Corso's strongest affiliations—close to faith and yet also close to doubt, the two poles of his poetry.

Corso's work, registered on a political or philosophical scale, is hard to quantify. As a historian or philosopher, he had lapses. As a political thinker, he was probably more of a puzzle than a guide. As a poet, however, Corso was peerless. Echoing Nietzsche's final lines in *The Birth of Tragedy*, we can only cry out, "Ah, but what suffering he must have endured to create such beauty!" (146).

Works Cited
Index

Works Cited

Altieri, Charles. *Canons and Consequences.* Evanston: Northwestern UP, 1990.

———. *Self and Sensibility in Contemporary American Poetry.* New York: Cambridge UP, 1984.

André, Michael. "Interview with Gregory Corso." *Unmuzzled Ox* 22 (1981): 123–58.

Aquinas, Thomas. *Summa Theologica.* Vol. 2. Trans. Daniel J. Sullivan. Chicago: Encyclopedia Britannica, 1952.

Aristotle. *Aristotle on Man in the Universe.* Ed. Louise Ropes Loomis. New York: Gramercy, 1971.

———. *The Poetics.* Trans. Stephen Halliwell. London: Duckworth, 1987.

Ashby, Romy. "Gregory and His Daughter." *Goodie Magazine* 9 (2001): 4–18.

Bainton, Roland. *Here I Stand: A Life of Martin Luther.* Nashville: Abingdon, 1950.

Bakhtin, Mikhail. *The Dialogic Imagination.* Austin: U of Texas P, 1991.

Barnstone, Willis. *The Other Bible.* San Francisco: Harper, 1984.

Breton, André. *Arcane 17.* Paris: Pauvert, 1971.

———. *Les Vases Communicants.* Paris: Gallimard, 1955.

Burke, Kenneth. *Attitudes Towards History.* 1937. Berkeley: U of California P, 1984.

———. *On Symbols and Society.* Ed. Joseph R. Gusfield. Chicago: Chicago UP, 1989.

———. *Surrealism Pro and Con.* New York: Gotham Book Mart, 1973.

Cawardine, Richard. "Christianity in North America from the Sixteenth Century." *Judaism and Christianity.* Ed. Leslie Houlden. London: Routledge, 1988. 195–202.

Chénieux-Gendron, Jacqueline. *Surrealism.* Trans. Vivian Folkenflik. New York: Columbia UP, 1990.

Chesterton, G. K. *Heretics.* London: John Lane, 1905.

———. *St. Francis of Assisi.* 1923. London: Hodder and Stoughton, 1960.

———. *St. Thomas Aquinas.* 1943. London: Hodder and Stoughton, 1956.

———. *The Victorian Age in Literature.* 1913. London: Oxford UP, 1966.

Corso, Gregory. *American Express.* Paris: Olympia, 1961.

———. *Earth Egg.* New York: Unmuzzled Ox, 1974.

———. *Elegiac Feelings American.* New York: New Directions, 1970.

———. *Gasoline.* San Francisco: City Lights, 1958.

———. *The Happy Birthday of Death.* New York: New Directions, 1960.

———. *Herald of the Autochthonic Spirit.* New York: New Directions, 1981.

———. "Interview with Robert King." *The Beat Vision: A Primary Sourcebook.* Ed. Arthur Knight and Kit Knight. New York: Paragon, 1987. 152–84.

———. *Long Live Man.* New York: New Directions, 1962.

———. *Mindfield: New and Selected Poems.* New York: Thunder's Mouth, 1989.

————. "Notes from the Other Side of April: With Negro Eyes, With White." *Esquire Magazine* (July 1964): 86–87.

————. "Radio Interview, 16 Aug. 1981." *Wings, Wands, Windows.* Englewood, CO: Howling Dog, 1982. 20–29.

————. "Some of My Beginnings—and What I Feel Right Now." *Magazine* 2 (1965): 36–41. Printed in substantially different form in *Poets on Poetry.* Ed. Howard Nemerov. New York: Basic, 1966. 172–81.

————. "Variations on a Generation." *A Casebook on the Beats.* Ed. Thomas Parkinson. New York: Cromwell, 1961. 88–97.

————. *The Vestal Lady on Brattle.* Cambridge: Richard Brukenfeld, 1955.

————. "When I Was Five I Saw a Dying Indian." *Evergreen Review* 11.48 (1967): 29–30, 82–87.

Corso, Gregory, and Allen Ginsberg. "Interview of William Burroughs." *Journal for the Protection of All Beings* 1 (1961): 79–83.

Couliano, Ioan. *The Tree of Gnosis.* Trans. H. S. Weisner and Ioan Couliano. San Francisco: Harper, 1992.

Deleuze, Gilles, and Félix Guattari. *Difference and Repetition.* Trans. Paul Patton. New York: Columbia, 1994.

————. *The Logic of Sense.* Trans. Mark Lester. New York: Columbia, 1990.

————. *A Thousand Plateaus: Capitalism and Schizophrenia.* Minneapolis: U of Minnesota P, 1987.

Dennett, Daniel. *Darwin's Dangerous Idea.* New York: Touchstone, 1996.

Derrida, Jacques. "'Eating Well,' or the Calculation of the Subject: An Interview with Jacques Derrida." *Who Comes After the Subject?* Ed. Eduardo Cadava. Trans. Peter Connell and Avital Ronell. New York: Routledge, 1991. 96–119.

Eberhart, Richard. "West Coast Rhythms." *On the Poetry of Allen Ginsberg.* Ed. Lewis Hyde. Ann Arbor: U of Michigan P, 1984. 24–25.

Eco, Umberto. *The Aesthetics of Thomas Aquinas.* Trans. Hugh Bredin. 1956. Cambridge: Harvard UP, 1988.

————. *Art and Beauty in the Middle Ages.* Trans. Hugh Bredin. 1959. New Haven: Yale UP, 1986.

Ferry, Luc. *The New Ecological Order.* Chicago: U of Chicago P, 1995.

Froula, Christine. *A Guide to Ezra Pound's Selected Poems.* New York: New Directions, 1983.

Gifford, Barry, and Lawrence Lee. *Jack's Book: An Oral Biography of Jack Kerouac.* New York: St. Martin's, 1994.

Ginsberg, Allen. *Deliberate Prose.* New York: Harper, 2000.

————. Interview. Found at http://levity.com/mavericks/gins.html.

————. Introduction. *Gasoline.* By Gregory Corso. 1958. San Francisco: City Lights, 1976. 7–10.

Glucksmann, André. *The Master Thinkers.* Trans. Brian Pearce. London: Harvester, 1980.

Gray, Richard. *American Poetry of the Twentieth Century.* London: Longman, 1990.

Hölderlin, Friedrich. *Remarques sur Oedipe, Remarques sur Antigone.* Trans. François Fédier. Paris: 10/18, 1965.

Honor, Hugh, and John Fleming. *A World History of Art.* London: Lawrence King, 1995.

Howard, Richard. *Alone with America.* New York: Atheneum, 1980.

Hunsberger, Bruce. "Kit Smart's Howl." *On the Poetry of Allen Ginsberg.* Ed. Lewis Hyde. Ann Arbor: U of Michigan P, 1984. 158–70.

Hyde, Lewis. *Trickster Makes This World.* New York: FSG, 1998.

Irenaeus. *The Writings of Irenaeus.* Trans. Alexander Roberts and W. H. Rambaut. Edinburgh: T. and T. Clark, 1883–84.

Jonas, Hans. *The Gnostic Religion.* Boston: Beacon, 1963.

Kazin, Alfred. *A Writer's America.* London: Thames and Hudson, 1988.

Kendrick, Donald F. Lecture. Found at www.mtsu.edu/~pyskip/Itlec13.htm.

Klossowski, Pierre. *La Monnaie Vivante.* Paris: Eric Losfeld, 1970. Preface by Michel Foucault. Marseille: Joëlle Losfeld, 1994.

———. *Nietzsche et le Cercle Vicieux.* Paris: Mercure de France, 1969.

———. *Ressemblance.* Marseille: Ryôan-ji, 1984.

———. *Sade Mon Prochain.* 1947. Paris: Editions du Seuil, 1967.

Klossowski de Rola, Stanislas. *Alchemy.* 1973. London: Thames and Hudson, 1992.

Knight, Arthur, and Kit Knight. *The Beat Vision: A Primary Sourcebook.* New York: Paragon, 1987.

Kuschel, Karl-Josef. *Laughter: A Theological Reflection.* Trans. John Bowden. New York: Continuum, 1994.

Laertius, Diogenes. *Lives of Eminent Philosophers Volume II.* Trans. R. D. Hicks. New York: Putnam's, 1925.

Lecercle, Jean-Jacques. "Alice and the Sphinx." *Real: Yearbook of Research in English and American Literature 13.* Ed. Herbert Grabes. 1997. 25–35.

———. *Philosophy of Nonsense: The Intuitions of Victorian Nonsense Literature.* London: Routledge, 1994.

Lenhart, Gary. "Whitman's Informal History of His Times." *The Teachers and Writers Guide to Walt Whitman.* Ed. Ron Padgett. New York: Teachers and Writers, 1991. 130–50.

Lewellyn, John. *The Middle Voice of Ecological Conscience.* London: MacMillan Academic, 1991.

Lewitzky, Anatole. "Le chamanisme." *Le Collège de Sociologie.* Ed. Denis Hollier. 1975. Paris: Gallimard, 1995. 577–605.

Logan, William Bryant. "Whitman's Own Way." *The Teachers and Writers Guide to Walt Whitman.* Ed. Ron Padgett. New York: Teachers and Writers, 1991. 79–83.

Lovejoy, Arthur. *The Great Chain of Being: A Study of the History of an Idea.* 1936. New York: Harper, 1960.

Lyotard, Jean-François. *Economie Libidinale.* Paris: Minuit, 1974.

———. *Postmodern Fables.* Trans. George Van Den Abbeele. Minneapolis: U of Minnesota P, 1996.

Mahoney, Edward P. "Lovejoy and the Hierarchy of Being." *Journal of the History of Ideas* 2 (April-June 1987): 211–30.

Martin, Mike W. "Humor and Aesthetic Enjoyment of Incongruities." *The Philosophy of Humor and Laughter.* Ed. John Morreall. Albany: State U of New York P, 1987. 172–86.

Marx, Karl. *Capital Vol. 1.* New York: International, 1974.

———. *A Contribution to the Critique of Political Economy.* Trans. Maurice Dobb. New York: International, 1970.

McClanahan, Thomas. "Gregory Corso." *American Poets Since World War II.* Ed. Donald J. Greiner. Detroit: Gale, 1980. Vol. 5 of *Dictionary of Literary Biography.*

Mead, G. R. S. *Fragments of a Faith Forgotten.* London and Benares: Theosophical, 1906.

Monnoyer, Jean-Maurice. *Le Peintre et Son Démon: Entretiens Avec Pierre Klossowski.* Paris: Flammarion, 1985.

Nietzsche, Friedrich. *The Birth of Tragedy and The Genealogy of Morals.* Trans. Francis Golffing. New York: Doubleday, 1956.

Oakley, Francis. "Lovejoy's Unexplored Option." *Journal of the History of Ideas* 2 (April-June 1987): 231–46.

O'Hara, Frank. *The Collected Poems of Frank O'Hara.* Berkeley: U of California P, 1995.

Orlovsky, Peter. *Clean Asshole Poems and Smiling Vegetable Songs.* Introduction by Gregory Corso. San Franciso: City Lights, 1978.

Otto, Walter F. *Dionysus: Myth and Cult.* Trans. and introduction by Robert B. Palmer. Bloomington: Indiana UP, 1995.

Pagels, Elaine. *Adam, Eve, and the Serpent.* New York: Vintage, 1988.

Parker, Derek. "Corso, Gregory." *Contemporary Poets.* Ed. Rosalie Murphy. Chicago: St. James, 1970. 236–37.

Parkman, Francis. *The Conspiracy of Pontiac.* 1908. London: Dent, 1944.

Penguin Modern Poets 5. London: Penguin, 1963.

Perkins, David. *English Romantic Writers.* New York: Harcourt, 1967.

Perloff, Marjorie. *Frank O'Hara: Poet Among Painters.* Chicago: U of Chicago P, 1997.

Philip, Jim. "Journey in the Mindfield: Gregory Corso Reconsidered." *The Beat Generation Writers.* Ed. A. Robert Lee. London: Pluto, 1996. 61–73.

Podhoretz, Norman. "A Howl of Protest in San Francisco." *On the Poetry of Allen Ginsberg.* Ed. Lewis Hyde. Ann Arbor: U of Michigan P, 1984. 34–35.

Polizzotti, Mark. *Revolution of the Mind: The Life of André Breton.* New York: FSG, 1995.

Rexroth, Kenneth. *Assays.* New York: New Directions, 1961.

Ridley, Matt. *The Origins of Virtue.* New York: Viking, 1996.

Rycroft, Charles. *Psychoanalysis and Beyond.* Ed. Peter Fuller. London: Hogarth, 1985.

Sarje, Kimmo. "A Romantic Turn in Visual Art?" *Art and Beyond: Finnish Approaches to Aesthetics.* Ed. Ossi Naukkarinen and Olli Immonen. Lahti, Finland: Finnish Society for Aesthetics, 1995. 126–39.

Saw, Ruth. "Sense and Nonsense in Aesthetics." *Aesthetics in the Modern World.* Ed. Harold Osborne. London: Thames and Hudson, 1968. 33–48.

Schwartz, Marilyn. "Gregory Corso." *The Beats: Literary Bohemians in Postwar America.* Ed. Ann Charters. Detroit: Gale, 1983. Vol. 16 of *Dictionary of Literary Biography.* 117–40.

Selerie, Gavin. "Interview with Gregory Corso." *The Riverside Interviews, 3, Gregory Corso.* London: Binnacle, 1982. 21–47.

Shattuck, Roger. *The Banquet Years.* New York: Vintage, 1968.

Skau, Michael. *A Clown in a Grave: Complexities and Tensions in the Works of Gregory Corso.* Carbondale: Southern Illinois UP, 1999.

Stauffer, Donald. "Gregory Corso." *Contemporary Poets.* Ed. Tracy Chevalier. Chicago: St. James, 1991. 178–79.

Stephenson, Gregory. *Exiled Angel: A Study of the Work of Gregory Corso.* London: Hearing Eye, 1989.

Tillotson, Kristin. "Beat Poet Gregory Corso Dies in Twin Cities." *Minneapolis Star-Tribune* Jan. 19, 2001.

Timm, Robert C. "Unleashing Language: The Post-Structuralist Poetics of Gregory Corso and the Beats." *Kerouac Connection* 27 (Winter 1995): 34–41.

Trilling, Diana. "The Other Night at Columbia: A Report from the Academy." *On the Poetry of Allen Ginsberg.* Ed. Lewis Hyde. Ann Arbor: U of Michigan P, 1984. 56–74.

Tuveson, Ernest Lee. *The Avatars of Thrice Great Hermes: An Approach to Romanticism.* Lewisburg: Bucknell, 1982.

Tytell, John. "The Legacy of Surrealism." *On the Poetry of Allen Ginsberg.* Ed. Lewis Hyde. Ann Arbor: U of Michigan P, 1984. 171–79.

Young, Julian. *Nietzsche's Philosophy of Art.* Cambridge: Cambridge UP, 1992.

Index

Abelard, Peter, 29
"Active Night" (Corso), 32–33, 92
"Ah . . . Well" (Corso), 99
"Alchemy" (Corso), 43
Althusser, Louis, 103
Altieri, Charles, 22, 105, 122
"American Express" (Corso), 36
"American Way, The" (Corso), 95
"America Politica Historia, in Spontaneity"
    (Corso), 106
"Amnesia in Memphis" (Corso), 161
"Ancestry" (Corso), 83
André, Michael, 10, 21, 27, 28, 47–48, 74–
    75, 89
Ansen, Alan, 106, 115
Aristotle, 39, 143, 145
"Army" (Corso), 105
Aron, Raymond, 140
Artaud, Antonin, 90
Ashbery, John, 125, 126, 128
Ashby, Romy, 110

Badiou, Alain, 169
Bainton, Roland, 108
Bakhtin, Mikhail, 17, 18, 20, 21, 53, 81
Barnstone, Willis, 95, 96, 150
Bartok, Bela, 20
Bataille, Georges, 79, 90, 140, 156
Baudelaire, Charles, 136
Baumer, Francis, 163
Benedetto, Roseanne, 116
Benne, Robert, 108
Berkeley, George, 87
"Berlin Zoo" (Corso), 37
Berry, Wendell, 44

"Birthplace Revisited" (Corso), 72
Blake, William, 71, 108, 124
Blanchot, Maurice, 140
Bloom, Harold, 146
"Bomb" (Corso), 10–11, 60, 105
"Bombed Train Station, 80 Killed" (Corso),
    60
"Botticelli" (Corso), 72
Brautigan, Richard, 136
Breton, André, 10, 16, 57, 58–59, 76–79,
    166; and his aversion to the family ex-
    perience, 136, 140, 147
Bryant, William Jennings, 26
Bundy, Ted, 142–43
Burke, Edmund, 161
Burke, Kenneth, 59, 63–64, 65, 67–68, 80,
    88, 99, 123, 155
Burroughs, William, 4, 30, 49, 66, 71, 97,
    101, 103, 105, 128; work ethic of, 124
"But I Do Not Need Kindness" (Corso),
    120–21, 131
Byron, George, 84–85

Cage, John, 161
Caillois, Roger, 140
"Cambridge, First Impressions" (Corso), 73
Carpocratians, 89, 145
Carrington, Leonora, 136
Carroll, Lewis, 25, 26, 28
Carruth, Hayden, 25
Cawardine, Richard, 9
Celine, Louis-Ferdinand, 125
Cellini, Benevuto, 20
Chénieux-Gendron, Jacqueline, 55, 56, 89,
    96

Chernovsky, Neeli, 127
Chesterton, G. K.: on St. Francis, 15, 18, 19, 20, 23, 153; on Spencer, 33; on Thomism, 31, 40
Clairvaux, St. Bernard de, 151
Cleveland, John, 125
"Clown" (Corso), 22, 122
Cocteau, Jean, 126
Coleridge, S. T., 70
"Columbia U Poesy Reading" (Corso), 83–84
Conrad, Joseph, 125
Copernicus, Nicolaus, 164
Couliano, Ioan, 91
Cox, Harvey: on Christ as jester, 30
Cros, Charles, 79
Curtius, E. R., 15

Dali, Salvador, 79, 136, 139
Darwin, Charles, 8, 14, 15, 59–60, 65, 66, 69, 70, 90, 155
"Dear Girl" (Corso), 6
"Dear Villon" (Corso), 103, 146–47
"Death" (Corso), 158
Deleuze, Gilles, 27, 38, 49, 50, 103, 105, 152
Dennett, Daniel, 56–58
Derek, Parker, 95
Derrida, Jacques, 45, 50
"Destiny" (Corso), 83
Dickinson, Emily, 25, 26–27, 125
"Difference of Zoos, A" (Corso), 37
Diogenes, 103, 150, 157
"Don't Shoot the Warthog" (Corso), 130, 142, 152
"Dreamed Realization, A" (Corso), 37
Duchamp, Marcel, 76

Eberhart, Richard, 23
"Ecce Homo" (Corso), 137–38, 141, 169
Eco, Umberto, 13–14, 15, 17, 53–54, 151, 163–65
"Elegiac Feelings American" (Corso), 117
Elmslie, Kenward, 125, 126
Ensor, James, 30
Epic of Gilgamesh, 75, 82
Epicurus, 96
Ernst, Max, 76

Fagin, Larry, 3
Faithful, Marianne, 170
"Feelings on Getting Older" (Corso), 170
feminism, 3
Ferlinghetti, Lawrence, 21, 23, 25, 63
Ferry, Luc: on ecofeminism and animal rights, 39–41
Fichte, Johann Gottlieb, 66, 69
"Field Report" (Corso), 5, 85–86, 161
"Fire Report—No Alarm" (Corso), 50–52, 170
Fleming, John, 148
"Food" (Corso), 37
food chain, 28–29, 35–50, 79, 168
"For John Lennon" (Corso), 170
"For Lisa, 2" (Corso), 138
"For Miles" (Corso), 73
Francis, Sam, 161
Francis of Assissi, Saint, 13, 15, 17, 18, 20, 23, 67, 164
Fraser, G. S., 25
Freud, Sigmund, 146, 156
Front de Libération Nationale, 12, 16
Frostin, Per, 108
Froula, Christine, 121
Fuller, John, 25

Galileo, 163
Gardner, Isabella: as thief of Corso's poetry, 44
"Geometric Poem" (Corso), 72–73, 75, 82, 86
"Giant Turtle" (Corso), 92
Gilbert of Hoyt, 18
Gilson, Etienne, 13
Ginsberg, Allen, 3, 4, 21, 23, 26, 27, 30, 31, 45, 49, 60, 63, 66, 70, 79, 89, 93, 97, 99, 101, 103, 105, 117, 121, 123, 125, 129, 131, 132; erudition of, 124
Glucksmann, André, 103
Gnosticism, 32, 48, 86, 88–99, 101, 134, 135, 145, 146, 154, 156
"God is a Masturbator" (Corso), 42, 69
"God? She's Black" (Corso), 98
Gray, Richard, 167
"Greenwich Village Suicide" (Corso), 20, 161
Guattari, Félix, 38

Guest, Barbara, 126
"Guide for My Infant Son, A" (Corso), 149–50

Haggard, H. Rider, 7, 11
"Hair" (Corso), 105
Hals, Franz, 126
"Happening on a German Train" (Corso), 166
"Heave the Hive with New Bees" (Corso), 159–60
Hegel, Georg, 55, 69
Heidegger, Martin, 35, 36, 42, 43, 49
Hölderlin, Friedrich, 5, 66, 151, 166; on poetry as the highest art, 169
Holquist, Michael, 19
Honor, Hugh, 148
"Horses" (Corso), 160
Howard, Richard, 7, 10, 132
"Howl" (Ginsberg), 131
Hugo, Victor, 13
Hunsberger, Bruce: on Franciscan imagery in Beat writing, 28
Hyde, Lewis, 65

"I Dream in the Daytime" (Corso), 100–101
"Immutable Moods" (Corso), 69
"Inter & Outer Rhyme" (Corso), 150–51
"In the Fleeting Hand of Time" (Corso), 134
"In the Morgue" (Corso), 81
Irenaeus, Bishop, 90, 91–92, 93, 145
Italian American, Corso as, 72, 101, 134
"Italian Extravaganza" (Corso), 72
"I Where I Stand" (Corso), 106–15, 119–20, 121, 123

Jarry, Alfred, 79, 136, 137, 149
Jonas, Hans, 91, 96

Kant, Immanuel, 35, 43
Kazin, Alfred, 26–27
Keats, John, 84
Kendrick, Donald, 41
Kennedy, John F., 41, 43, 63
Kerouac, Jack, 4, 44, 49, 63, 66, 69, 71, 76, 81, 99, 117, 124, 128, 129
King, Robert, 43, 112
Klee, Paul, 34

Klossowski, Pierre, 92, 139, 140, 141, 143, 144, 145–46
Klossowski de Rola, Stanislas, 101
Koch, Kenneth, 125, 126
Korzybski, Count Alfred, 71
Kuschel, Karl-Josef, 170; on Easter laughter, 24–25; on the fool in Christianity, 29–30; on hellish and heavenly laughter, 132–33

Laakso, Sami, 36
Laertius, Diogenes, 150
Lambda, Jacqueline, 57
Langerman, Sheri, 170
"Last Gangster, The" (Corso), 72
"Last Night I Drove a Car" (Corso), 64–65, 79
Laughlin, James, 21
Lautréamont, Comte de, 136
"Leaky Lifeboat Boys, The" (Corso), 97–98
Lear, Edward, 25, 28, 103, 105
Leary, Timothy, 60
Lecercle, Jean-Jacques, 169; on Mrs. Jellyby, 25, 28
Leibniz, Gottfried, 55, 163
Lenhart, Gary, 127
Lennon, John, 22
Leonardo da Vinci, 125
Leo XIII, Pope, 8
Levinas, Emmanuel, 35, 36, 42, 43, 49
Lewellyn, John, 35
Lewitzky, Anatole, 156, 158, 161
"Life is a Battlefield" (Corso), 37
Lincoln, Abraham, 63
Lindsay, Vachel, 24, 25, 26
"Lines Written Among the Euganean Hills" (Shelley), 114–15, 118–19
"Lines Written Nov. 22, 23—1963—in Discord" (Corso), 42, 63
Logan, William, 126
Lovejoy, Arthur: on the great chain of being, 29, 55–56, 64–65
LSD, 4, 60
Luther, Martin, 108, 165–66, 168
Lutheranism: as a rebirth of the Dionysian, according to Nietzsche, 139, 165–66
Lyotard, Jean-François, 103, 140, 143, 157–58, 160–61, 168

MacBeth (Shakespeare), 114
Magus, Simon, 95
Mahoney, Edward P., 151–52
"Man About to Enter Sea" (Corso), 56–57
Manicheanism, 17–18, 43, 95
"Many Have Fallen" (Corso), 60
Mao Tse-tung, 104
Marcos, Imelda, shoes of, 154
Marinetti, Tomasino, 63
"Marriage" (Corso), 6–11, 79, 105, 109, 113
Martin, Mike, 150
Marx, Groucho, 103
Marx, Harpo, 102
Marx, Karl, 104, 130, 141, 144–45
McClanahan, Thomas, 99
Mead, G. R. S., 90
Melville, Herman, 73
Monnerot, Jules, 89
Monnoyer, Jean-Maurice, 140, 146
Moore, Marianne, 25
Mozart, Amadeus, 20
Mussolini, Benito, 71

Nancy, Jean-Luc, 46
Naropa Institute, 2, 16, 99, 111, 115, 120, 124, 125
Newton, Isaac, 163
Nietzsche, Friedrich, 50, 52, 139, 143, 152, 165, 168, 171; on vegetarianism, 49
"Notes from the Other Side of April: With Negro Eyes, with White" (Corso), 4
Notre Dame (Paris), 12–13, 16
Novalis, Friedrich von, 65, 96

Oakley, Francis, 163
"Of One Month's Reading of English Newspapers" (Corso), 43
O'Hara, Frank, 125, 126; on Corso, 127, 128
Olson, Charles, 105
Oppenheim, Meret, 76
Orlovsky, Peter, 17, 126, 128
Ostade, Adrien von, 126
Otto, Walter, 152, 156, 168

Pagels, Elaine, 90
Palmer, Robert B., 152
Parker, Charlie, 27
Parker, Derek, 25

"Pastoral Fetish, A" (Corso), 21, 33, 34
Perkins, David, 119
Perloff, Marjorie, 125, 127, 128
Philip, Jim, 27–28, 105
Picasso, Pablo, 76
Pilate, Pontius, 145
Plato, 145, 146, 157; on nature as outside logos, 45, 48, 69
Plotinus, 29, 90, 96
Podhoretz, Norman: on Franciscan imagery of the Beats, 28
Poe, Edgar Allan, 2, 3
"Poem Jottings in the Early Morn" (Corso), 92, 95
Polizzotti, Mark, 76–77, 136, 147
"Poor Bustard, The" (Corso), 67–69
Pound, Ezra, 10, 70, 105, 121, 122, 128
"Power" (Corso), 105
Presley, Elvis, 21
"Puma in Chapultepec Zoo" (Corso), 37
Pythagorus, 2, 145

Queneau, Raymond, 79

Rabelais, Francois, 79
"Radio Interview" (Corso), 17, 19
"Requiem for Bird Parker" (Corso), 73
"Return" (Corso), 94
Rexroth, Kenneth, 25, 33, 162
Ridley, Matt, 155
Rimbaud, Arthur, 75, 136
Rothschild, Jocelyn, 3
Rouault, George, 30
Runyan, Damon, 101
Rycroft, Charles, 110–13, 115–17, 120–21, 122, 124, 129, 138, 154, 166–67

Sade, Marquis de, 87, 89, 136, 138, 146, 155
"Saint Francis" (Corso), 38
Sandburg, Carl, 24
Sanders, Edward, 170
Sarje, Kimmo, 66
"Sausages, The" (Corso), 35
Saw, Ruth, 140
Sayre, Nora, 127
Schelling, Friedrich, 55–56, 69, 96
Schlegel, Friedrich von, 64, 66, 96
Schopenhauer, Arthur, 150

Schuyler, James, 126
Schwartz, Marilyn, 1, 106, 119, 162
"Sea Chanty" (Corso), 21, 33, 37
Selerie, Gavin, 43–44
Shakespeare, William, 70, 125
Shattuck, Roger, 137
Shelley, Percy Bysshe, 20, 52–53, 61, 66, 69, 85, 108, 109, 120, 121, 122, 124, 125, 151, 171
Skau, Michael, 1, 4, 5, 49, 62–63, 79–80, 81, 97, 111, 116, 120, 127, 128, 168; on the superiority of Corso to Ginsberg, 25
Snyder, Gary, 25, 27, 30, 31, 52, 71, 105, 150; on the need to confront Corso, 44–45
"Song" (Corso), 21, 33
Soupault, Philippe, 79, 105, 136
Spencer, Herbert, 33
"Spirit" (Corso), 153–54
"Spontaneous Requiem for the American Indian" (Corso), 46–47
Stalin, Joseph, 104, 115
Stauffer, Donald, 105
Stephenson, Gregory, 1, 6, 33–34, 49, 67, 72–73, 75–76, 89, 127
Stone, Christopher D.: rights for plants, 40
"Suburbia Mad Song" (Corso), 76
Suckling, John, 125
"Sunrise" (Corso), 43, 53
surrealism, problem with the mother image in, 136
Swift, Jonathon, 79
Swinburne, Charles, 25

Tannu Tuva, 7
Tennyson, Alfred, 25
Tertullian, 140
"They" (Corso), 133
"This Was My Meal" (Corso), 35–36
Thomas Aquinas, Saint, 8, 9, 11–14, 17, 29, 43, 54, 148, 164, 165; and his reactionary attitude to women, 39; on resurrection's effect on the body, 160
"Thought" (Corso), 93
Tielhard de Chardin, Pierre, 58
Tillotson, Kristin, 170
Timm, Robert C., 6, 7
"To a Common Prostitute" (Whitman), 62
Tocqueville, Alexis de, 167

"To Die Laughing (?)" (Corso), 82
Trilling, Diana, 131
Trotsky, Leon, 78
Trungpa, Choygam, 120
Turpin, Ben, 139
Tuveson, Ernest Lee: on Hermes Trismegistus, 61–62, 69, 151
Tytell, John: on Ginsberg's interest in surrealism, 79
Tzara, Tristan, 133

Uccello, Paolo, 28
"Uccello" (Corso), 72, 74, 122, 161
"Upon My Refusal to Herald Cuba" (Corso), 2, 109
Urmuz, 133

Vaché, Jacques, 133
van Doren, Mark, 127–28
Van Gogh, Vincent, 20
"Variations on a Generation" (Corso), 102
"Vermeer" (Corso), 74
Villon, François, 20, 70, 146–47

Warhol, Andy, 125
"What the Child Sees" (Corso), 104–5
"When I Was Five I Saw a Dying Indian" (Corso), 1, 4–5
"When We All" (Corso), 170
Whitman, Walt, 24, 62–63, 67, 108, 124, 126, 128, 150
"Whole Mess . . . Almost, The" (Corso), 23
Willeford, Charles, 136
Williams, William Carlos, 126, 128
"Wisdom" (Corso), 104
Wittgenstein, Ludwig, 168
Wodehouse, P. G., 82
Wordsworth, William, 61, 69
"Writ in Horace Greeley Square" (Corso), 149
"Writ on the Eve" (Corso), 80, 148–49
"Written in Nostalgia for Paris" (Corso), 12–16

Young, Julian, 139
"Youthful Religious Experiences" (Corso), 97, 134–35

"Zizi's Lament" (Corso), 98

Kirby Olson is an assistant professor in the humanities department at State University of New York at Delhi. His essays, poetry, and stories have appeared in many publications, from *Partisan Review* to *Exquisite Corpse*. He is the author of *Comedy after Postmodernism: Rereading Comedy from Edward Lear to Charles Willeford.*

DATE DUE

HIGHSMITH #45115